Also by Adam Rome

*The Bulldozer in the Countryside: Suburban Sprawl
and the Rise of American Environmentalism*

The Genius of Earth Day

The Genius of Earth Day

How a 1970 Teach-In

Unexpectedly Made

the First Green Generation

Adam Rome

Hill and Wang *A division of Farrar, Straus and Giroux New York*

Hill and Wang
A division of Farrar, Straus and Giroux
18 West 18th Street, New York 10011

Copyright © 2013 by Adam Rome
Printed in the United States of America
First edition, 2013

Library of Congress Cataloging-in-Publication Data
Rome, Adam, 1959–
    The genius of Earth Day : how a 1970 teach-in unexpectedly made the first
green generation / Adam Rome.
        p.   cm.
    Includes bibliographical references and index.
    ISBN 978-0-8090-4050-6 (hardcover : alk. paper)
    1. Earth Day—History.   2. Environmentalism—History.   I. Title.

GE195 .R65 2013
333.72—dc23
                                                                2012034728

www.fsgbooks.com
www.twitter.com/fsgbooks • www.facebook.com/fsgbooks

10 9 8 7 6 5 4 3 2 1

For Donald Worster

Contents

A photographic insert follows page 164.

● Preface

I've come to believe that the first Earth Day is the most famous little-known event in modern American history. Environmentalists and scholars long have recognized that Earth Day 1970 was critical in the rise of the environmental movement. Indeed, many people argue that Earth Day 1970 inspired a decade of far-reaching legislation to control air pollution, restore the health of rivers and lakes, ensure safe drinking water, regulate hazardous waste disposal, protect endangered species, and much more. Yet *The Genius of Earth Day* is the first in-depth study of the subject.

How is that possible?

Historians have assumed that the force of Earth Day 1970 essentially was symbolic: Millions of Americans demonstrated that they cared about the environment, and the unprecedented size of the demonstration convinced lawmakers to take the issue more seriously. That assumption makes most of the details of the story irrelevant. If all that mattered was the scale of the event, why look closely at how Earth Day was organized, or how it was celebrated across the country, or what people said in Earth Day speeches?

For years, I myself had little curiosity about Earth Day. I lectured about Earth Day, but I relied on a handful of short accounts of the event, and those accounts all derived from just a few sources. Even after I decided to write about Earth Day, I did not expect to make new claims about why Earth Day mattered. I simply was excited by the narrative challenge of bringing a history-making event to life.

I soon discovered that the story of Earth Day was more complex and compelling than I'd thought. Even the phrase "Earth Day" turned out to be misleading. In many places, the event lasted a week, not just a day, and the extended celebrations had many names. In Birmingham, Alabama, Earth Day was part of Right to Live Week. Cleveland, Ohio, celebrated Crisis in the Environment Week. In some places, Earth Week didn't even include Earth Day: The events were in late March or early April.

The more I learned about Earth Day, the more improbable the story seemed. The basic facts still amaze me. In September 1969, Senator Gaylord Nelson of Wisconsin vowed to organize a nationwide environmental teach-in in spring 1970, and his call to action inspired thousands of events across the country. Roughly 1,500 colleges and 10,000 schools held teach-ins. Earth Day activities also took place in hundreds of churches and temples, in city parks, and in front of corporate and government buildings. The teach-ins collectively involved more people than the biggest civil-rights and antiwar demonstrations in the 1960s.

But the numbers do not begin to tell the story. The first Earth Day had a freshness and intensity that are difficult to imagine today. Because Earth Day 1970 was unprecedented, the organizers had to plan everything from scratch, and the effort often was life-changing. Tens of thousands of people spoke on Earth Day— and many had never spoken publicly about environmental issues before. The discussions at Earth Day teach-ins sometimes were soul-searching: Many participants truly were struggling to get to the roots of "the environmental crisis."

That freshness and intensity gave Earth Day 1970 tremendous power. Thousands of organizers and participants decided to devote their lives to the environmental cause. Earth Day built a lasting eco-infrastructure: national and state lobbying organizations, environmental-studies programs, environmental beats at newspapers, eco sections in bookstores, community ecology centers.

The Genius of Earth Day ultimately is about the making of the first green generation.

The prologue describes a teach-in at the University of Michigan six weeks before Earth Day. The Michigan teach-in was the first sign that Earth Day would be a stunning success, and the prologue introduces the major themes of this book. Chapter 1 considers the prehistory of Earth Day. In the 1950s and 1960s, a variety of Americans became more concerned about environmental issues, but their efforts were fragmented until Earth Day. Chapter 2 is about the thousands of organizers who made Earth Day happen. Chapter 3 illustrates the variety of Earth Day events. Because Nelson allowed local organizers to make their own plans, no two events were the same, and the local adaptations ensured that Earth Day would be much more than a huge demonstration. Chapter 4 profiles seven Earth Day speakers to suggest the intellectual energy of the event. Chapter 5 analyzes the institutional legacies of Earth Day. The epilogue tells the stories of four people whose lives were changed by Earth Day.

I have not considered every aspect of the Earth Day story. When I began my research, I planned to include a chapter about how African-Americans, union members, conservative intellectuals, and corporate executives reacted to Earth Day. I also planned to write about media coverage. But I eventually decided that those topics did not fit. They shed light on the strengths and weaknesses of the environmental movement, but they did not help to explain why Earth Day was a transformative event, and that is my focus.

Though I did not try to be comprehensive, this book took much longer to write than I expected, but I never tired of the subject. I found the story of Earth Day energizing. Inspiring, really. I hope you will too.

The Genius of Earth Day

● Prologue: "Give Earth a Chance"

The first sign that Earth Day would be a history-making event came on March 11, 1970, in Ann Arbor, Michigan.

Nearly 14,000 people were at the University of Michigan's basketball arena for the kickoff of a teach-in on the environment. The kickoff began with the cast of the musical *Hair* singing "Let the Sunshine In." The governor of Michigan spoke briefly, and then the president of the university. Then biologist Barry Commoner stepped to the podium to give the keynote.[1]

Commoner was used to speaking in public—he was a professor and a well-traveled activist—but he was momentarily awed. Fourteen thousand people! He had never spoken to so large a crowd before. No environmentalist had.

Six weeks earlier, Commoner had appeared on the cover of *Time*. "The Paul Revere of ecology," the magazine called him. But Commoner knew that the huge turnout was not just a sign of his new renown. The environment had become a hot issue, and students everywhere were gearing up for Earth Day.[2]

"I am deeply honored to appear before what must surely be the world's largest seminar on ecology," Commoner began. "What a wonderful thing you have done! At a time when the whole country has begun to ask why, in the wealthiest, most scientifically advanced nation in the history of man, the heavens reek, the waters below are foul, children die in infancy, and we and the world which is our home are threatened with nuclear annihilation—you have shown us how to take off our blindfolds, pull out our earplugs and shout 'We're not gonna take it!' "[3]

Commoner was especially moved by the young teach-in organizers. They were leading "the nation's new fight for survival," he argued. Their resolve gave Commoner heart.

Commoner was right to be impressed by the organizational effort. The teach-in committee at first was only six graduate students in the School of Natural Resources. The organizers took the name ENACT—Environmental Action for Survival—and decided on a teach-in slogan: "Give Earth a Chance." In October 1969, the first teach-in planning meeting drew 350 people, and more than 1,000 eventually helped to make the teach-in happen. The planning was not all peace and love. The campus black-power organization threatened a boycott because the organizers were not devoting enough attention to the problems of the ghetto, while members of Students for a Democratic Society mocked the "not-so-liberal liberalism" of the featured speakers. But the event blossomed. The organizers raised $50,000. The teach-in became four days, with more than 125 activities.[4]

To raise environmental consciousness in the community, housewives hosted teas and businessmen sponsored lunches. High-school students urged consumers at Ann Arbor grocery stores to boycott pesticides. On campus, a guerrilla theater troupe put a 1959 Ford sedan on trial for crimes against the environment. At a "scream-out," participants debated whether the environment would deflect attention from the Vietnam War, the civil-rights struggle, and the movement for woman's liberation. One workshop provided a Republican take on the environmental crisis, while another offered a socialist perspective. Technical sessions focused on everything from the future of the Great Lakes to the role of engineers in preventing pollution. A U.S. House of Representatives subcommittee on conservation and natural resources held a hearing at the teach-in. The headliners included the most prominent environmentalists in the U.S. Senate, Gaylord Nelson and Edmund Muskie; Friends of the Earth director David Brower; consumer activist Ralph Nader; United Auto Workers president Walter Reuther; entertainers Arthur Godfrey and Eddie Albert; several renowned scientists; the chief executives of Dow Chemical and Consolidated Edison; environmental economist Kenneth Boulding; radical eco-philosopher Murray Bookchin; environmental lawyer Victor Yannacone; and Richard Hatcher, one of the nation's first black mayors. The attendance topped 50,000.[5]

Because the Michigan teach-in offered a preview of Earth Day, the week's activities received national attention. A television crew even came from Japan. ABC and CBS reported on the event on the nightly news. The teach-in also was the subject of a documentary shown on network television just before Earth Day. *Business Week*, *Science*, and *The Nation* ran feature stories, and *Saturday Review* published Commoner's reflections on the teach-in. Syndicated columnist Joseph Kraft reported on the teach-in. So did reporters for big-city newspapers from across the country. *The New York Times* positively gushed about the event, calling it "one of the most extraordinary 'happenings' ever to hit the great American heartland: Four solid days of soul-searching, by thousands of people, young and old, about ecological exigencies confronting the human race."[6]

The energy of the teach-in continued to flow through the community after March 1970. To provide a focal point for local activism, ENACT members helped to found the Ann Arbor Ecology Center. (ENACT veterans later established an ecology center in Washington, D.C., as well.) The School of Natural Resources added master's degrees in environmental advocacy and environmental communication. The school also hired two new faculty members; one became a leader in the environmental-justice movement. The teach-in organizers at the high school formed an environmental-action club. In the early 1970s, club members lobbied the state legislature for a ban on DDT, a bottle bill, and a measure to protect wild and scenic rivers. The outdoor writer for *The Ann Arbor News* began a weekly "Eco-Action" column. Two ENACT organizers put together a collection of essays by teach-in contributors: *Recycle This Book!*[7]

Years later, the four principal organizers of the teach-in still had vivid memories of the event. All four—co-chairs Doug Scott and David Allan, finance director Art Hanson, and publicity director John Turner—were changed by the experience. Though they already were interested in environmental issues, the teach-in shaped their careers in significant ways.

John Turner, the publicity director, was most affected. He grew up in a conservative ranching family in Wyoming, and he was working toward a Ph.D. in wildlife ecology. He might have gone back to the ranch or become a professor. Instead, the teach-in convinced Turner to enter politics. "I was challenged daily," he recalled. "I was targeted as a supporter of Nixon, a lackey, a Republican." The attacks shook him but ultimately gave him new resolve. He became convinced of the need for leaders who were levelheaded and practical, not bomb throwers. He ran successfully for the Wyoming legislature. In nineteen years as a state representative and senator, he was a forceful advocate for environmental protection. He then served as director of the U.S. Fish and Wildlife Service under George H. W. Bush, president of the Conservation Foundation in the Clinton years, and assistant secretary of state for global environmental issues under George W. Bush.[8]

The legacies were subtler for Scott, Allan, and Hanson. Scott felt a deeper determination to pursue a career in environmental politics. He had written a master's thesis on the legislative history of the Wilderness Act of 1964, he had worked for a summer as a lobbyist for the Wilderness Society, and he devoted his life to the cause: He now is a grassroots organizer for the Campaign for America's Wilderness. Allan became a professor of stream ecology. The teach-in pushed him to do more policy-oriented research, not just the straight science he did in graduate school. Hanson also earned a Ph.D. in science, but he became an academic entrepreneur: He ultimately directed an international institute on sustainable development. "For me, the most important legacy was a sense of empowerment," Hanson recalled. "The teach-in gave me the sense that if you really wanted to do something, you could. Just go ahead and do it."[9]

1 ● The Prehistory of Earth Day

Earth Day was not the work of a well-established movement. Indeed, commentators did not begin to speak about "the environmental movement" until the run-up to Earth Day. Though many Americans had sought to address environmental issues before 1970, their efforts were fragmented. Few organizations worked on both rural and urban problems. The old conservation groups focused on wildlife and wilderness. The fight against air pollution largely was led by single-issue organizations, from Stamp Out Smog in Los Angeles to Citizens for Clean Air in New York. The only "environmental" organization in the late 1960s—the Environmental Defense Fund—essentially was a handful of lawyers and scientists who pursued high-profile lawsuits. The Natural Resources Defense Council was a month old on Earth Day.[1]

Because the environmental movement still was inchoate in the 1960s, Earth Day had no obvious precursors. That made Earth Day quite different from the biggest civil-rights and antiwar demonstrations of the era. The 1963 March on Washington for Jobs and Freedom was the culmination of nine years of activism: the Montgomery bus boycott, the Greensboro sit-ins, the arrest of Martin Luther King Jr. in Birmingham. The 1969 Moratorium to End the War in Vietnam came after four years of protests, from the antiwar teach-ins of 1965 to the 1967 march on the Pentagon.

The lack of antecedents reveals much about the significance of Earth Day. Earth Day did not just mobilize activists to demonstrate the growing power of their cause. In several ways, Earth Day helped to create the movement. Earth Day gave environmental activism a name. Earth Day also convinced many Americans that pollution, sprawl, nuclear fallout, pesticide use, wilderness preservation, waste disposal, and population growth were not separate issues: All were facets of a far-reaching "environmental crisis." Perhaps most important, Earth Day brought together activists who had worked separately before.

The new movement drew support from a variety of people, but members of five groups were critical. In the course of the 1950s and 1960s, many liberal Democrats, scientists, middle-class women, young critics of American institutions, and conservationists became more concerned about environmental issues. Though the activists in those groups did not become a concerted force until Earth Day brought them together, they made Earth Day possible.[2]

Liberals

In the mid-1950s, a handful of Democratic intellectuals began to reconsider the liberal agenda, and their efforts intensified after Adlai Stevenson's defeat in the presidential election of 1956. What could liberalism offer in a time of unprecedented affluence? Many Democratic policy advisers and elected officials soon concluded that one answer to that question was a commitment to environmental protection. In coming to that conclusion, they were influenced by the arguments of experts in a growing number of professions concerned about the environment. They also were responding to growing grassroots activism. But the Democratic intellectuals and politicians were leaders as well as followers. By making environmental issues part of a broad new liberal agenda, they fundamentally changed the terms of debate.

The most influential advocates of the new liberalism were the historian Arthur Schlesinger Jr. and the economist John Kenneth Galbraith. The two Harvard professors were unusually well positioned to shape political debate. Both wrote speeches for Stevenson in 1952 and 1956, and both were founders of Americans for Democratic Action. Both also served on the domestic policy committee of the national Democratic party. In the late 1950s, both men became advisers to John F. Kennedy, and their influence in Democratic politics continued into the 1960s.[3]

For Schlesinger and Galbraith, a liberal agenda for the 1960s followed from two related ideas about the nation's postwar prosperity, and both ideas provided a powerful new justification for expanding the role of government in protecting the environment. First, liberals needed to move beyond the basic goals of the New Deal. In an age of abundance, government could and should do more than ensure that Americans enjoyed a minimum of material comfort. Schlesinger put the point succinctly: "Instead of the quantitative liberalism of the 1930s, rightly dedicated to the struggle to secure the economic basis of life, we need now a 'qualitative liberalism' dedicated to bettering the quality of people's lives and opportunities." Second, liberals needed to address what Galbraith called "the problem of social balance." Though the postwar economic boom enabled people to buy more and more consumer products, the private sector could not satisfy the increasing demand for a number of vital community services. Accordingly, the challenge for liberals was to offer a compelling vision of the public interest.[4]

Though neither Schlesinger nor Galbraith was a noted conservationist, both pointed to environmental problems to support their argument for a new liberalism. The state of the environment clearly affected the quality of life. If the nation's

streams were polluted, then fewer people could enjoy the pleasures of fishing or boating. The quality of the environment also
was a classic example of a public good, since consumers could
not simply buy fresh air, clean water, or sprawl-free countrysides.

Schlesinger addressed the issue first. "Our gross national
product rises; our shops overflow with gadgets and gimmicks;
consumer goods of ever-increasing ingenuity and luxuriance
pour out of our ears," he wrote in a 1956 essay on the future of
liberalism. "But our schools become more crowded and dilapi-
dated, our teachers more weary and underpaid, our playgrounds
more crowded, our cities dirtier, our roads more teeming and
filthy, our national parks more unkempt, our law enforcement
more overworked and inadequate."[5]

In *The Affluent Society*—a bestseller in 1958—Galbraith used
more evocative language. "The family which takes its mauve and
cerise, air-conditioned, power-steered, and power-braked automobile out for a tour passes through cities that are badly paved,
made hideous by litter, blighted buildings, billboards, and posts
for wires that should long since have been put underground,"
he wrote. "They pass into a countryside that has been rendered
largely invisible by commercial art . . . They picnic on exquisitely
packaged food from a portable icebox by a polluted stream and
go on to spend the night at a park which is a menace to public
health and morals. Just before dozing off on an air mattress,
beneath a nylon tent, amid the stench of decaying refuse, they
may reflect vaguely on the curious unevenness of their blessings.
Is this, indeed, the American genius?" Those lines would become
the most famous in the book.[6]

The fame of the passage was not due simply to Galbraith's
acerbic style. In a few nauseating images, Galbraith had caught a
growing concern about the deterioration of the nation's environment. By the time *The Affluent Society* appeared, many Americans
no longer could take for granted the healthfulness of their milk,
because radioactive fallout from nuclear testing had contami-

nated dairy pastures. Across the country, people had begun campaigns to save "open space" from the sprawl of suburbia. The smog over California's exploding cities had become a symbol of the perils of progress, and federal health officials had organized a national conference on the hazards of air pollution. Thousands of homeowners in new subdivisions had watched in shock as detergent foam came out of their kitchen faucets. As Galbraith suggested, countless families also had come face-to-face with pollution while trying to enjoy new opportunities for outdoor recreation.[7]

Sputnik also gave bite to Galbraith's words. Even before the Soviet satellite orbited the earth in 1957, a handful of social critics had begun to question the fruits of abundance, and the stunning Soviet success turned those lonely voices into a resounding chorus of self-doubt. Had the United States become too comfortable? The question helped to provoke a spirited end-of-the-decade debate about the nation's mission. The Rockefeller Brothers Fund commissioned a series of studies of "the problems and opportunities confronting American democracy," and the studies appeared with great fanfare under the title *Prospect for America*. In 1960, Dwight D. Eisenhower appointed a presidential commission on national goals. The editors of *Life* and *The New York Times* asked Americans to reflect on "the national purpose."[8]

Much of the debate focused on the Schlesinger/Galbraith argument about the imbalance between private wealth and public poverty. In a series of articles early in 1960, *The New York Times* reported that many officials in Washington had concluded that "the most important continuing issue of American policy and politics over the next decade will be the issue of public spending—what share of America's total resources should be devoted to public as distinct from private purposes." Though Americans enjoyed more consumer goods than any people in the history of the world, the newspaper summarized the liberal side of the argument, that the public sector of society was impoverished: "Education is underfinanced. Streams are polluted. There remains a shortage of hospital beds. Slums proliferate, and there is a gap in middle-income housing. We could use more and better parks, streets, detention facilities, water supply. The very quality of American life is suffering from these lacks—much more than from any lack of purely private goods and services."[9]

As *The New York Times* summary suggests, the problem of pollution was cited again and again by the advocates of a more expansive public sphere. The problem of suburban sprawl also figured often in "the great debate." In the *Life* series on the national purpose, two of the ten contributors wrote about the deteriorating environment. The political scientist Clinton Rossiter argued that the private sector was not equipped to deal with "the blight of our cities, the shortage of water and power, the disappearance of open space, the inadequacy of education, the need for recreational facilities, the high incidence of crime and delinquency, the crowding of the roads, the decay of the railroads, the ugliness of the sullied landscape, the pollution of the very air we breathe." Adlai Stevenson agreed. Though the nation's manufacturers were providing cars and refrigerators in abundance, the booming private economy could not protect against "the sprawl of subdivisions which is gradually depriving us of either civilized urban living or uncluttered rural space. It does not guarantee America's children the teachers or the schools which should be their birthright. It does nothing to end the shame of racial discrimination. It does not counter the exorbitant cost of health, nor conserve the nation's precious reserves of land and water and wilderness. The contrast between private opulence and public squalor on most of our panorama is now too obvious to be denied."[10]

In the report of the presidential commission on national goals, the urbanist and housing advocate Catherine Bauer Wurster gave considerable attention to the problems of "vanishing open space and spreading pollution." Wurster also offered a shrewd psychological explanation for the reluctance of taxpayers to accept a rise in community spending. Because the average citizen often had no chance to participate directly in the large-scale decisions that shaped the public environment, she argued, the public world was less satisfying than the private sphere. "Since he has more sense of personal power and choice in the consumer goods market, he tends to spend more money on . . . automobiles than on public services, and is likely to vote down higher taxes even though a park, or less smog, might give him more personal pleasure than a second TV set."[11]

The bestselling social critic Vance Packard made similar arguments about pollution, sprawl, and national purpose in *The Waste Makers*. Packard already had questioned the consumerism of the 1950s in *The Hidden Persuaders* and *The Status Seekers*, and *The Waste Makers* extended the critique. In addition to the insights of a few conservationists, Packard drew on the arguments of both Schlesinger and Galbraith. As the nation entered a new decade, Packard wrote, the great unmet challenges all involved the provision of public goods. "A person can't go down to the store and order a new park," he explained. "A park requires unified effort, and that gets you into voting and public spending and maybe soak-the-rich taxes." But the effort was essential. The consumption of ever-greater quantities of "deodorants, hula hoops, juke boxes, padded bras, dual mufflers, horror comics, or electric rotisseries" could not ensure national greatness. Instead, Americans needed to improve the quality of the environment, to stop the spread of pollution and "the growing sleaziness, dirtiness, and chaos of the nation's great exploding metropolitan areas."[12]

Though the national-purpose debate was bipartisan—the conservative columnist Walter Lippmann wrote often about the need to give a higher priority to public goods—the Democrats seized the issue of the deteriorating quality of the environment. When *Life* asked both presidential candidates in 1960 to define the national purpose, only John F. Kennedy mentioned environmental problems. "The good life falls short as an indicator of national purpose unless it goes hand in hand with the good society," Kennedy wrote. "Even in material terms, prosperity is not enough when there is no equal opportunity to share in it; when economic progress means overcrowded cities, abandoned farms, technological unemployment, polluted air and water, and littered parks and countrysides; when those too young to earn are denied their chance to learn; when those no longer earning live out their lives in lonely degradation."[13]

In the White House, Kennedy's top domestic priority was a growth-boosting tax cut. But he took a few important steps to address the issue of environmental quality. He supported a new federal program to assist local and state governments in acquiring open space, and he endorsed a measure to preserve wilderness. In 1962, he held a White House Conference on Conservation, the first since Franklin D. Roosevelt's presidency. After the publication of Rachel Carson's *Silent Spring*, Kennedy instructed his science advisers to report on the use of pesticides. He also appointed an activist secretary of the interior, Stewart Udall, who energetically promoted the cause of environmental protection.[14]

Like Kennedy, Udall borrowed from Schlesinger and Galbraith. He argued again and again that "the new conservation" was a vital effort to improve "the quality of life." He also argued that the nation's deteriorating environment was a sign of "the disorder of our postwar priorities." In *The Quiet Crisis*—a 1963 call to action—he began by pointing out the stark contrast between the economic and environmental trends of the postwar decades. "America today stands poised on a pinnacle of wealth and power," he wrote, "yet we live in a land of vanishing beauty, of increasing ugliness, of shrinking open space, and of an overall environment that is diminished daily by pollution and noise and blight."[15]

The growing Democratic interest in the environment went

beyond the Kennedy administration. By 1961, the California chapter of Americans for Democratic Action had deemphasized the old economic issues of unemployment and workmen's compensation; instead, the group was focusing on "quality of life" issues, including the preservation of open space and the planning of metropolitan growth. In the early 1960s, a new breed of policy entrepreneurs in Congress sought to establish national reputations by championing consumer and environmental legislation, and Senator Edmund Muskie of Maine soon earned the nickname "Mr. Pollution Control."[16]

After Kennedy's assassination, Lyndon B. Johnson resolved to finish the unfinished environmental business of the Kennedy administration. But he hoped to do more. Johnson had a more personal stake in the issue than Kennedy. His wife had a keen interest in nature. In the field of conservation—as in so many areas of policy—Johnson sought to surpass the achievements of Franklin D. Roosevelt. Like his mentor, Johnson wanted to go down in history as a great conservation president.[17]

The decision to give a higher priority to environmental protection made perfect sense to Johnson's domestic advisers. Early in Johnson's presidency, they proposed "the Great Society" as the overarching theme that would give historic weight to the 1964 campaign, and the roots of their vision lay in the Schlesinger/Galbraith call for a qualitative liberalism. The historian Eric Goldman and the speechwriter Richard Goodwin especially found inspiration in the arguments of the late 1950s about the challenge of abundance.[18]

As the president's house intellectual, Goldman asked Galbraith to serve as "the quality of American life" adviser to the Johnson brain trust. He had written admiringly of Galbraith's contribution to the debate over national purpose in 1960, and he spoke several times in the next few years about the proper goals of a "post-affluent" society. "Material concerns were still pressing—particularly the disgraceful and dangerous economic position of the Negro—but the nation had reached a general affluence which permitted it to give attention not only to the quantity but to the quality of American living," he argued in 1964. The next generation of Americans at last could escape the burdens of the "dull society," the "overmaterial society," and the "ugly society."[19]

Goodwin recognized that a part of the Johnson agenda needed to do what the New Deal had not done to guarantee a modicum of comfort and security for all Americans. But he concluded that the great opportunity for going beyond the old liberalism lay in acknowledging "that private income, no matter how widely distributed, was only a foundation; that private affluence, no matter how widely distributed, could not remedy many of the public conditions that diminished the possibilities of American life." For Goodwin, that meant tackling the issues of pollution, suburban sprawl, and environmental health.[20]

In a speech written by Goodwin, President Johnson spoke to those issues in May 1964. The speech was the president's first attempt to define the Great Society, and he addressed only a few points. The Great Society required the abolition of poverty and racial injustice, he argued, "but that is just the beginning." The Great Society would spark the imagination, offer stimulating forms of leisure, and provide the satisfactions of true community. "It is a place where man can renew contact with nature," the president continued. "It is a place where men are more concerned with the quality of their goals than the quantity of their goods." Perhaps because the occasion for the speech was a college graduation, the president spoke passionately about the need to ensure that "every child can find knowledge to enrich his mind and enlarge his talents." But the rest of the speech focused on the problems of the metropolis and the countryside. The president decried the social and environmental costs of suburban growth, including the loss of open space. He also called for action to protect the natural splendor of the nation. "We have always prided ourselves on being not only America the strong and America the free, but America the beautiful," he explained. "Today that beauty is in danger. The water we drink, the food we eat, the very air that we breathe, are threatened with pollution. Our parks are overcrowded, our seashores overburdened. Green fields and dense forests are disappearing."[21]

The speech was not merely talk. Johnson made the environment a major focus of the Great Society. Though scholars have paid much more attention to the civil-rights acts, the War on Poverty, and the expansion of health and education programs, Johnson himself considered the environmental agenda no less important. As historian Robert Dallek concludes, "he had no real priority" among the Great Society initiatives—"he wanted them all." Johnson aggressively used the power of the presidency to draw public attention to environmental problems. He convened a White House Conference on Natural Beauty, and he asked the President's Science Advisory Committee to report on ways to restore the quality of the environment. He devoted several major addresses to his environmental proposals. The result was a torrent of legislation: Johnson signed almost 300 conservation and beautification measures. The most important bills addressed the problems of air and water pollution, solid-waste disposal, wilderness preservation, and endangered species. The Johnson initiatives also created national lakeshores and seashores, increased the number of national parks, and provided funds to state governments for land and water conservation.[22]

To be sure, the legislation of the mid-1960s was not enough to solve the most serious environmental problems. In the fight against pollution, the truly landmark acts did not come until the early 1970s. But the achievements of the Great Society were critical in the evolution of the environmental movement. Before the 1960s, the problem of pollution was not a principal concern of the federal government. In 1960—just before leaving office— President Eisenhower vetoed a clean-water act with a blunt declaration that water pollution was "a uniquely local blight." John F. Kennedy and Lyndon B. Johnson both rejected that view, and the legislation of the mid-1960s firmly established the principle of federal responsibility for the quality of the nation's air and water. That responsibility was institutionalized in two new agencies with the ability to research and publicize environmental problems. The Federal Water Pollution Control Administration and the National Air Pollution Control Administration both helped to strengthen the demand for tougher legislation to protect the environment. The new bureaucracies were agenda setters.[23]

Scientists

When *Time* published a special issue on the environment before Earth Day, the magazine put biologist Barry Commoner on the cover. The magazine could have chosen a number of people to symbolize the environmental movement. The decision to use Commoner acknowledged the critical role of scientists in the surge of concern about environmental degradation. Though members of many professions contributed to the new movement, scientists were especially active.[24]

For some scientists, the cause largely was pedagogical. They introduced environmental issues to the classroom, and their courses inspired a generation of eco-activists. Other scientists put environmental issues on the public agenda by speaking at community meetings, testifying at hearings, writing essays for popular periodicals, and organizing groups to seek action. A few scientists became famous author/activists. Paul Ehrlich—author of *The Population Bomb* and founder of Zero Population Growth—even became a frequent guest on *The Tonight Show*.[25]

The environmental activism of scientists was both surprising and predictable. Unlike landscape architects or civil engineers or doctors, scientists had no commitment to the ideal of service. Just the opposite: They prided themselves on their detachment. As *The New York Times* argued in a profile of Ehrlich, "scientists as a group have long disdained direct political action and propagandizing, feeling it compromised their objectivity." Yet almost every environmental problem had a scientific component. Once scientists decided to speak publicly, they often addressed what many called "the environmental crisis," not just one or two issues.[26]

Commoner did more than anyone to rally scientists to the cause. He argued repeatedly that scientists had a duty to provide citizens with the scientific knowledge needed to make informed decisions about environmental issues. He helped to establish influential institutions dedicated to the public-information mission. His 1966 book *Science and Survival* became a classic—a call for "a new conservation movement" that would focus on preserving "life itself," not just forests or soils or places of sublime beauty.[27]

Commoner intended to be an activist long before the environment became an issue. As a graduate student in the 1930s, he was active in the American Association of Scientific Workers, a leftist group keen to ensure that science served the public good. That organization focused on social justice, not the environment. But Commoner began to be concerned after World War II about the unintended environmental consequences of technological development. The fallout issue drove the danger home. The testing of atomic weapons in the deserts of the Southwest caused radioactive rain to fall over a vast region. Because radiation settled on dairy pastures, milk became contaminated. Yet the tests continued without a thorough understanding of the environmental consequences—and with little discussion of the wisdom of aboveground testing. To Commoner, that was appalling.[28]

At first, Commoner pressed the American Association for

the Advancement of Science to act. In 1956 and again in 1960, he chaired AAAS committees that called for scientists to take part in public debate about the potentially destructive effects of science. Both committees argued that the vastly greater control over nature afforded by modern science brought unprecedented risks as well as wondrous opportunities. "In some situations our enhanced ability to control nature has gone awry and threatens serious trouble," the 1956 committee concluded. To ensure that science served society, scientists no longer could remain mute. They had to concern themselves with "social action." The 1960 committee recommended that the AAAS make public information a priority.[29]

The AAAS did not rise to the challenge, but Commoner pressed on. In 1958, he joined a group of St. Louis women to form a grassroots organization to draw attention to fallout. The Greater St. Louis Citizens' Committee on Nuclear Information soon earned a national reputation for effective activism. In addition to organizing local events, the committee invited parents to send baby teeth to St. Louis to be tested for radioactivity, and the response was overwhelming. The committee also published a newsletter, *Nuclear Information*, that evolved into the first magazine devoted solely to environmental issues: *Environment*.[30]

With several veterans of the AAAS committees, Commoner formed a national organization, the Scientists' Institute for Public Information, in 1963. "Scientists today," he explained, "are the first to live with the knowledge that our work, our ideas, and our daily activities impinge with a frightening immediacy on national politics, on international conflicts, on the planet's fate as a human habitation." Affiliate organizations soon formed in several cities, and observers began to speak about a public-information "movement" among scientists.[31]

The new movement helped to make activists of many graduate students. At Rockefeller University in New York, chemist Glenn Paulson heard about the local committee from several professors, and he soon was devoting much of his time to public science. Though his dissertation was about pesticides, he became an expert on several other environmental issues, from air pollution to nuclear power. In the late 1960s, he talked to PTA groups, testified at City Hall, and spoke with journalists. He co-authored a well-publicized report on the carbon monoxide hazard of a proposed Manhattan expressway. He led a campaign to reduce lead poisoning among city children. He also worked with the Oil, Chemical and Atomic Workers Union to publicize both occupational and environmental threats to health. In 1970, he helped to organize Earth Day events.[32]

Though a few scientists had no hesitation about speaking publicly, many only reluctantly became activists. Some were goaded to action by the fallout issue. Many more began to question the ideal of detachment after the publication of Rachel Carson's *Silent Spring* in 1962.

With a clarity no one had managed before, Carson warned that the human power to alter nature had become profoundly dangerous:

> During the past quarter century this power has not only increased to one of disturbing magnitude but it has changed in character. The most alarming of all man's assaults upon the environment is the contamination of air, earth, rivers, and sea with dangerous and even lethal materials. This pollution is for the most part irrecoverable; the chain of evil it initiates not only in the world that must support life but in living tissues is for the most part irreversible. In this now universal contamination of the environment, chemicals are the sinister and little-recognized partners of radiation in changing the very nature of the world—the very nature of its life. Strontium 90, released through nuclear explosions into the air, lodges in soil, enters into the grass or corn or wheat grown there, and in time takes up its abode in the bones of a human being, to remain until his

death. Similarly, chemicals sprayed on croplands or forests or gardens lie long in the soil, entering into living organisms, passing from one to another in a chain of poisoning and death. Or they pass mysteriously by underground streams until they emerge and, through the alchemy of air and sunlight, combine into new forms that kill vegetation, sicken cattle, and work unknown harm on those who drink from once pure wells. As Albert Schweitzer once said, "Man can hardly even recognize the devils of his own creation."

Silent Spring became both a bestseller and a subject of intense controversy.[33]

For life scientists, the debate over Carson's work was both technical and moral. Was she right? If she was, what responsibility did biologists have to help avoid the threats she made so vivid?

Silent Spring was especially troubling to members of the Ecological Society of America. Though the society was established in 1915, ecology still was a young discipline. The first celebrated textbook in the field only appeared in 1953, and the first academic departments of ecology were established in the mid-1950s. What kind of enterprise was ecology going to be? Carson's book made a powerful case that citizens needed to understand ecology, but would ecologists assume roles as educators of the public? In 1963, the ESA created a public affairs committee. The society's ecology study committee—charged with assessing the future of the discipline—also made "public welfare and policy" a major focus of its 1965 report.[34]

"The question of Society participation in public affairs has been a contentious issue for years," the study committee wrote. "There are members of the Society who still doubt the wisdom or necessity of becoming involved in controversial issues, but there are clearly areas of public interest which ecologists can no longer avoid, either as individuals or as a Society." The human impact on ecosystems had increased tremendously, and the public needed to understand that impact. "Ecologists have a definite obligation to make their views known when they can provide information which might avert environmental disaster," the committee argued. "While members of the Society have testified as individuals, ecologists have never collectively brought their influence to bear on the range of environmental problems that are properly within their area of competence. It is the feeling of the Ecology Study Committee that they should and must . . . Rachel Carson's book *Silent Spring* created a tide of opinion which will never again allow professional ecologists to remain comfortably aloof from public responsibility."[35]

The committee acknowledged that spelling out the details of that responsibility would not be easy. The tax code barred lobbying by tax-exempt nonprofit organizations, so the society could only offer counsel, not organize campaigns to pass legislation. On some important issues, the society could not speak with one voice. Though most academic ecologists were concerned that pesticides might reduce biological diversity, the committee noted, many applied ecologists did not share that concern. ESA members also might disagree about the limits of ecological expertise. The profit motive had become a driving force in many ecosystems, the committee argued, but the ESA might not be able or willing to offer an ecological assessment of capitalism. Still, the committee concluded, the society needed "to furnish the best possible data and to contribute the most responsible, scientific judgment that is possible" on relevant issues of public import.[36]

The debate about the social obligation of ecologists went beyond the in-house publications of the ESA. In 1964, for example, the journal *BioScience* devoted a special issue to the future of ecology, and the issue editors made clear that they were prompted by concern about the environmental impact of modern technologies. For the first time, they argued, we faced the possibility that we could contaminate the environment "beyond its capacity to support life." They cited the hazards of fallout and DDT, and they illustrated the issue with a series of photographs that collectively formed an essay on environmental degradation. Almost all of the contributors called for ecologists to become more involved in public life. But they offered different assessments of what specifically ecologists needed to do. Eugene Odum made a boosterish argument that ecology should be a basic tool of ecosystem "management." Paul Sears, in contrast, argued that ecology was "a subversive science," a phrase that became a rallying cry for many ecologists later in the decade. "By its very nature, ecology offers a continuing critique of man's operations within the ecosystem," Sears wrote. As he understood the field, ecology cast doubt on "the current glib emphasis on economic 'growth' as the solution of all ills." The editors did not try to resolve the disagreements. But they argued that ecologists had "a responsibility, a challenge, an obligation to revised and/or extended thinking." By 1970, many ecologists had accepted that argument.[37]

Paul Ehrlich ultimately became the most famous activist to draw inspiration from *Silent Spring*. He began to worry about pesticides long before Carson's work appeared: As a teenager, he feared that pesticides were killing butterflies, his great passion. When he was a graduate student in the late 1950s, he joined the Chicago Society for Exterminating Exterminators, a group formed to protest the U.S. Department of Agriculture's campaign to eradicate the fire ant. But he did not speak publicly about the environment until 1965. By then he had become a tenured professor at Stanford. He also had come to see the pesticide issue as part of a broader challenge. Humans had become vastly more adept at manipulating the environment, and that ability had led to vastly greater human numbers. Yet meeting the needs and wants of an exploding population—more food, more power, more water, more living space—threatened environmental catastrophe.[38]

The ever-increasing scale of human endeavor imposed new burdens on scientists, Ehrlich concluded. Scientific research no longer was academic. Scientists needed to "consider the consequences of their activities." How would their results be used? But the responsibility of scientists went beyond their own work. "We *must* come out of our ivory towers and take an active part in the political life of our society," Ehrlich argued. "Following Rachel Carson's lead we must fight abuses wherever they occur."[39]

Once freed from the shackles of scientific dispassion, Ehrlich quickly developed a prophetic voice. His talks in San Francisco attracted raves. After hearing Ehrlich speak, Sierra Club executive director David Brower invited him to write a short book about the population issue. Ehrlich took just three feverish weeks to produce *The Population Bomb*, which appeared as a paperback original in May 1968. By Earth Day, Ehrlich's tract had sold almost a million copies.[40]

The tone of the book was unlike anything Ehrlich had written before. If we failed to meet the challenge of exploding population, he wrote, "mankind will breed itself into oblivion." Hundreds of millions of people would starve. The quality of life of the survivors would be reduced drastically, because population growth was eroding the world's most fertile soils, poisoning the water and the air, destroying the habitats of countless species, and even changing the climate. Because the trends all pointed toward self-destruction, every nation needed to control population—by voluntary means if possible, but otherwise by compulsion. People also needed to act immediately "to reverse the deterioration of the environment before population pressure permanently ruins our planet." No task was more urgent. "Somehow we've got to change from a growth-oriented, exploitative system to one focused on stability and conservation," Ehrlich concluded. "Our entire system of orienting to nature must undergo a revolution."[41]

Critics called Ehrlich an alarmist, and Ehrlich did not

shrink from the charge. "I *am* an alarmist," he told *Playboy*, "because I'm very goddamned alarmed. I believe we're facing the *brink* because of population pressures." Though some scientists were appalled by Ehrlich's "unscientific" rhetoric, many others were inspired. By the summer of 1969, a year after *The Population Bomb* was published, journalists were reporting on "the new Jeremiahs," the growing number of scientists who were warning of environmental catastrophe.[42]

Like grassroots activists, most scientists had to educate themselves about environmental issues. The AAAS contributed to that process of self-education. Though the association did not directly support activism, the AAAS encouraged members to learn more about the most pressing problems.

The association's 1966 meeting explored "How Man Has Changed His Planet." Because the annual meetings rarely had themes, the decision to focus on the environment underscored the importance of the subject. (The last AAAS conference with a theme was 1948, when the meeting celebrated the association's centennial.) "The Historic Roots of Our Ecological Crisis" was the subject of one keynote address. In a second keynote, insurance executive Thomas Malone called for scientists to take the lead in warning the nation's leaders about the possible consequences of global climate change. "The point is that there is still time for reflective thought, for setting objectives, for weighing alternative courses of action—in short, to act responsibly," he concluded. One plenary interdisciplinary symposium focused on pollution, and a series of three sessions explored population growth. Hundreds of specialized sessions addressed environmental issues as well. Many conference participants argued that scientists had to become activists.[43]

In the late 1960s, the AAAS journal *Science* effectively became a continuing education course in environmental studies. A cross between a news magazine and a scholarly publication, *Science* had everything from editorials to research reports. Because the environment was relevant to so many scientific disciplines, almost every issue addressed the subject in some form.

For some scientists, *Science* even became the road to Damascus. Geneticist Wes Jackson exemplifies the journal's influence. In 1967, keen to make his introductory biology class more relevant, he began to clip the journal's environmental material. The more he clipped, the more concerned he became about the future. He soon remade the bio course into an "ain't it awful?" survey of environmental problems. He pressed his college administration to make "survival studies" a focus of the curriculum. In 1970, he turned his course materials into a pioneering environmental reader: In the first edition of his *Man and the Environment*, roughly half of the readings came from *Science*. He also helped to organize the college's Earth Day events, and he began to speak prophetically about the environmental crisis. He was one of many.[44]

Middle-Class Women

The environmental activism of middle-class women did not begin in 1960. In the Progressive Era, women actively supported the conservation movement. They also lobbied for smokeless skies, clean water, pure food, and urban parks, and they often justified their efforts as "municipal housekeeping." Women continued to press for environmental protection in the decades after World War I. For several reasons, however, the number of women active in the environmental cause increased dramatically in the late 1950s and 1960s. In some cases, the activists worked through old conservation or women's organizations. More often, women formed ad hoc groups to stop pollution, save open spaces, or protect wildlife. The activism of women was crucial in making the environment an issue in communities across the nation.[45]

The League of Women Voters played a vital role in the battle against water pollution. One of the first popular books about the issue—Donald Carr's *Death of the Sweet Waters*—was dedicated to the league's members. The national leadership of the league made water a focus for education and activism in 1956, and many local chapters soon launched clean-water campaigns. To win support for a sewage-treatment plant in Idaho Falls, Idaho, league members put flyers about polluted drinking water in every restaurant menu in town, convinced milkmen to distribute leaflets to every milk box, painted slogans on sidewalks, and erected road signs to direct people to the Snake River sewage outlet: "It's a shocker!" By 1960, the league had become a major player in the debate about the federal responsibility for water quality, and league members continued to lobby for government action throughout the 1960s. Their effectiveness was especially evident at the end of the decade, when the league organized a coalition of almost forty labor, municipal, and conservation groups to wage the Citizens Crusade for Clean Water.[46]

Activist women often became identified with the rivers and lakes they sought to save. In the mid-1960s, Marion Stoddart of Massachusetts earned the epithet "Mother Nashua" after forming a group to save one of the nation's most polluted rivers: The Nashua River Clean-up Committee played a key role in the passage of the Massachusetts Clean Water Act in 1966. The campaign of Verna Mize to stop a mining company from polluting Lake Superior became a national symbol of effective citizen action. In one account of her campaign, the author even imagined the lake offering Mize words of thanks.[47]

In many cities, women worked aggressively to stop air pollution. New Yorker Hazel Henderson organized a group called Citizens for Clean Air by passing out leaflets to mothers during her daily walks in the park with her infant daughter. The group soon had more than 20,000 members; roughly 75 percent were women. Despite the obstacles to success, Henderson wrote in a

1966 article in *Parents' Magazine*, the work was satisfying for a young mother. "You are exercising the responsibilities of citizenship, and you are setting an example to your children, at the same time that you are working for their health and welfare," she explained. "Best of all, you are learning firsthand about one of the most exciting frontiers of our growing knowledge and technology—how to manage our natural heritage so that it can support the needs of our increasing population, and at the same time remain orderly and beautiful, a fitting and joyous setting for future generations."[48]

Women also organized in the 1960s to address new forms of pollution. On November 1, 1961, approximately 50,000 "concerned housewives" went on strike to protest the hazards of the arms race. Instead of cooking and cleaning, the women lobbied elected officials, picketed nuclear installations, and marched in the streets. In all, the founders of Women Strike for Peace organized events in sixty cities, including New York, Philadelphia, Baltimore, Washington, Cleveland, Cincinnati, Detroit, St. Louis, Denver, San Francisco, and Los Angeles. Many of the marchers pushed baby carriages or held photographs of children. Though a number of the women called for a ban on nuclear weapons and a halt to the arms race, the immediate goal was to stop atmospheric weapons testing, since radioactive fallout from nuclear tests posed a threat to life. "This movement was inspired and motivated by mothers' love for children," one Women Strike for Peace member explained. "When they were putting their breakfast on the table, they saw not only the Wheaties and milk, but they also saw strontium 90 and iodine 131." In the months after the strike, the membership of Women Strike for Peace grew rapidly, as women rallied to the cause: "Pure Milk," they demanded, "Not Poison."[49]

Like nuclear fallout, the wanton use of pesticides inspired women to act. Women's organizations helped to make Rachel Carson's *Silent Spring* both a bestseller and a political force.

Though Carson took pains not to appeal solely to women—she used a variety of arguments and rhetorical strategies—she recognized that women were likely to be quicker to share her concerns. "I believe it is important for women to realize that the world of today threatens to destroy much of that beauty that has immense power to bring us a healing release from tension," she argued in a speech to Theta Sigma Phi, a national sorority of women journalists. "Women have a greater intuitive understanding of such things. They want for their children not only physical health but mental and spiritual health as well. I bring these things to your attention because I think your awareness of them will help, whether you are practicing journalists, or teachers, or librarians, or housewives and mothers." Carson cultivated a network of women supporters—and women eagerly championed her work. They used *Silent Spring* as a basis for educational pamphlets, wrote letters to the editor, and lobbied politicians. The most active were the American Association of University Women, the National Council of Women, the Garden Club of America, and the General Federation of Women's Clubs. Carson also had support from members of the League of Women Voters and from women in wildlife conservation and animal-rights groups.[50]

In many communities, women also led campaigns to preserve open space. Often, the activists sought to save undeveloped woods or fields where children played. But some of the open-space campaigns were more ambitious. In California, a trio of Berkeley faculty wives—including Catherine Kerr, the wife of the university's president—organized the Save San Francisco Bay Association in the early 1960s. The group soon helped to secure passage of one of the first state laws regulating land use. Because the open-space campaigns often succeeded, journalists in the mid-1960s began to point to the activism of women as a model for a new kind of conservation. A short guide to open-space preservation published in 1964 began with the story of one woman's successful campaign to preserve a marsh from development. "The war Ruth Rusch has been waging in her little corner of suburbia contains immense significance for all of us," the author wrote. "For it shows not only that we can win the fight to save our landscape from the despoilers but also specifically how to go about it."[51]

The list could go on and on. Lady Bird Johnson worked as First Lady to protect and restore "natural beauty," and her efforts led to the Highway Beautification Act in 1965. After the Santa Barbara oil spill in 1969, women were the driving force behind Get Oil Out, a grassroots group that sought to end offshore drilling. A Seattle housewife collected over 250,000 signatures on a petition to halt the development of the supersonic transport. From New York to California, activist women campaigned to stop construction of power plants in scenic areas. No matter what the issue, environmentalism at the grass roots depended on a volunteer corps of women.[52]

The women active in the environmental movement were overwhelmingly white. More often than not, they were in their thirties and forties, they lived in metropolitan areas or college towns, and they were well educated. Most were married to white-collar or professional men, and most had children. At a time when the percentage of married women working outside the home was rising sharply, the women activists usually described themselves as housewives.

Though women often were attracted to the environmental cause for the same reasons as men, the predominance of women at the grass roots was very much a function of gender expectations. As their children grew more independent, many housewives sought new ways to use their talents, and the environmental cause seemed to some to be more challenging and important than traditional volunteer work. For many other women, the decision to become active came in response to an environmental threat that hit home. That was especially true in the fast-growing suburbs.

The residents of postwar suburbs lived in the most rapidly changing environment in the nation. Every year, a territory roughly the size of Rhode Island was bulldozed for metropolitan development. Forests, marshes, creeks, hills, cornfields, and orchards all were destroyed to build subdivisions. Though some of the environmental consequences of suburban development were invisible to untrained observers, others were obvious. Again and again, the destruction of nearby open spaces robbed children of beloved places to play. The suburbs also were a kind of sanitation frontier. Beyond the range of municipal sewer systems, the residents of postwar subdivisions often depended on septic tanks for waste disposal, and widespread septic-tank failures in the 1950s and 1960s caused a host of health and environmental problems.[53]

Because the suburbs were domestic places—and women traditionally were caretakers of the domestic—threats to environmental quality in suburbia were threats to "the woman's sphere." The stakes were the sanctity of the home and the well-being of the family. For many middle-class women, the environmental cause seemed a natural extension of their concerns as housewives and mothers.[54]

In the early 1960s, the major women's magazines all published pieces about water pollution, and the articles highlighted the threat to domestic life. *Redbook* offered a primer on what readers needed to know "to protect your family," while *American Home* grabbed attention by describing water-related health problems in children. *Good Housekeeping* extolled the antipollution efforts of the League of Women Voters in traditional terms. "Here is where intelligent and aroused women can do the most important job," the magazine concluded. "The clean-up of our rivers to safeguard our precious water supply—this is the biggest housekeeping chore facing the nation today."[55]

Even in 1970—after the publication of Betty Friedan's *The Feminine Mystique*, after the formation of the National Organization for Women, after the first women's liberation protests—

women in environmental groups often appealed directly to housewives and mothers. Betty Ann Ottinger used traditional arguments to make the case for environmentalism in *What Every Woman Should Know—and Do—About Pollution: A Guide to Good Global Housekeeping.* The environmental cause "is one that the American woman can really sink her teeth into," she argued. As housewives, women determined "how more than two-thirds of our consumer dollars are spent. This in itself is a major weapon which is made even more potent by the influence we exert over the decision as to how most of the remaining dollars are allocated." As mothers, women shaped "the attitudes and lifestyles of the coming generation which will play the key role in choosing whether we follow the road to environmental sanity or strangle in the products of our own affluence." Eventually, Ottinger hoped, women would work to protect the environment as politicians and business leaders. (Ottinger was the wife of U.S. Representative Richard Ottinger, a liberal Democrat from New York.) But Ottinger concluded that the immediate opportunity for women to make a difference was at home. In the domestic sphere—unlike the world of politics and business—women did not have to wait for men to lead the way.[56]

Though often attracted to the environmental cause as an extension of their traditional roles as housewives and mothers, many women found the work liberating. Sylvia Troy is a good example. Until her late thirties, Troy was content to be the wife of a doctor. She had little interest in politics. But in 1960 she went to a dinner meeting of the Indiana Save the Dunes Council, and she was impressed by the spirit of the group: "They were all nature lovers—non-political, non-activist, not organizers, not joiners, not cause-oriented." She became active in the organization, and she soon realized that she had the skills to be a leader. She could network, lobby, recruit, motivate, and negotiate. When the group's first president stepped down, Troy was chosen to succeed her. She then served as president for more than a decade. "The

Save the Dunes Council experience changed me dramatically," she recalled. "It became a vehicle for my personal growth. I learned a lot about my own capabilities, my own strengths, and my own assertiveness in behalf of a cause."[57]

Even for women who did not become leaders of organizations, environmental activism often was consciousness raising. In the group Women Strike for Peace, Amy Swerdlow concludes, "thousands of women who had identified themselves only as housewives found to their surprise that they could do serious research, write convincing flyers and pamphlets, speak eloquently in public, plan effective political strategies, organize successful long-range campaigns, and challenge male political leaders . . . to whom they had previously deferred." The result was a new sense of self-worth, a new willingness to take risks, even a new understanding of the ways women were limited by traditional gender roles.[58]

Again and again, women in environmental organizations struggled against the condescension of men in positions of power. When a group of California housewives met with officials in 1966 to argue against the construction of a highway, a project engineer dismissed a member of their group with a blunt put-down: "Get back in your kitchen, lady, and let me build my road!" The comment only intensified the desire of one of the women to fight on. Because many men considered women irrational, women often found that speaking at a public forum was a trying test. Yet many responded to the challenge with a new resolve. As air-pollution activist Michelle Madoff explained, "I didn't want to go and testify and be branded as another idiot housewife—hysterical Squirrel Hill housewife in tennis shoes, as we're referred to—you know, uninformed, emotional."[59]

The environmental movement also helped women to find vocations beyond the home. For some women, environmental activism led to elected office. Michelle Madoff drew on her experience as a founder of Pittsburgh's Group Against Smog and Pollution to win election to the city council. The environmental study groups of the League of Women Voters were particularly good jumping-off places for careers in politics. Other activists moved from volunteer work to paid employment. Many became staff members of environmental groups or consultants to government agencies. After a decade of volunteer work with the Sierra Club in California, Claire Dedrick was appointed the state's secretary of resources in 1975. Hazel Henderson's struggle to address the air-pollution issue in New York laid the foundation for a pioneering career in the field of environmental economics.[60]

In different ways, then, the environmental movement benefited from the gender constraints of the postwar decades. For some college-educated housewives, environmental activism resolved a tension between traditional expectations and unfulfilled ambitions. Because they acted to protect the home and the family, they could enter the public sphere—they could be more than "just" housewives—without rejecting the claims of domesticity. For other women, environmental activism was the first step toward a new sense of mission. As they became more involved, they became more confident of their abilities and more determined to change the world.

The Young

At the end of the 1960s, journalists began to report that concern about the environmental crisis was exploding on college campuses. "American youth has found a new supercause," the Associated Press reported in November 1969. "So far, the young ecologists are not a full-fledged movement. They are unorganized, largely unknown." That soon would change.[61]

The environmentalism of the young owed much to the postwar economic boom. For the first time in American history, millions of children grew up in settings designed to bring people into harmony with nature. In the new suburbs, kids often could play in forests and fields just beyond the edge of development. The newly affluent families of the 1950s often vacationed outdoors: Hunting, fishing, and camping became more popular after 1945. Then an unprecedented number of the baby boomers went to college, to spend four years walking across tree-lined quadrangles.[62]

The environmentalism of the young also owed much to the Bomb. Many baby-boom children had nightmares about atomic war. Would humanity survive? The mounting evidence of environmental degradation in the 1960s provoked similar anxieties about "survival," a word that appeared again and again in environmentalist discourse. In 1969, when Joyce Maynard read Paul Ehrlich's shocking bestseller, *The Population Bomb*, she immediately felt the kind of fear she had felt during the Cuban missile crisis: "Not personal, individual fear but end-of-the-world fear, that by the time we were our parents' age we would be sardine-packed and tethered to our gas masks in a skyless cloud of smog." Maynard's response was common. In a 1969 discussion of the generation gap, Margaret Mead argued that growing up in the shadow of the Bomb made the young more likely to understand the environmental crisis. "They have never known a time when war did not threaten annihilation," Mead wrote. "When they are given the facts, they can understand immediately that continued pollution of the air and water and soil will soon make the planet uninhabitable and that it will be impossible to feed an indefinitely expanding world population."[63]

Though the environmental movement drew young people from all parts of the ideological spectrum, the new cause appealed especially to critics of the nation's cultural and political institutions. For many rebels against the soul-deadening artificiality of consumer culture, nature became a source of authentic values. For many members of the New Left, the degradation of the environment became a powerful symbol of the exploitive character of capitalism. The horrors of Vietnam also led many people to question "the war against nature." By 1970, the effort to protect the environment seemed to many activists to be part of a larger movement to affirm Life.[64]

The countercultural roots of environmentalism went deepest. In the late 1950s, the Beat writers began to tout the open spaces of nature as a kind of antidote to the poisonous conformity of suburbia. In Jack Kerouac's 1958 novel *The Dharma Bums*, the narrator joins the fictionalized Gary Snyder and Allen Ginsberg on a quest for truth in the mountains of California. At one point, the Snyder character, Japhy Ryder, dreams out loud about a new generation refusing to stay "imprisoned in a system of work, produce, consume, work, produce, consume." "I see a vision of a great rucksack revolution," he tells his friends, "thousands or even millions of young Americans wandering around with rucksacks, going up to mountains to pray, making children laugh and old men glad, making young girls happy and old girls happier, all of 'em Zen Lunatics who go about writing poems that happen to appear in their heads for no reason and also by being kind and also by strange unexpected acts keep giving visions of eternal freedom to everybody and to all living creatures."[65]

Within a few years, Ryder's dream was becoming reality as thousands of young suburbanites turned their backs on middle-class life. Many fled to countercultural enclaves in cities. By 1967, dozens of hippie communes also had sprung up in rural areas, and the number increased dramatically in the last years of the decade. "Right now, I'm trying to keep from being swallowed by a monster—plastic, greedy American society," a nineteen-year-old wrote to the members of one rural commune. "I need to begin relating to new people who are into taking care of each other and the earth."[66]

The hippies hoped to feel the flow of the seasons, to grow things, to enjoy the beauty of sunrise, to walk naked. Drugs helped. Indeed, the desire to return to nature was a driving force in the drug culture of the 1960s. In the words of historians Maurice Isserman and Michael Kazin, "LSD made it possible to have a decent conversation with a tree." The experience of writer Geoffrey O'Brien was typical. On drugs, he went to "the wilderness." He felt in tune with the rhythms of the "stars, migratory patterns, planting cycles, the chirping of insects." Nature talked and he listened, in ecstatic communion. "The planet is a sentient companion! Everything that lives is taking in everything and communicating its response *back* to everything, without stopping, constantly!"[67]

Especially in the countryside, however, many of the hippies were not just seeking to commune with nature. They also were motivated by apocalyptic visions of the collapse of industrial civilization. Smog alerts, water shortages, pesticide scares, power outages, traffic tie-ups—all suggested that the urban environment soon would be deadly to both body and soul. As one commune member explained, "Our ecological sophistication told us that the cities and everybody in them were doomed. 'Don't drink the water and don't breathe the air' is pretty sound advice these days in the places where most Americans live."[68]

Though most of the late 1960s countercultural communities did not last long, the hippies inspired many young people to think more deeply about the earth. Hippie communes typically were open. Anyone could stop by to get a taste of the simple life, and thousands did: According to one scholarly estimate, half a million Americans spent some time at rural communes in the late 1960s and early 1970s. Because the mainstream media gave tremendous attention to the counterculture, the hippie argument that the nation needed to find a less environmentally destructive way of life reached a wide audience. The hippies themselves often sought to spread their gospel. Some started countercultural restaurants, with menus that proclaimed the virtue of natural food. Others performed street theater. In New

York, a troupe sprayed black mist and passed out blackened flowers at a "soot-in" in front of the Consolidated Edison building. A group of hippies in Eugene, Oregon, formed CRAP—Cyclists Revolting Against Pollution—"to show people there are ways to move other than foul automobiles spewing death." Throughout the nation, the underground press regularly enjoined readers to "revere nature." In a variety of ways, then, the counterculture helped to put the environment on the protest agenda.[69]

For the New Left, the path to environmentalism was more difficult. The first student radicals had little interest in the environment. Unlike the hippies, the founders of Students for a Democratic Society were theoreticians: They were inspired by sociology, not poetry. *The Port Huron Statement* did not discuss nature at all. The only reference to the environment in the 1962 SDS manifesto was a warning about the unrestrained exploitation of natural resources at a time of rapidly expanding world population. Even in 1970, as millions of young Americans readied for the first Earth Day, many New Leftists dismissed environmentalism as a diversion from the pressing issue of social justice. But the skepticism was not universal. In the course of the 1960s, a minority within the New Left began to articulate a radical interpretation of the environmental crisis.[70]

The young radicals at first followed the lead of Ralph Nader. In a chapter of his 1965 exposé of the automobile industry, *Unsafe at Any Speed*, Nader challenged "the power to pollute," and a few New Left theorists soon joined Nader in attacking corporate polluters. As long as business interests ruled, SDS member Richard Flacks argued in 1966, the quality of the nation's land, air, and water would continue to deteriorate. By the end of the decade, that argument had become more common, and more radical. The authors of works about "the politics of ecology" and "the ecology of capitalism" called for assaults on concentrated corporate power. In 1969, a Berkeley activist started "Earth Read-Out," a radical report on environmental issues that soon appeared regularly in more than fifty underground papers. To save the earth, a typical "Earth Read-Out" report insisted, people needed to challenge a "corrupt economic system" and an "unresponsive, undemocratic government." The editors of the New Left magazine *Ramparts* also argued aggressively for radical change. "Like the race crisis and the Vietnam War," one wrote in 1970, "the ecological impasse is not merely the result of bad or mistaken policies that can be changed by a new Administration or a new will to do better. It is, rather, the expression of a basic malfunction of the social order itself, and consequently cannot be dealt with on a piecemeal, patchwork basis."[71]

The Santa Barbara oil spill prompted many radicals to think harder about the environment. In January 1969, a disastrous leak at a Union Oil well became national news, and photographs and television images of oil-covered beaches outraged people across the country. The angry response of Santa Barbarans suggested that the issue of environmental degradation had the potential to radicalize people. A group of college students attacked the office of a bank with strong ties to Union Oil—and a number of gas stations owned by the polluters of Santa Barbara Bay. The response of the city's adults was even more heartening. In a normally Republican community, thousands of people took part in rallies, pickets, and demonstrations against the unchecked power of Big Oil. As one local radical wrote, "It became clear that more than petroleum had leaked out from Union Oil's drilling platform. Some basic truths about power in America had spilled out along with it."[72]

The battle over People's Park in 1969 also was a critical turning point. In April, a group of Berkeley students and residents began to plant flowers and trees on a vacant lot owned by the University of California. The site quickly became a rallying place for people trying to imagine alternatives to traditional concepts of property ownership. For many, the park also offered the hope of creating a new kind of relationship with the nonhuman world. "The most revolutionary consciousness," Gary Snyder argued there, "is to be found among the most oppressed classes—animals, trees, grass, air, water, earth." To the university, however, the construction of the park was a form of trespass. When the university used the National Guard to clear the site in May, a young man was killed. For the first time, the state had attacked people attempting to improve the quality of the environment, and the use of force made the environmental fight seem more like the struggles for peace and justice: All challenged the brute power of a repressive establishment. "The park has brought the concept of the Whole Earth, the Mother Earth, into the vocabulary of revolutionary politics," a contributor to the leftist magazine *Liberation* wrote. "The park has raised sharply the question of property and use; it has demonstrated the absurdity of a system that puts land title above human life; and it has given the dispossessed children of the tract homes and the cities a feeling of involvement with the planet, an involvement proved through our sweat and our blood."[73]

The Vietnam War contributed in a very different way to the rise of environmental protest. By the late 1960s, the news media had begun to report that U.S. forces in Vietnam were fighting a war against nature as much as a war against people. American troops had sprayed one-eighth of the country with chemical defoliants. Though the herbicide spraying mostly targeted forests, rice fields were targets too. The air war was just as devastating to the landscape. To many observers, the heavily cratered wastelands created by "saturation" bombing looked like the moon. Automated artillery fire also turned forests into biological deserts. Throughout the field of operations, the military used gigantic bulldozers to clear the terrain of potential cover for enemy troops. Even napalm was used to destroy vegetation. In the view of many scientists and activists, the United States was committing "ecocide."[74]

For many intellectuals, therefore, the movement to end the

war and the movement to protect the environment became aspects of one all-encompassing struggle. Many critics pointed to the complicity of the corporate world in environmental devastation abroad and at home. The same companies that profited from the defoliation campaign in Vietnam also profited from the wanton use of toxic chemicals in the United States. To some critics, the war and the environmental crisis both followed from the deadly logic of technocracy. In Vietnam, we destroyed towns in order to "save" them; here, we degraded the environment in order to make "progress." According to other critics, the heart of the problem lay instead in the Western drive to conquer the world, to remake societies and landscapes at will. The war in Vietnam was akin to the war Americans had waged against Indians and wilderness. "The white race *is* the cancer of human history," the radical critic Susan Sontag wrote in 1966; "it is the white race and it alone—its ideologies and inventions—which eradicates autonomous civilizations wherever it spreads, which has upset the ecological balance of the planet, which now threatens the very existence of life itself."[75]

For many activists, too, the war and the environmental crisis were related causes. In 1969, the magazine of the War Resisters League devoted a special issue to the environment. At the November 15 antiwar rally in Washington, one participant reported, many of the protesters spent free moments rapping about the environment. The strongest student eco-action groups formed at schools in the forefront of antiwar activism. The first environmental teach-in was held at the University of Michigan. At UCLA, a group of antiwar activists turned "eco-freaks" staged a sit-in to protest campus interviews for manufacturers of automobiles and chemical pesticides because their products polluted the air and endangered the health of both people and wildlife. At the University of Wisconsin, the Ecology Students Association focused on water pollution and waste disposal in Madison—and defoliant use in Vietnam.[76]

The founders of the Youth International Party—the Yippies—also joined antiwar activism and environmentalism. At a news conference early in 1968 to announce plans for a Yippie "Festival of Life" to counter the Democratic "Convention of Death" in Chicago, Allen Ginsberg touted the event as a way to protest the threats of "violence, overpopulation, pollution, [and] ecological destruction." Both Abbie Hoffman and Jerry Rubin spoke about starting ecology schools. Ed Sanders soon suggested that the Festival of Life might include a "Yippie Ecological Conference," where people would "spew out an angry report denouncing scheiss-poison in the lakes and streams, industrial honkey-fumes from white killer industrialists, and exhaust murder from a sick hamburger society of automobile freaks." The eighteen-point manifesto that the Yippies distributed in Chicago demanded both the end of the war and the elimination of pollution.[77]

Though the Yippie flame quickly burned out, the effort to counter Death with Life became common. The war machine was just one horrid component of a life-denying "system"—as critics often called the nation's ruling institutions. What kind of society exalted the deadening cycle of getting and spending? What kind of culture made schools into soul-killing "knowledge factories"? What kind of government relied for national defense on the threat of annihilation? What kind of economy depended on relentless destruction of the environment? For a growing number of people, the questions suggested the overriding importance of protecting all the spontaneous, organic, and creative energies of the world.[78]

To a greater extent than historians of the sixties have recognized, the struggle to affirm Life bridged the divide between the counterculture and the New Left. By 1970, several countercultural writers had begun to contemplate radical action to save the planet. In a series of "revolutionary letters," the poet Diane di Prima even imagined blowing up petroleum lines and destroying Dow Chemical plants. At the same time, a number of radicals began to sound more like hippies. To counter the argument that student protesters were "nihilists," the Columbia activist James Kunen opened *The Strawberry Statement* with a short affirmation of the blessings of life: "I, for one, strongly support trees (and, in a larger sense, forests), flowers, mountains and hills, also valleys, the ocean, wiliness (when used for good), good, little children, people, tremendous record-setting snowstorms, hurricanes, swimming underwater, nice policemen, unicorns, extra-inning ball games up to twelve innings, pneumatic jackhammers (when they're not too close), the dunes in North Truro on Cape Cod, liberalized abortion laws, and Raggedy Ann dolls, among other things." The SDS leader Paul Potter found in the ecological concept of interconnectedness a powerful metaphor for community. Instead of seeing ourselves as independent individuals, Potter argued, we needed to acknowledge our dependence on other people and other creatures, so that "all life lives within us"— and so that "we live in all life, seeing with its eyes and feeling with all of its senses."[79]

The increasing overlap between countercultural and radical thinking was part of a larger trend that pollster Daniel Yankelovich termed "the new naturalism." In a series of studies of college students in the late 1960s and early 1970s, Yankelovich discovered a widespread conviction that everything artificial was bad, while everything "natural" was good. As Yankelovich noted, that ideal was open to many interpretations. For some people, the concept meant rejecting hypocrisy; for others, emphasizing cooperation. But the core ideas clearly included a new wariness about the attempt to master nature—and a new willingness to restrain economic growth and technological development in order to preserve the natural environment.[80]

The most dramatic expression of that new generational sensibility came on Earth Day.

Conservationists

The conservation movement in 1950 was weak and fragmented. In 1954, a sympathetic political scientist suggested that "movement" was a misnomer, because most conservation organizations focused on a single concern. The biggest groups consisted of people who hunted and fished. Then came "groups interested in bird preservation, wildflowers, soil conservation, national parks, and wilderness preservation." No conservation organization fought against air pollution. The only conservation group with a strong record of opposition to water pollution—the Izaak Walton League—was faltering. The league had 175,000 members five years after its establishment in 1922, but membership in 1950 was just 40,000. That still beat the combined total for the National Audubon Society and the Sierra Club. Though both organizations were roughly fifty years old in 1950, neither had a national reach. Audubon's 17,000 members almost all lived in the East. The Sierra Club truly was a club—two members had to endorse applicants for membership—with 7,000 members, mostly in California.[81]

In the 1950s and 1960s, however, the conservation movement became much bigger and broader. The Audubon Society and the Sierra Club both had more than 100,000 members in 1970. Membership in several smaller organizations increased tenfold between 1950 and 1970. The most successful groups took on many new issues. By 1970, almost all the old conservation groups were pursuing a more "environmental" agenda.[82]

The transformation of the conservation movement was not inevitable. The Izaak Walton League changed little from 1950 to 1970. In most organizations, some members resisted any redefinition of purpose. Because the organizations had different traditions and missions, they took different paths. In some groups, a visionary leader charted a new course. In other groups, the process of change was more organic: The group recognized new threats to cherished places or creatures and then decided that responding to those threats required a new approach. The histories of the National Wildlife Federation, the National Audubon Society, and the Sierra Club illustrate the different routes to rebirth.

The National Wildlife Federation was the first conservation organization to remake itself. Founded in 1936, the federation essentially was the Washington representative of thousands of local hunting and fishing groups. The founding charter limited the organization to efforts to promote appreciation and protection of "wildlife resources." In 1960, when newly hired executive director Tom Kimball began to transform the organization, the local hunting and fishing groups claimed roughly two million members. Because the local groups were a political force in many states, the federation commanded respect. President John F. Kennedy spoke at the dedication of the federation's national headquarters in March 1961. Yet the federation was institutionally limited. Individuals could not join: The only members were state wildlife federations, which represented the local groups. The state federations provided little financial support, so the national organization relied on donations and merchandise sales. The federation also lacked a way to mobilize members of the local groups.[83]

Kimball hoped to lead "a great army" of conservationists. He was convinced that the federation could attract people concerned about the destruction of natural beauty and the threat of environmental degradation. "America was suddenly awakening to the fact that something was rotten in the environment," he argued. "Recreation areas were smelling and so were the rivers. You couldn't fish in them or swim in them. Air pollution was so bad it was just like fog, particularly in our larger cities." In 1961, at Kimball's urging, the federation opened the door to members who did not hunt or fish. The federation created a membership category for individuals and revised its mandate:

Henceforth, the federation would work to protect natural resources of all kinds, including places of aesthetic value.[84]

To attract members, Kimball inaugurated a publishing program. A bimonthly magazine, *National Wildlife*, debuted at the end of 1962. The federation started to publish newsletters about conservation issues and legislation in 1963. The first issue of *Ranger Rick's Nature Magazine* appeared in 1967, with two goals: "to give boys and girls a year-round program of activities, adventure and knowledge which will help them appreciate and enjoy nature" and to encourage children to "know and respect all things that grow and creatures that move, that all may desire to conserve and wisely use the vital natural resources of the world."[85]

Kimball's strategy worked. By 1965, the federation had 250,000 individual members, and membership reached 540,000 in 1970. As Kimball hoped, many of the members did not belong to a local hunting or fishing group.[86]

From the first, *National Wildlife* was more than a "nature" magazine. The second issue included a five-page analysis of the controversy over pesticides. The last issue of volume one reported on water pollution: "America's Shame." In the mid-1960s, *National Wildlife* was the only conservation magazine to devote considerable space to pollution of all kinds.[87]

Though the federation eventually gained a reputation as the most conservative environmental group, *National Wildlife* strongly supported the Great Society conservation agenda. Editor John Strohm argued early in 1964 that the presidency of John Kennedy "marked the launching of conservation's 'third wave'"—a worthy successor to the efforts of the two Roosevelts. Strohm predicted that Lyndon B. Johnson similarly would be a great conservationist. Because anything that seemed like lobbying could jeopardize the federation's nonprofit status, *National Wildlife* rarely endorsed specific legislation. But the magazine repeatedly touted campaigns to clean up the nation's air and water, save open space, and preserve natural beauty. Almost every report on environmental problems closed with a call for citizen action. "ISN'T IT ABOUT TIME YOU DID SOMETHING?" a 1964 report on water pollution concluded.[88]

National Wildlife also encouraged readers to adopt an environmental ethic. The December–January issue usually included a reflection on our obligations to the rest of creation. The philosophical essays occasionally seconded Aldo Leopold's call for an "ecological conscience." More often, they argued in religious terms. One essay—"God and Man and Natural Resources"— began with quotations from the biblical books of Genesis, Joel, and Luke. Another simply asked: "Is Man a Faithful Steward?"[89]

To give substance to the ideal of stewardship, *National Wildlife* updated the Progressive concept of "wise use." For the conservationists of Gifford Pinchot's day, that phrase meant scientific forestry and river engineering. But *National Wildlife* argued that wise use required keeping some open spaces in sprawling metropolitan areas, saving some streams "in their wild, free state," and setting aside some wilderness areas. "People must live and work and drive," the magazine argued in 1965, "but they need something to live for, and work toward, and drive to." In the mid-1960s, *National Wildlife* also defined water pollution as a problem of wise use: Because Americans had misused so many rivers and lakes, the nation soon might face shortages of water for many essential purposes.[90]

By 1970, *National Wildlife* had begun to use a recognizably environmentalist rhetoric. In a twelve-page report in 1969, the magazine introduced a yearly Environmental Quality Index, a pioneering effort to assess the nation's air, water, soil, forests, wildlife, and mineral resources. The federation judged the overall environmental quality to be "poor," with air and water particularly bad. The wildlife section epitomized the federation's shift from the rhetoric of conservation. "Like the miner's canary, wildlife is a sensitive indicator of a healthy human environment," the section began. "We are concerned for wildlife, not as sentimentalists or hunters or fishermen, but as humans who know that the presence of healthy wildlife means we are sharing a healthy environment. Unfortunately, some 40 species of birds and mammals have been lost in the U.S. in the last 150 years. Presently 89 more are on the 'Endangered Species List.' An ominous omen indeed for the future of man!" The federation soon distributed more than 100,000 reprints of the inaugural index, which drew praise from both Gaylord Nelson and Richard Nixon.[91]

The National Audubon Society's transformation was slow, stressful, yet ultimately profound. The society was founded in 1905 to stop hunters from shooting plumage birds. When anti-hunting laws proved inadequate, the society developed a system of wildlife sanctuaries and a program in nature education. Neither endeavor required a crusading spirit. In the decades after World War II, however, Audubon officials and members began to appreciate that birds faced new threats. Pesticides, large-scale development, oil spills, pollution—all harmed birds. By 1969, the society had broadened its focus to "the total environment."[92]

The pesticide issue hit home first, and the reckoning with pesticides made Audubon members more ecologically sophisticated. Audubon officials began to warn about the potential hazards of widespread use of DDT as soon as World War II ended. In 1946, president John Baker argued that broadcasting DDT would open a Pandora's box of troubles. Yet Audubon struggled to define an institutional response to the growing use of pesticides. At first, the staff hoped that public education would suffice. Audubon urged caution and more research. But beyond that, what could the society do? The sanctuary system offered no refuge from persistent, mobile chemicals. By the early 1960s, a few staff members were pressing for Audubon to endorse a DDT ban. Yet the board of directors had no stomach for a direct assault on pesticide use. The U.S. Department of Agriculture and the chemical industry were far more powerful enemies than plume hunters. Even after the publication of *Silent Spring* in 1962, the society was torn. Audubon finally took a stand against DDT in 1967. But the society still was not willing to lead the charge: Instead, Audubon decided to help a legal challenge to DDT by the newly formed Environmental Defense Fund.[93]

The prospect of jetport development also pushed Audubon in new directions. Jets still were new in the 1960s, and a desire to accommodate bigger and faster aircraft led many communities to expand old airports or build new facilities. Often the construction was in marshland—a critical habitat for many birds. Though a single jetport never threatened ecological disruption on a large scale, the forces that led to one proposed facility surely would lead to more. Jetports were symbols of modernity, of the ever-greater ability of humans to remake the world to suit our convenience. Because air travel was a consumer good, not just a part of the business world, Audubon concluded that disputing the need for more jetports required challenging assumptions about progress.[94]

The society began to question the relationship between technological progress and "the good life" early in 1967, when officials proposed a jetport in New Jersey's Great Swamp. "There is a new battle to be waged—to keep man's technology in check while promoting the welfare of man himself," declared an editorial in *Audubon* magazine. "The conservationist—in his struggle to halt the dirtying of our air and water, in his efforts to bring man and his environment into better harmony—is in a farsighted camp. And he is not fighting progress when he questions the need for a new jetport, a new highway or new industry. It is a case of progress for whom and toward what?"[95]

The Great Swamp proposal never got off the ground, but a proposed jetport in the Florida Everglades finally forced Audubon to mobilize in 1969. The Everglades were almost sacred ground for Audubon: The society was established to save the egrets and herons and spoonbills there. The airport would be a massive island in the middle of the river of grass, with runways six miles long. Highways and pipelines would tie the airport to Miami, and planners predicted that a booming center of commerce would rise from the swamp. The ecological disruption would be devastating. Audubon had a field representative in Florida, Joe Browder, who put together a grassroots coalition in 1969 to oppose the project. Audubon also rallied conservationists nationally. To Audubon, the issue was not just the fate of the Everglades but the survival of humankind. As a call to battle in *Audubon* argued, the Everglades jetport resulted from "the same philosophy that allows industry to pollute air and water to the brink of disaster, agriculture to use poisons like DDT long after the hazards are known, the Army Engineers to dam rivers and dig canals with no concern for the total environment."[96]

In July 1969, *Audubon* debuted "The Audubon Cause," a section devoted to grassroots activism. One subsection—"The Bulldozer"—focused on controversies over development. "The Audubon Cause" also included commentaries on issues, reports on legislation, and updates on ongoing campaigns. With every issue, the section argued for a new kind of commitment. Because the threats to the environment no longer were isolated or infrequent, members needed to be ever vigilant.

The Sierra Club was slower than the National Wildlife Federation or the National Audubon Society to redefine its mission. Though the board of directors debated issues ranging from population growth to nuclear power, the club's conservation agenda remained focused on national parks and wilderness until fall 1969, when the board voted to make "environmental survival" a priority. But executive director David Brower changed the club in the 1960s from a hiking group to a crusading army—and that transformation led to phenomenal growth, especially in the second half of the decade.[97]

To save wilderness in a time of sprawl and technological

hubris, Brower concluded at the end of the 1950s, conservationists needed to act boldly and uncompromisingly. Brower first demonstrated the club's new militance in campaigns in the mid-1960s to establish a redwood national park and to stop two proposed dams in the Grand Canyon. Working with a hip advertising agency, Brower took out full-page ads in *The New York Times* and other newspapers. The ads were not just aggressive; they mocked the timber industry and the dam proponents, and they directly challenged the president and the secretary of the interior to defend America's greatness. After the first Grand Canyon ad, the Internal Revenue Service threatened to revoke the club's tax-exempt status, but the club did not back down. Thousands of people sent money to help David topple Goliath. The media began to describe the club in a new way. The "Fighting Sierrans," *Newsweek* termed them, while *Time* reported that the club "was willing to fight at the drop of a tree." By 1967, reporters routinely identified the club as the most powerful, imaginative, and devoted conservation group in the country.[98]

The club's growth also owed much to Brower's innovations in proselytizing. To bring the gospel of wilderness into urban and suburban homes, he produced a series of "exhibit-format" coffee-table books. (The first in the series—*This Is the American Land*, published in 1960—began as a museum exhibit.) Several of the exhibit-format books were philosophic: The bestselling *In Wildness Is the Preservation of the World* joined the words of Henry David Thoreau and the photographs of Eliot Porter. Most of the club's books were calls to defend particular places. But even the "battle books," as Brower called them, warned against sacrificing natural beauty to "the false gods of progress and growth."[99]

Brower worked especially hard to attract young people. In 1967, the club published *On the Loose*, a photo essay by two twentysomething Californians, Terry and Renny Russell, who celebrated self-reliance and self-discovery in the wilderness— and who railed against those who would reduce "oceans of beauty" to "scattered puddles, muddy and drying up." The book eventually sold more than a million copies. The club also joined the poster revolution in 1967: Now students could express themselves by putting images of wilderness on their walls. The same year, the club arranged with Ballantine to publish paper-back editions of the bestselling exhibit-format books, and soon almost every campus bookstore had copies of *In Wildness Is the Preservation of the World*. In 1969, the club became the first conservation organization to have a staff person devoted to campus outreach.[100]

By 1970, thousands of young people had joined the club. They were not just attracted by Brower's marketing genius. The club's attacks on the shallowness of materialist values spoke power-fully to the counterculture. Brower also inspired students eager to speak truth to power. As one young admirer wrote in 1969, Brower's militance "appealed to the growing activism of the de-cade, and his outrage at the rape of the land by big government and big business dovetailed nicely with its morality."[101]

The new members often pushed their older counterparts to pursue a more radical agenda. In Madison, Wisconsin, for ex-ample, a young activist ran as a petition candidate for the board of the local Sierra chapter, and his petition was unsparing:

We haven't realized the radical nature of our cause: that we stand squarely athwart the economic-political ideology of this country; that amid an age that revels in smothering the spirit in convenience, comfort, and ugliness that we live to excite that spirit in challenge and Beauty; that in a country which mea-sures growth primarily in terms of ever bigger numbers, we can stand no more human beings. Our cause is doomed to fail—swallowed up in the oil sludge of a reckless age—unless we act as radicals to change the basic values of this nation. The 2-child—*and no more*—family must become the accepted norm. Warring in Asia must be stopped immediately so that serious

> warring against all the pollutions of our exploitive economy
> can begin. Children must be taught that Beauty is more valu-
> able than Dollars, that forests and parks are needed more than
> highways and parking lots.

The activist won. His victory accompanied a national shift in the
club's direction. The club began to challenge big business more
directly, and to take stands on a broader range of issues.[102]

The dialectic of young and old was especially important in the
run-up to Earth Day. In fall 1969, just after Gaylord Nelson proposed a national environmental teach-in for spring 1970, Brower
decided to sponsor a teach-in handbook. By then, Brower had
left the Sierra Club and founded Friends of the Earth, and the Sierra Club soon followed his lead. *The Environmental Handbook*
appeared in January 1970, and the Sierra Club's *Ecotactics* came
out in April. Both books were largely the work of the young. Both
were huge hits. Sales of the handbook reached 1.5 million, while
Ecotactics sold 500,000 copies. To many commentators, the handbook was the distilled essence of Earth Day.[103]

2 ● Organizers

Earth Day began modestly. On September 20, 1969, in a speech at the annual symposium of the Washington Environmental Council in Seattle, Senator Gaylord Nelson of Wisconsin announced plans to organize a nationwide teach-in on the environment in spring 1970. The venue was a strange choice for a major announcement. Though Seattle had hosted a world's fair, the city was not yet the trendsetting home of Starbucks, grunge rock, and Microsoft. The national media did not cover the event. Nelson's assignment simply was to inspire his hosts. He had introduced legislation to ban DDT, and the Washington Environmental Council was working to bar use of the pesticide in the state. The council also hoped to add a conservation bill of rights to the state constitution. That night, though, Nelson decided to do more than anyone expected. He had begun to think about the environmental teach-in a few weeks before, and he was ready to give voice to the idea. "I am convinced that the same concern the youth of this nation took in changing this nation's priorities on the war in Vietnam and on civil rights can be shown for the problems of the environment," he said. "That is why I plan to see to it that a national teach-in is held." Several accounts of the symposium did not mention Nelson's announcement. But the *Seattle Post-Intelligencer* published a story about Nelson's plan, and the Associated Press sent a few paragraphs about the teach-in over the national wire.[1]

How did a few words at a conference 3,000 miles from the nation's political and media centers become the greatest demonstration in U.S. history? Years later, Nelson often said that Earth Day "organized itself." That was false modesty. Nelson worked tirelessly to promote the teach-in. When he saw that Earth Day was becoming too big for his staff to handle, he established a nonprofit organization, Environmental Teach-In, Inc., and hired a group of twentysomething activists to run the operation. But Nelson was right that the national organizers did not really organize Earth Day. Earth Day happened because thousands of local people organized events across the country.[2]

The great protests of the 1960s were organized very differently. The organization of the 1963 March on Washington for Jobs and Freedom was top-down. With the quiet support of the Kennedy administration, the "big six" civil-rights organizations picked the speakers, provided guidelines for members to use in recruiting attendees, and raised the money. The event drew roughly 250,000 people to the National Mall. The 1969 Vietnam Moratorium, in contrast, began with little support from the powerful. The two national coordinators were young veterans of Eugene McCarthy's insurgent presidential campaign in 1968, not leaders of established organizations. Though the coordinators publicized the event and sought endorsements, the moratorium organizing effort was decentralized, with hundreds of rallies and vigils around the nation. Perhaps two million people participated. That turnout was impressive—but still far short of the turnout for Earth Day.[3]

Earth Day was so successful because the organizing effort joined the power of the Establishment and the energy of the grassroots. As a senator, Nelson commanded attention. He could attract money and talented people. But Nelson was astute enough to recognize that his connections alone were insufficient to make the teach-in a history-making success. He found a way to allow thousands of local people to take ownership of Earth Day. Because the local organizing effort was empowering, the involvement of so many organizers also helped to ensure that Earth Day left a lasting legacy.

The Senator

Gaylord Nelson's environmentalism was rooted in liberalism.

As a boy, Nelson was endowed with a faith that government could do good. He grew up in a small town in northern Wisconsin, and his parents revered the state's Progressive leaders, Robert "Fighting Bob" La Follette and his son Robert Jr. When Nelson was ten, in 1926, his father took him to hear the younger La Follette give a speech. Fighting Bob had died the year before, and Young Bob had succeeded him as a Wisconsin senator. After the speech, Nelson's father asked if Gaylord had any interest in entering politics. "I would," the boy answered, "but I'm afraid by then Bob La Follette may not have left any problems for me to solve."[4]

Nelson was a political natural. He was affable and athletic, and his childhood nickname was "Happy." Because his father was a doctor, the family knew everyone in Clear Lake. The town was so tiny that Gaylord would have known everyone anyway. His high-school class had thirty-nine students. He was chosen to be one of the two student speakers at his graduation in 1934, and he planned to talk about the New Deal. But Nelson never gave the speech: He had an attack of nerves and stayed home. His first unhesitating step toward a political career came five years later, when he entered the University of Wisconsin Law School. While he was a law student, he campaigned for La Follette. He also led both liberal organizations on campus, the Young Progressives and the Young Democrats. He loved to listen to the political talk at bars near the capitol. As he recalled, Madison still had "a few old-fashioned, give-'em-hell, rough-and-tumble, no-holds-barred newspaper editors and a good collection of colorful, creative, self-made politicians mixed in with the practical political operatives who made the system work."[5]

Nelson's liberal instincts were strengthened in the 1940s. During World War II, he served as one of four white officers in charge of an all-black company in the army's quartermaster corps, and he encountered racial segregation for the first time. He became a supporter of civil rights. When he returned to Wisconsin after the war, he worked as a lawyer for a Madison firm that represented a union of government employees. Much of his work involved organizing workers and negotiating contracts. In 1948, union support helped him to win a seat in the state senate.[6]

After a decade in the legislature, Nelson was elected governor. Like many northern Democrats in the late 1950s, he sought to adapt liberalism to the needs of affluent times. In the spirit of Arthur Schlesinger and John Kenneth Galbraith, he argued that Wisconsin needed to redress the imbalance between private and public spending. His inaugural address challenged the state's citizens to support the services that only government could provide: "To those who would neglect our schools, our colleges, our public welfare activities and institutions, our highway and conservation resources, I would say this—you spend more money on cigarettes, liquor, cosmetics and other luxuries than the total cost of your state government. If we have not completely lost our sense of values . . . the question in its proper perspective is really this—are you willing to give up a few personal luxuries in exchange for a more creative investment in our future?"[7]

In 1959, Nelson did not yet have a special interest in environmental issues. Conservation was just one of fourteen responsibilities of state government that he addressed in the gubernatorial campaign. But Nelson left office with a reputation as "the conservation governor." The issue that started him on the path to Earth Day was outdoor recreation.

Nelson became convinced that Wisconsin faced an outdoor recreation crisis. With the sprawl of metropolitan Milwaukee and Chicago, rural land in southeastern Wisconsin was fast becoming housing developments, roads, and shopping centers. Without state action, Nelson feared, open space would disappear. At the same time, the new affluence of the 1950s dramatically increased the number of urban and suburban residents eager to get away to the country. Fishing surpassed baseball as the state's most beloved form of recreation. Family camping doubled in Wisconsin from 1950 to 1958. In the summer, Wisconsin's parks sometimes resembled open-air tenements. The July Fourth weekend in 1960 was a vivid demonstration of the inadequacy of the state's outdoor recreation facilities. Every park in the state was jammed—in some cases, to the point of squalor.[8]

For Nelson, the outdoor recreation crisis hit home. Clear Lake was surrounded by woods, fields, and water, and he spent a lot of time outdoors as a boy. In the summer, he swam and hiked and camped. In the winter, he skied and sledded and skated. He sometimes amused himself by fooling with turtles migrating from one lake to another. He also loved to catch wild creatures, from rabbits to gophers. In one archetypal photograph, circa 1930, Gaylord stood on the sand by a lake with a captured snake around his neck. Unlike many North Country boys, however, Nelson rarely fished or hunted. He did not join a rod-and-gun club until he became governor. As a friend explained in 1959, "Gaylord is all for the woods and wilderness. But for him it is enough to *be* in the woods. He doesn't have to do much of anything to enjoy himself."[9]

What could the state do to ensure that the next generation of Wisconsin families had some of the opportunity to commune with nature that Nelson enjoyed as a boy? In 1961, Nelson proposed a pioneering program to preserve the state's woods, lakes, rivers, and marshes. With funding from a one-cent tax on cigarettes, the Outdoor Recreation Act Program—ORAP— provided $50 million over ten years for land acquisition and development. "The choice we are faced with, quite simply, is now or never," Nelson told the legislature. "Wisconsin's entire recreational future will continue to be undercut, month by month, unless we start immediately on a program of wise and prudent investment in our outdoor assets."[10]

ORAP was a political success. The cigarette industry opposed the one-cent tax, but otherwise the only interest-group opposition came from tourism promoters in one county who preferred private development to more state parks. Some individuals also wondered why their taxes should subsidize the pastimes of a privileged few. If Nelson was willing to improve hunting and fishing, they argued, the state also should pay to help bowlers and stamp collectors! But in fact outdoor recreation no longer was limited to the well-to-do, and Nelson correctly foresaw that ORAP would have bipartisan appeal. In the Democratic cities, many families now had the time and money to take vacations, while many rural residents—largely Republican—always had loved the outdoors. Republican officials tried to defeat ORAP, but only because they hoped to get credit for passing a similar bill.[11]

The ORAP victory brought Nelson national attention. Though California and New York had passed open-space-acquisition bills the year before, the Nelson legislation had several innovative elements. The Wisconsin program also provided much more money per capita. The new secretary of the interior, Stewart Udall, called ORAP "the boldest conservation step ever taken on a state level." Because the loss of open space was becoming a concern across the country, ORAP became a model for other states.[12]

Nelson saw a similar opportunity for leadership at the national level. When he won election to the Senate in 1962, he went to Washington determined to make a mark as a conservationist. "I think the most crucial domestic issue facing America . . . is the conservation of natural resources," he told *The Christian Science Monitor* in January 1963. "We only have in this country now, in my judgment, another ten years in which to preserve a significant amount of the outdoor resources that we have. They're being destroyed carelessly and criminally throughout the nation by the pollution of our waters, the drainage of wetlands, the rapid growth of cities eating up land all around them." Nelson hoped that the federal government soon would begin a massive program to acquire outdoor recreation sites.[13]

As a first-year senator, Nelson urged President Kennedy to make a conservation tour. If the president traveled the country speaking about conservation, Nelson believed, the media would see the importance of the issue, and the resulting news reports and editorials would rally people to the cause. In August 1963, Nelson sent Kennedy a lengthy memo with suggestions for making the tour a success. "The question is how to maximize the effect—how to hit the issue hard enough to leave a permanent impression after the headlines have faded away—how to shake people, organizations and legislators," he wrote. Since World War II, the nation had destroyed and polluted the natural landscape faster than ever before. The baby boom ensured that the demand for resources would grow tremendously in future decades. Without decisive action, Nelson argued, Americans faced a cramped, impoverished, and ugly future. The next decade was the "last chance" to protect the nation's "vital resources." The urgency of the issue easily could be demonstrated with "a mass of bone chilling statistics," and Nelson hoped the president would take inspiration from Rachel Carson's work, which was "a perfect example of the kind of impact that can be made with specifics." The interest in conservation transcended "party lines, economic classes and geographic barriers," Nelson concluded. All that was missing was political leadership.[14]

Despite Nelson's high hopes, the conservation tour was a bust. In late September, Kennedy visited eleven states in five days, but the tour was not a crusade. The itinerary had less to do with dramatizing the conservation issue than helping the Democrats in the 1964 election. Much of the time the president seemed bored. On the day the tour began, he signed the nuclear test-ban treaty, and he was more interested in talking about foreign policy than wilderness. He often departed from his prepared texts. In Billings, Montana, he abandoned conservation altogether and spoke instead about the need for the nation to be strong enough to secure peace. In Duluth, Minnesota, he spoke about the depressed economy of the northern Great Lakes, and he promoted his major domestic proposal of the year, a tax cut to stimulate the economy. Those comments became the headlines the next day. When Kennedy stuck to his conservation message, the audience response mostly was tepid. The reporters covering the tour also asked many more questions about the Cold War than conservation—a subject few knew much about.[15]

Even if the president had shown more excitement, the tour almost certainly would have disappointed Nelson. Unlike Earth Day, the tour was totally top-down, yet presidential action never is enough to build a movement. The tour also depended almost entirely on the media. Though the crowds reached 10,000 in some places, the president directly addressed only a tiny fraction of the citizenry. But the biggest problem was more basic. In 1963, the word "conservation" evoked old efforts to ensure wise use of forests and protect places of great natural beauty, not new concerns about pollution and environmental degradation.

Nelson's memo to Kennedy showed how far conservationists still had to go to become environmentalists. The crusading rhetoric of the memo was new, yet Nelson still framed the conservation challenge largely in terms of outdoor recreation. Though he invoked *Silent Spring*, he did not truly appreciate the originality of Carson's work. He did not follow Carson in calling for a new environmental ethic. Though he mentioned the poisoning of the nation's air and water, he did not argue that pollution threatened public health. He attacked pollution as a destroyer of outdoor recreation sites. Though he argued that conservation was of great concern to many people, he still imagined that support for the cause would come largely from the old vanguard of sportsmen and nature lovers.

In the mid-1960s, however, Nelson escaped the conceptual constraints of ORAP. He continued to speak about outdoor recreation, but he began to address environmental problems that could not be solved just by acquiring land. His standard speech from 1965 on decried the devastation wrought by strip-mining, the poisoning of birds, and the killing of fish, which suffocated in lakes and rivers deprived of oxygen by pollution. He called the speech "America's Last Chance."[16]

The problem of water pollution was especially important in the evolution of Nelson's thinking. His first speech as a senator was in support of a bill to ban phosphate detergents. Hardly anyone heard the speech—the Senate chamber was nearly empty—and the bill failed. But Nelson's words later seemed prescient. The rise of detergent pollution of lakes and rivers showed the need for "a comprehensive and nationwide program to save the national resources of America," he said. "We cannot be blind to the growing crisis of our environment. Our soil, our water, and our air are becoming more polluted every day. Our most priceless natural resources—trees, lakes, rivers, wildlife habitats, scenic landscapes—are being destroyed."[17]

By 1965, Nelson had come to see the degradation of the Great Lakes as a symbol of the nation's self-destructiveness. Though the lakes had become more polluted decade by decade, "we paid little attention because we thought these lakes were so vast that even Americans could not destroy them." Unfortunately, the Great Lakes were not big enough to wash away the sins of urban growth and industrial development. Lake Michigan, in stretches, was "a cesspool." Lake Erie was "a disgusting, disgraceful chemical tank." Their fates portended much worse. All of the nation's lakes and rivers would die eventually if the government failed to act. In 1966, Nelson introduced a series of water-pollution bills of unprecedented scope. The effort to restore water quality would cost $50 to $100 billion over the next generation, he argued, but that was a necessary and affordable investment in the nation's long-term well-being. Few of Nelson's colleagues were ready to invest that much money: Congress did not pass a strong clean-water act until 1972.[18]

The threat to water quality also was important in Nelson's decision to seek a ban on DDT in 1966. The evidence of pesticide contamination of surface and groundwater grew more troubling year by year. In Wisconsin, a state study found DDT in the tissues of fish taken from thirty lakes. The levels of pesticides in Lake Michigan were especially frightening. Nelson knew that Wisconsin was not exceptional. Pesticides had contaminated seas, lakes, and streams across the world. From reindeer in Alaska to penguins in Antarctica, many creatures besides fish now bore toxic chemicals in their bodies. Humans too. "The long range biological effects of this global contamination, which is building up every day that the use of DDT continues, are not yet known," Nelson argued, "but the potential is present for a national calamity." Again the bill died.[19]

The legislative defeats gnawed at Nelson. What could he do to build a new movement? Though Congress had approved several important environmental measures since he joined the Senate in 1963, the nation still was losing ground. What could lead the government to act, boldly and decisively, to protect the environment? By 1969, Nelson was more resolved than ever to be a catalyst. Environmental issues had played no role in the 1968 presidential election. Yet when Nelson gave speeches about pollution, people were engaged. On college campuses, only the

Vietnam War was a hotter topic than the environment. Why wasn't Washington getting the message?

Nelson ultimately found inspiration in the antiwar movement. He had expressed doubts about the escalation of the U.S. involvement in Vietnam in 1965, and he had voted against war appropriations since 1967. He hoped that grassroots opposition to the war would convince the president to make peace. At first, though, he did not see any connection between his opposition to the war and his passion for the environment. His aha moment came in August 1969, when he read about the antiwar teach-ins while flying home from California after his first chance to see the damage done by the Santa Barbara oil spill. Still thinking about the oil-scarred beaches, Nelson wondered whether the teach-ins might be a model for environmentalists.[20]

The potential was not obvious. The first teach-ins were in 1965, and the antiwar movement had abandoned the teach-in as a tactic. Though organized by opponents of the war, the teach-ins were not demonstrations. They were extracurricular seminars that allowed antiwar activists to challenge the assumptions of the war's supporters. But Nelson concluded that the intense discussions were empowering. The antiwar teach-ins pushed students and faculty to think more clearly, and then to act. An environmental teach-in, Nelson thought, would be even more likely to empower people.[21]

Because Nelson was not a radical young academic, the next steps also were unclear. Could a senator—a pillar of the Establishment—organize a nationwide teach-in? In considering that question, Nelson was helped tremendously by a veteran Democratic Party operative, Fred Dutton. Dutton had worked for John F. Kennedy in the White House, served as chief of staff for California governor Pat Brown, and played a key role in Robert Kennedy's brief campaign for president in 1968. He was a member of the University of California Board of Regents, so he also knew something about academic life. After Dutton and Nelson discussed the teach-in idea, Dutton prepared a detailed prospectus.[22]

Dutton suggested that Nelson establish a teach-in office near Capitol Hill and hire a small staff. The staff director should be youngish "but experienced, hard-driving, knowledgeable about both student movements and Washington, D.C." Four young people, willing to "volunteer" for a subsistence wage of $250 a month, would work as regional organizers. They would line up student and faculty coordinators at campuses across the country. Ideally, two of the organizers would be women, and one would be black. The staff would be part of a steering committee chaired by Nelson, perhaps with the head of the National Student Association as co-chair. Dutton hoped that Nelson could find "a first-rate publicist" willing to donate half of his or her time to the effort. A fund-raiser and a lawyer with expertise in environmental issues also might serve on the steering committee. Dutton proposed a tentative budget of $55,000. In addition to philanthropic individuals, the financial sponsors might include unions, foundations, public-spirited corporations, trade associations without direct ties to "plunderers," and publications such as *Reader's Digest* and *National Geographic*. In the best of all worlds, Joan Baez, Jefferson Airplane, Simon and Garfunkel, or another group would agree to give benefit concerts in Los Angeles and New York.[23]

Once the office was open, Dutton argued, the next critical task would be to rename the event. "Teach-in" was generic. Instead, the name should be unique, evoking "a simple, unmistakable image. I do not like the possibilities which immediately come to mind, but they suggest the direction in which some brainstorming might be done: Last Chance Day . . . Mission: Earth Rescue . . . Nature Day . . . etc."

Dutton envisioned a much more centralized event than Earth Day became. The teach-ins would follow a national model, adapted to meet local conditions. The ideal event would grab students—and not let go. "Controversy is absolutely essential," Dutton wrote. One session should include a representative of a local industry "charged with despoiling the environment." Another session might be just students, since young people were more likely to blast away than older experts, who often equivocated or pointed out complications. In addition to offering suggestions about the structure of panels, the teach-in guidelines should include a list of "leading but provocative questions" to help "assure that the teach-ins are lively, move along and keep to mainstream issues." Dutton also argued that the model teach-in needed to include dramatic visual demonstrations to break up the talk. At least one session should be outdoors, perhaps a "meditation with sky and nature" or a "communion with the air and wind." Though the outdoor events would differ from place to place, all should aim to encourage participants to make a more emotional connection and commitment to the environmental cause.

Forty schools would be flagships, Dutton suggested. The regional organizers each would identify ten schools, with a mix of big and small, public and private, religious and nonsectarian. Each flagship school needed to have a student and a faculty coordinator "screened, designated, and operating" by January 1. The national office would prepare a guide to organizing a teach-in. To ensure that the flagship campuses could attract impressive keynoters, the staff would create a speaker's bureau. In addition, the national office would provide participating campuses with films and reports on environmental issues. If no suitable films were available, Dutton wrote, the staff might commission a teach-in production, perhaps by the National Wildlife Federation or the Sierra Club. The issue reports would be prepared by expert task forces, and initially released in a series of news conferences.

Dutton also outlined a public-relations blitz. He was convinced that the environment was a harder sell than opposition to the war, and he urged Nelson to visit as many campuses as possible before spring 1970. He should not just give speeches—he should meet with students, faculty, and local activists who might organize teach-ins. Early in the fall, Nelson should pitch environmental stories and programs to the media, especially the television networks. Ideally, one network would agree to broadcast a made-for-TV teach-in during prime time just before the big day. To keep the teach-in in the news, the national staff should plan a variety of special events, some traditional and some not. Dutton suggested the formation of a national board of sponsors, which would host a miniconference in February. The sponsors might include such luminaries as feminist Gloria Steinem, civil-rights leader Jesse Jackson, consumer advocate Ralph Nader, United Auto Workers leader Walter Reuther, and oceanographer Jacques Cousteau, as well as student activists, university presidents, and professors. Dutton also suggested that the national staff make a list of environmental "villains" and organize nonviolent protests against especially "recalcitrant" polluters. "Negatives are needed in this project as well as affirmations," he wrote.

Nelson took many of Dutton's suggestions. But Nelson rejected the proposal for a top-down event. He understood that the teach-in could not be an extension of his will. Though he conceived the idea, he was willing to let go. Not all at once, not of everything, and not without a struggle in some cases. But Nelson did not try to control the teach-in. That decision allowed Earth Day to engage the creativity of thousands of people.

Launching the teach-in still was a daunting task. The essential first steps—putting together a steering committee, establishing a tax-exempt organization, raising seed money, hiring a staff director, opening the office, getting the attention of the national media—took three manic months. Much of that work fell to Nelson's legislative director, John Heritage.

Though only thirty-one, Heritage had several years of experience with environmental issues. He had begun to ponder the costs of progress in 1960 as a cub reporter at *The Atlanta Constitution*. "Driving to work," he recalled, "I went up and down a valley, it was beautiful, it had dogwood, a stream ran through it, and I got a certain amount of peace going through that road. And then one day I saw bulldozers—by golly, they wiped that stretch of road out, destroyed the stream and the trees, and built homes. And that's when it hit me." While working as a congressional aide in the mid-1960s, Heritage took a keen interest in the Great Society antipollution initiatives. When he returned to journalism after the defeat of his employer, he convinced his bosses at *The Minneapolis Tribune* to let him start an environmental beat. In 1968, he wrote an award-winning series about Minnesota's deteriorating environment, "Assault on the Land." Nelson hired him to work on environmental issues early in 1969.[24]

"I turned into a ball of fire," Heritage said. "I was working 16 hours a day, and I worked those hours for months." No matter how much he did, the to-do list got longer. Write to every governor—and two hundred mayors—to urge their support for the teach-in. Arrange a meeting for Nelson with conservationists. Travel to San Francisco to attend a national conference of student activists. Contact general-interest, professional, and student publications. Identify potential members of the steering committee. Draft news releases, speeches, articles. Prepare a brief about how to organize a teach-in to send to interested students and faculty members. Answer the seemingly endless requests for information. "The phone was just ringing and ringing," Heritage recalled, and the tempo became more feverish, week after week, as more people heard about the teach-in.[25]

Nelson did a lot too. During the fall, he touted the teach-in at every opportunity: a meeting of the AFL-CIO's industrial-union committee, a symposium of young professionals concerned about the environmental crisis, a convention of the American Society for Engineering Education, a congressional conference on the environment. Nelson met in New York City with executives of the four television networks. He raised money. He donated all the honoraria he received for giving speeches to the teach-in—more than $18,000 in all. At Nelson's urging, Walter Reuther arranged for the UAW to contribute $2,000. Not to be outdone by a rival for leadership of the labor movement, George Meany's AFL-CIO gave $1,000—and another $5,000 after Earth Day to help erase a budget deficit. Conservationist Laurance Rockefeller provided almost $18,000. John Gardner, head of the liberal Urban Coalition, offered office space at no charge.[26]

On November 11, Nelson announced the date of the teach-in, a decision that shaped Earth Day in many ways. Because the original emphasis was on college and university events, a Wednesday was appealing. Class attendance was highest in midweek, while a weekend day would mean more competition with nonacademic activities. No one considered what would be best for working adults. Late April fit the academic calendar. At most schools, April 22 was after spring break and before final exams. The date also promised mild weather everywhere. But April 22, 1970, was the one hundredth anniversary of the birth of Vladimir Lenin! Anticommunist crusaders quickly seized on the coincidence to attack Earth Day as subversive. Nelson responded with typical grace and humor. "On any given day, a lot of both good and bad people were born," he said. "A person many consider the world's first environmentalist, Saint Francis of Assisi, was born on April 22. So was Queen Isabella. More important, so was my Aunt Tillie." The attacks continued. A few conservative public officials even refused to sanction April 22 events.[27]

On November 11, Nelson also made the teach-in bipartisan: He announced that Representative Paul (Pete) McCloskey, a California Republican, would co-chair the steering committee. Before entering politics in 1967, McCloskey had been a lawyer with a reputation as a conservationist. He became a local hero by fighting a David-versus-Goliath battle to stop the Atomic

Energy Commission and the Pacific Gas and Electric Company from building aboveground power lines through the scenic town of Woodside. The issue, he argued, was beauty or blight. He also fought against construction of a quarry and garbage dump, and against development of a part of San Francisco Bay. Though he held traditionally Republican views on many issues, he often was called a maverick. In his first campaign, he argued that poverty and racial discrimination were the most important issues the nation faced. He took a strong stand against the Vietnam War—and he eventually campaigned as an antiwar candidate against Richard Nixon in the 1972 Republican presidential primaries. He faced a primary challenge in 1970, and his conservative opponent argued that one of McCloskey's sins was "lending the dignity of his office to Earth Day." McCloskey continued to champion the environmental cause.[28]

The steering committee at first included only one other member: Sydney Howe, president of the Conservation Foundation. The choice of Howe was institutional as well as personal. Unlike the Sierra Club, the National Audubon Society, and the National Wildlife Federation, the Conservation Foundation was not a membership organization, and Nelson did not want to single out one membership organization and risk offending members of the other groups. The foundation had a reputation as a neutral think tank. Founded in 1948 to disseminate expert information about the relationship of resource use and population growth, the foundation had begun to move in compelling new directions in the mid-1960s. Howe's predecessor had commissioned Ian McHarg's landmark manifesto about ecology and planning, *Design with Nature*. Howe was hired in 1965 to help the foundation develop closer ties with grassroots activists, including the League of Women Voters. Like many conservationists, he loved to fish, but he hoped the movement would move beyond the world of privileged enthusiasm for the outdoors. When he became president, he pushed the foundation to devote more attention to urban issues, and especially to the relationship between environmental problems and social justice. His grandfather had founded a college for African-Americans in Virginia, the Hampton Institute, and his father led the school when Howe was growing up, so his commitment to social justice was as much a part of his background as his concern for conservation. Several board members worried about Howe's support of Earth Day, and their skepticism turned out to be a sign that Howe's tenure would be short: He was caught between a conservative board and an increasingly progressive staff, and he resigned in 1973. But in 1970 he was a great help. In addition to offering wisdom, he volunteered to loan the teach-in $10,000, and the foundation's loan was critical in opening the teach-in office.[29]

At the first meeting of the steering committee on November 20, Nelson, McCloskey, and Howe voted to add five members. Paul Ehrlich was one. Another was Harold "Bud" Jordahl, a University of Wisconsin professor of regional planning who had advised Nelson on conservation issues since ORAP days. The other three members were students. Doug Scott was one of the organizers of the University of Michigan's teach-in on the environment, which already was far along by late November. He provided a memo about the planning of the Michigan event that Heritage sent to everyone who inquired about the national teach-in. Glenn Paulson, a Ph.D. student in environmental science at Rockefeller University, was working with the Oil, Chemical, and Atomic Workers on occupational health issues. Charles Creasy was a student leader at Federal City College, a new school in Washington, D.C. Before the second meeting of the steering committee, one more member was added, Wall Street investor Daniel Lufkin, who led the fund-raising effort.[30]

By the end of December, Environmental Teach-In, Inc., finally had flesh and blood. The office opened on the eighth, with a temporary staff. One of Nelson's legislative assistants, Linda Billings, moved to the new office. On December 18, the steering committee approved the hiring of five staff members: the staff director, a press coordinator, a high-school organizer, and two people "to do general staff work for the month of January."[31]

Despite the delay in organizing the office, the teach-in was growing exponentially. In the first twelve days of December, fifty-seven schools inquired about the teach-in. That nearly doubled the number of calls and letters to that point. The pace continued to quicken. On December 16, the mail brought inquiries from twelve schools: Fullerton Junior College, the University of Minnesota, Cedar Crest College, Fresno State College, Cabrillo College, the University of South Dakota, Wheaton College, Albion College, the University of Delaware, Polk Junior College, Swarthmore College, and Yale University. By January, ten inquiries a day was the norm.[32]

The steering committee's decision to hire a high-school organizer was another sign of the teach-in's benign weediness. Even where no one planted seeds, the idea spread with amazing speed. Though Nelson was focused on colleges and universities, K–12 students, teachers, and administrators were inspired. "I've been hearing about this teach-in idea of yours which I think will be great," a Wisconsin student wrote Nelson on November 25, 1969. "Is this just for College or can High Schools do it too. It seems like it would get people thinking." The interest did not just come from individuals. A young National Education Association staff member, Rozanne Weissman, read about the teach-in and decided that schoolteachers ought to be involved. She sent a memo on November 4 to the publication editors of every state NEA affiliate to suggest that they consider publishing stories tied to the event. Many students were angry about pollution, keen to "return to nature," and skeptical about the profit motive, she wrote, and the teach-in offered teachers a chance to make classes more relevant. Weissman sent another memo on November 24 and, after interviewing Nelson, another on December 23. Her third memo suggested that editors publish the Nelson Q & A as well as a statement by NEA president George Fischer endorsing the teach-in. Many followed her suggestion. By early 1970, thousands of NEA members were preparing to involve their classes.[33]

The media also had become more and more interested. Nelson's idea kept popping up—here, there, and then almost everywhere. The teach-in was the lead in a short piece in the October 10, 1969, issue of *Time* about the rise of environmental activism:

> Wisconsin Senator Gaylord Nelson is convinced that the hottest growth stock in U.S. protest is conservation. In fact, Nelson himself is toiling to make the nation's campuses erupt next spring—in a giant, peaceful teach-in about environmental evils. As he has been telling audiences across the country for the past month: "The new generation is not satisfied with coming out on the losing end of man's drive for progress and profit."

On November 30, the new environmental correspondent of *The New York Times*, Gladwin Hill, predicted in a front-page story that the teach-in would be the "D-Day" of a new campus movement. Because student concern about the environment was surging, Hill concluded, the teach-in "could be a bigger and more meaningful event than the antiwar demonstrations." The *Times* also editorialized in support of "The Ultimate in Teach-Ins." *Newsweek* published a report on student environmentalism, "New Bag on Campus," in December. In 1969, when Americans had far fewer news sources than today, the pieces in *Time*, *The New York Times*, and *Newsweek* were the triple crown. As John Heritage recalled, "We climbed some kind of media ladder in the fall."[34]

Nelson kept up the pressure. In January, just before the president delivered the State of the Union address, Nelson spoke to Congress about "the state of the environment." He collaborated with *Country Beautiful* magazine to produce a lavishly illustrated book about the environmental crisis, *America's Last Chance*. He wrote about the teach-in for the April 1970 issue of *Reader's Digest*. He appeared on television talk shows. He received approximately 1,000 speaking invitations, and he accepted dozens. In a sprint to the finish in April, he went on a two-week, seventeen-stop speaking tour. In addition to teach-ins across the country, he addressed the United Auto Workers convention and the Pennsylvania and Massachusetts legislatures. He touted the tour as "a call for political action for environmental sanity." On Earth Day, at last, he could speak about the new day coming.[35]

The Teach-In Staff

Perhaps even more than Nelson, the teach-in staff became personifications of Earth Day. The media viewed the environmental movement as a "youthquake," and the teach-in office was run by young idealists. Everyone was twentysomething. Of the seven most visible staff members, all but one had taken time off from college to travel or try to make the world a better place. All had played a role in the historic campaigns of the sixties. All were convinced that young people could change the direction of society.

For national coordinator Denis Hayes, Earth Day was the unexpected end of a long quest. He grew up in Camas, Washington, a gritty town dominated by the paper mill where his father worked. As a kid, he reveled in the forests and streams of the Cascades. But in his teenage years, his driving ambition was to escape. In 1964, after two years at a community college, he jumped ship. He spent three of the next four years far from home. "I became very, very uptight about the war," he explained in 1970. "I had to get away from the patterns of my life. I had to get away from America. I knew there was a tremendous world out there." He made his way to Hawaii, saved enough money from odd jobs to go to Japan, worked at the Tokyo American

Club, then traveled to the Soviet Union, Eastern Europe, the Middle East, and Africa. He had read Karl Marx and Frantz Fanon, and he was keen to see what kind of societies their ideas had produced. In the Namib Desert one night, when he was stranded, cold, hungry, and exhausted, he finally saw his destination. He would front the essential problems of his time. To do that, he concluded, he needed to study at one of the nation's elite universities. He was accepted at Stanford. After a year there, however, he returned to Japan. Then, finally, he was ready to finish school. Indeed, he was determined to make his mark. In his last year at Stanford, he served as student-body president, and his experience in office helped prepare him for Earth Day. In April 1969, he defused a potentially explosive protest against classified military research. Students occupied the Applied Engineering Laboratory, and Governor Ronald Reagan threatened to send the National Guard to campus. After nine days, Hayes convinced the students to end the occupation by calling an all-school meeting to debate the issue of classified research. The meeting drew 8,000 students, faculty, and administrators, and the overwhelming majority ultimately agreed that classified research betrayed the mission of the university. Two weeks later the trustees endorsed that sentiment. Hayes graduated with a B.A. in history and entered a new Harvard graduate program in public policy for students who also were pursuing professional degrees; his degree would be in law. Near the end of his first semester, he read about the teach-in. Though he had no experience as an environmental activist, he had taken a course in ecology, he had read *Silent Spring* and *The Population Bomb*, and he saw a chance to do something important. He flew to Washington for a ten-minute meeting with Nelson. Their conversation lasted two hours, and Nelson hired him a week later as staff director. Hayes then changed his job title to national coordinator.[36]

Hayes brought two colleagues from Harvard, Andrew Garling and Stephen Cotton. The public-policy program required students to do an off-campus project in January, and Garling and Cotton initially were hired just for that month. Both stayed for the duration. Garling became the Northeast coordinator and recruited several other staff members. Cotton ultimately served as the media coordinator. (The first media coordinator, Phil Taubman, a Stanford student who now works for *The New York Times*, stayed for only two months.) Neither Garling nor Cotton had worked on environmental issues before. They both saw the teach-in as a way to prod middle-of-the-road folks to question the nation's priorities.[37]

Garling was the son of a doctor in Muncie, Indiana, the subject of the celebrated "Middletown" sociological studies in the 1920s and 1930s. His family was straight Republican, but he had little interest in politics as a kid. As an undergraduate at Yale, he took a year off to roam the world by steamship, and his travels politicized him. He majored in sociology and political science. When he went to Harvard Medical School, he resolved to do more than just take classes. He worked with community activists to stop the university from expanding through the bulldozing of poor neighborhoods. He also raised money to go to Vietnam and study civilian casualties. "That *really* politicized me," he recalled. After he returned, he organized Medical Peace Action, a Boston-area group of students. The dean of the medical school soon invited Garling to serve on the Harvard Community Health Plan board of directors. Then the dean recommended him for the public-policy program. If Hayes had not suggested the teach-in as a way to fulfill the program's off-campus requirement, Garling never would have chosen an environmental project. But he agreed that the environment might be a better issue than Vietnam or poverty, because people had not yet had time to harden their positions.[38]

Cotton was a veteran of the civil-rights movement. He grew up in Hyde Park, home of the University of Chicago—an island of privilege in a sea of poverty. Less than 20 percent of the students at his high school were white, and the experience of being a minority sensitized Cotton to the issue of race. At Harvard, he took a year off to work for *The Southern Courier*, a weekly civil-rights newspaper in Alabama started in 1965 by Harvard students who had gone south for Freedom Summer. The *Courier*'s biracial staff reported stories that few southern papers would touch. Cotton returned to Harvard with a powerful faith that journalism could make history. He became editorial page editor of *The Harvard Crimson*, and he worked in the summers for *Newsweek* in Atlanta and London. Because he saw himself as a reporter rather than an activist, he did not join the protests of the day. In his first year at Harvard Law School, however, he led a campaign to change the grading system to pass/fail. "The idea of every man for himself, clawing his way to the top and some Wall Street job over someone else, can't be allowed to dominate legal education any more," he told *The New York Times*. "Law schools shouldn't be trying to teach young lawyers that what matters is making it, and the hell with everyone else." That campaign led to the opportunity to join the public-policy program. When Hayes and Garling suggested the teach-in project, Cotton was skeptical. He saw little evidence that the environment had become the new bag on campus, and he worried that establishment leaders would use the issue to sap the energy of the antiwar and civil-rights movements. But he decided that he could help make the teach-in a more radical event.[39]

Hiring the other coordinators took a few weeks. High-school coordinator Bryce Hamilton and Midwest coordinator Barbara Reid already were working in Washington. Western coordinator Arturo Sandoval came from New Mexico; Garling called him on the recommendation of a former Yale professor who had moved there. Southern coordinator Sam Love was recommended by a Mississippi newspaper editor Cotton had met while working at *The Southern Courier*.[40]

Hamilton was one of the first Peace Corps volunteers. He was not a rebel, yet he had left behind the expectations of his family in Tipton, Iowa, a town of about 3,000. His father headed the county agricultural-extension office and served in the state legislature as a Republican. "Dad keeps asking me when I'm going to settle down and start making some money," he told a reporter in 1970. "But I'm really interested in what I'm doing and I'm not sure that he understands. Dad and I are sort of at opposite ends of the political spectrum." At first, Hamilton planned a career in business. Then John F. Kennedy's call to service inspired him. He took a leave from the University of Iowa to join the Peace Corps, and his experience in Guatemala opened his eyes to the issue of social justice. After he graduated, he "wanted to do his part to make the world a better place." He was working for the American Freedom from Hunger Foundation in Washington when he read about Nelson's plans for the environmental teach-in. The idea wowed him. Not long before, he'd read *The Population Bomb* and become convinced that environmental issues were critical. "I felt the teach-in was cutting-edge," he recalled. "This was so exciting and important and timely." He immediately called Nelson's office, and he jumped at the chance to join the teach-in staff despite the much lower salary.[41]

Reid came to the teach-in office from the Conservation Foundation. She was the only coordinator with conservation credentials—she tracked innovations in environmental education—but she had not made a commitment to the cause. In truth, she was drifting. As a teenager in suburban Detroit, she imagined a career in the state department. (She had become interested in foreign affairs in the sixth grade, when Chrysler transferred her dad to Venezuela and her family moved there.) At the University of Michigan, she studied politics and learned Russian. But the escalation of the Vietnam War derailed her plans. Though never a campus activist, she opposed the war, and she volunteered in Robert Kennedy's presidential campaign in 1968. The campaign engaged her heart and soul: She worked for Kennedy in Indiana, Oregon, and California. "When he was killed," she recalled, "I thought my life was over, and America was going to the dogs, and I was just going to crawl into a hole." After graduating, in despair, she worked for several months for the National Security Agency before taking the job at the Conservation Foundation. Her boss told her about the teach-in. She began to help, unofficially. By January, she was convinced that the teach-in was a rare opportunity, and Hayes and Garling were delighted to hire her. She was skilled—and she was a woman.[42]

For defenders of the Old South, Love was a cold-sweat nightmare. He came from a respectable family in small-town Alabama—his father owned a gas distributorship, and his mother taught school part-time—but he defied southern convention again and again. At Mississippi State University, he befriended the few black students. He registered black voters. In 1968 he was a member of the Mississippi challenge delegation to the Democratic National Convention in Chicago, where he sat alongside Fannie Lou Hamer and other civil-rights leaders. As editor of the student newspaper, he joined a lawsuit challenging a campus ban on civil-rights speakers. During his tenure as editor, the newspaper won renown outside the university for in-depth reporting of "hard issues." He graduated from ROTC, but he filed for conscientious-objector status and refused to go on active duty. He then moved to Greenville, Mississippi, to work for the *Delta Democrat-Times*, and he helped to organize the antiwar moratorium events there in fall 1969. In addition to reporting, he wrote columns that challenged readers. In one, he argued that the nation needed to regain the rebellious independence of 1776. Just before he left town, he tried to unionize the newspaper: Though the editor was liberal on civil rights, the company fired several workers who supported the union. When Garling called about the teach-in, Love was feeling boxed in. He needed a lawyer to fight the army, and he thought he was more likely to find someone in Washington than Greenville. But he felt a pull as well as a push. He always had had a secondary interest in environmental issues. He read Rachel Carson in high school, and he belonged to a campus outdoor recreation and conservation group in college. He became more concerned about the hazards of modern life when a train derailment near Greenville led to a potentially disastrous chemical fire that forced the evacuation of 30,000 people. The teach-in offered a fresh start and a grand cause: Ten days after talking with Garling, Love was in Washington, working hard as the southern organizer.[43]

Sandoval was a child of the "sacred earth" of New Mexico's Espanola Valley. Decades after Earth Day, he wrote that he was raised as much by place as by family and community. His parents did not have a television until he was ten, and he had few store-bought toys. Instead, he played in the vast open spaces of the nearby Santa Clara Pueblo. He talked with birds, danced with trees, and swam in the Rio Grande. "Magicians prowled through my neighborhood at night, disguised as snakes and owls," he remembered. " 'Place' dirtied my clothes, wrung sweat out of my boy's body, made me late for supper, waited up all night for me, and made me whole." In 1970, however, he did not see himself as a defender of the land: He was a Chicano activist. After a year at the University of New Mexico, he joined VISTA, and his VISTA work put him at the center of a controversy over land claims. One of the most fiery defenders of Chicano rights, fundamentalist preacher Reies López Tijerina, even led an armed assault on a county courthouse in 1967 because the district attorney had arrested people for attending public meetings. Three months after the raid, Sandoval returned to the university ready to organize the Chicano community. He worked to form the United Mexican American Students. He pushed the administration to create a Chicano studies program. He also helped the university's physical-plant workers to fight discrimination. When Garling offered him a coordinator position, he consulted his colleagues in UMAS, and all encouraged him to accept.[44]

Though the seven coordinators were the only staff members in the public eye, many other people helped to make the office go. The size of the support staff fluctuated, but typically numbered ten or twelve. The office also attracted dozens of volunteers, from high-school students to middle-aged housewives. The volunteers were supervised by office manager Kent Conrad, a Stanford student from North Dakota who had managed a campaign in his home state to lower the voting age to nineteen (and who later became a U.S. senator).[45]

The staff quickly made a fateful decision. Like Dutton, they thought "environmental teach-in" lacked punch, and they asked New York advertising guru Julian Koenig to suggest a new name for the event. "Earth Day" was one of Koenig's suggestions. The staff debuted the new name on January 18 in a full-page ad in *The New York Times*. In bold, in the paper's biggest font size, the top left of the ad had four words: "April 22. Earth Day." "A disease has infected our country," the ad continued in smaller but still supersized type. "It has brought smog to Yosemite, dumped garbage in the Hudson, sprayed DDT in our food, and left our cities in decay. Its carrier is man." The text then offered a rationale for the event.

On April 22 we start to reclaim the environment we have wrecked.

April 22 is the Environmental Teach-In, a day of environmental action.

Hundreds of communities and campuses across the country are already committed.

It is a phenomenon that grows as you read this.

Earth Day is a commitment to make life better, not just bigger and faster; to provide real rather than rhetorical solutions.

It is a day to re-examine the ethic of individual progress at mankind's expense.

It is a day to challenge the corporate and governmental

leaders who promise change, but who shortchange the necessary programs.

It is a day for looking beyond tomorrow. April 22 seeks a future worth living.

April 22 seeks a future.

The rest of the ad introduced Environmental Teach-In, Inc. Senator Gaylord Nelson had proposed the teach-in and then passed the torch to the group's young staff members, who were "working seven days a week to help communities plan for April 22." The ad ended with a pitch for money. The coupon to accompany donations was a cloud from a smokestack.[46]

Like many activists of the time, Hayes, Cotton, and the rest of the staff had a keen sense of the power of symbols, and many of their early decisions were driven by concern about the teach-in's image. They wanted Earth Day to be a force for social transformation, not just for environmental reform. Though they hoped to attract folks who did not see themselves as radical, their overriding priority was to ensure that young people did not see April 22 as a cop-out.

Hayes immediately decided that a well-appointed office near Capitol Hill would give the wrong impression. A youthful movement for social change needed something dingy, even run-down. Hayes rented a ten-room office near DuPont Circle—at the time a high-crime neighborhood. To *Life* magazine, the area simply was a ghetto. Not long after the staff moved, the space below became a greasy spoon, Buffalo Bill's, that quickly became a haven for rough characters and lost souls. "Druggies, run-aways, pushers and hustlers occasionally stumbled upstairs . . . looking for a john," Cotton wrote; "drunks just used the staircase." No reporter could miss the message: The teach-in headquarters was no citadel of privilege. The interior reinforced the outsider image. The walls were covered with protest posters. "War is not healthy for children and other living things," one proclaimed.

Another poster revised a prowar slogan to define a new patrio-
tism: "Earth—Love it or Leave it!" A third declared, "Pollution
is a form of violence." Though the office contained equipment
capable of producing 30,000 pieces of mail a week, the efficiency of the operation was obscured by seemingly chaotic
piles of paper.[47]

On January 20, Hayes made the cop-out issue the focus of his
first news conference. He defined the new cause as "a movement
concerned with life." He then debunked three "myths." Myth
number one was "that environmental concerns will be a quieting
force—stilling troubled campuses and healing the wounds of a
divided nation." That was "wishful thinking," he said. "There are
fundamental value conflicts between those who seek a better
world, and those who care only for size, speed, and profit." Myth
number two was "that the environment movement will co-opt
people from other pressing social concerns to march on pollution." Not at all. "For ecology is concerned with the total system—
not just the way it disposes of its garbage. Our goal is not to clean
the air while leaving slums and ghettos, nor is it to provide a
healthy world for racial oppression and war. We wish to make the
probability of life greater, the quality of life higher. Those who
share these goals cannot be 'co-opted'; they are our allies—not our
competitors." Myth number three was "that the environment issue will defuse the anti-war movement." People can focus on more
than one issue at a time, Hayes argued, and in any case the fate of
the antiwar movement would be shaped by developments in
Washington, Vietnam, and Paris, the site of peace talks. Then
Hayes concluded by reflecting on the history of environmental
reform. Many of the concerns of 1970 were not new. Henry David
Thoreau, Theodore Roosevelt, and many others had called for
Americans to protect the environment. But the earlier efforts had
failed to prevent poisoned rivers, polluted air, scarred countrysides,
and deteriorating cities. The goal of Earth Day was "to involve an
entire society in a rethinking of many of its basic assumptions."[48]

The day after the news conference, the staff dumped the name "Environmental Teach-In, Inc." To hard-core activists, teach-ins were archaic: The first antiwar teach-in was in 1965, and that seemed like ages ago. "Teach-in" suggested that people just would talk, talk, talk. The word also suggested that April 22 would be campus-bound. The staff wanted something more forward-looking. They settled on Environmental Action. Though the legal name of the organization could not be changed, the group's stationery and publications highlighted the new name.[49]

In different ways, the staff also distanced Environmental Action from the Establishment. The group publicly rejected contributions from Mobil, Ford, and Standard Oil of New Jersey. Hayes ridiculed Richard Nixon's 1970 environmental agenda as smoke blowing. When Nixon aide John Ehrlichman invited Hayes to the White House, Hayes refused the invitation. As Cotton explained, too many politicians thought they could look good simply by expressing an interest in the environment, and Environmental Action didn't want to contribute to that sham. Though no one on the staff dissed Nelson, Hayes and Cotton often declared their independence. The teach-in steering committee didn't do any steering, they told reporters. That was not entirely true. The committee periodically discussed the budget, which ultimately reached $124,000. After Hayes attacked Nixon's legislative proposals, the committee warned that further comments might jeopardize the group's tax-exempt status. But otherwise the staff had real freedom.[50]

In the original plan for the teach-in, the national office was to serve as "an organizational stimulus, a communications clearinghouse, and a service center for the campus teach-ins," and Environmental Action worked hard to meet all three mandates. But the effort proved far more challenging than Dutton or Nelson foresaw. Every week, Earth Day grew bigger, and the office became more frenzied.[51]

Hamilton had the most straightforward job. The sheer

number of schools meant that he could not work closely with students and teachers. But he was deluged with requests for help. Most were from students. "Please send me all the information you have on Earth Day," wrote one. "I am in the fifth grade and would like to organize my community. The teachers and adults of my area are less aware of the urgency of this problem than the children and I would like to make them aware. I will send some money when I can." Hamilton answered the queries with a six-page letter. He offered almost forty suggestions for Earth Day activities, some purely educational and some more activist:

2. Make a local pollution inventory and establish "a pollution dis-honor roll."
7. Ask teachers to make the environment their subject on April 22.
13. Create an environmental corner in the library.
20. Write anti-pollution songs or skits.
25. Hold a well-publicized "mourn-in" for a polluted stream.
28. Set up environmental booths in your community's business district.
37. Encourage people to walk or ride bicycles instead of driving cars on April 22.

Hamilton also provided a brief guide to ecology books, a list of environmental organizations that provided educational materials, and ordering information for environmental films.[52]

For the regional coordinators, the overriding task turned out to be building a database. Where were Earth Day efforts under way? Who was involved, and what were they planning? Reid, Garling, Sandoval, and Love spent hour after hour calling student leaders, faculty members, and administrators. They called community groups. They also followed up every inquiry about how to organize a college or community teach-in. As Environmental Action received more publicity, the flow of communication became two-way: Without prompting, many local organizers sent the office information about their plans. "We were the PR office for what was happening," Reid recalled. "We kept track of everything."[53]

At first, the regional coordinators hoped to be catalysts as well as information gatherers. They encouraged their contacts to plan events that would engage diverse groups, reach beyond campus, and involve more than intellectual exchange. But the immensity of Earth Day soon overwhelmed the staff. In a time without computers and cell phones, just keeping up with the evolving plans of the ever-growing number of local organizers took enormous effort.

With very little time for organizing, the coordinators focused on big cities. The cities offered the best chance, they thought, to demonstrate that environmental issues were not just a concern of affluent white kids. The city focus became even more emphatic in March, when Environmental Action realized that New York's celebration would be much bigger than they expected. Many other cities also had dramatic plans, but many did not. Would the media judge Earth Day a failure if some of the nation's great cities did nothing?[54]

The organizing effort failed in several cities, but the staff pulled a rabbit out of the hat in Chicago. In January and February, Reid spoke several times with a young Chicago attorney, Joe Karaganis, who had become a vocal critic of the city's air-quality program and who had tried to unite local college students in a group called Help Stop Pollution. But in March, Chicago still had no plans for a downtown event on April 22. With help from native son Cotton, Reid invited civic leaders, labor representatives, social activists, and students to a coalition-building meeting on March 22. Though several groups were planning Earth Day programs, she wrote, "What is needed is a massive effort to mobilize the people of Chicago. Time and again groups have told me that Chicago is an environmental catastrophe—that its air is polluted, its lake is polluted, its South and West side are unlive-able, its public housing is unbearable, its major industries are unconcerned, and its local government unresponsive. April 22 is a day of action. It is a day when people throughout the city—and throughout the country—will be watching." About twenty-five people attended the meeting, and the group agreed to form the Chicago Earth Day Committee, chaired by Karaganis. In the next month, the committee managed to organize a noontime rally at the city's civic center plaza that drew between 4,000 and 7,000 people.[55]

In addition to direct contacts, the staff communicated with local organizers through a newsletter, *Environmental Action: April 22*. The preliminary teach-in budget did not provide for a publication, but Hayes decided that a newsletter was a critical organizing tool. The UAW offered to print the newsletter, which ranged from six to twelve pages—a huge in-kind contribution. The inaugural issue was mailed on January 31 to 7,000 individuals and organizations. After that issue, Love volunteered to serve as editor. By early March, the newsletter was appearing weekly. Every issue included "action notes" about Earth Day plans across the country. The newsletter reported in detail on the January 23 "teach-out" at Northwestern and the March teach-in at the University of Michigan, which drew huge crowds. Almost every issue included a list of eco-films as well as information about useful and cheap publications. (By the end of March, most of the films were booked for Earth Week.) To encourage Earth Day planners to emphasize political action, several issues included notes about pending environmental legislation.[56]

Beyond help with Earth Day planning, the newsletter aimed to give a sense that local organizers were part of a movement. Every issue sought to define the new movement by example. Several articles offered case studies of grassroots activism. In Chicago, for example, the Campaign Against Pollution was pressuring Commonwealth Edison to reduce harmful emissions, and the newsletter recommended the group's publications to anyone "challenging a corporate polluter." Other articles told about the rise of environmental law, the efforts of union members to stop pollution, and the campaign led by Ralph Nader to win seats on the General Motors board of directors for representatives of the environmental, consumer, and civil-rights movements. After Love settled into the job, the newsletter included articles about specific issues, including several topics rarely covered in traditional conservation publications—from lead paint and ghetto children to mass transit and highway funding. The newsletter also displayed the playful, satiric, countercultural side of the movement. Every issue featured underground cartoons from Ron Cobb's collection *Raw Sewage*. One issue included an essay on "ecological living," and another reprinted the *Chicago Seed*'s guide to making do after the environmental apocalypse. The newsletter even offered mock renditions of Mother Goose rhymes and "America the Beautiful."[57]

The media coverage of Environmental Action reinforced the idea that a powerful movement was emerging. "America's Youth Rallies to the War on Pollution," UPI reported on February 22. CBS News aired a special on "The Environment Crusade" two days later. *The New York Times* reported on March 2 that the young activists were organizing a "wide environmental protest." On March 15, *The Washington Post* summarized plans for Earth Day in a story entitled "Ecology: Protests to Mount." Countless other reports, columns, and editorials made the same point. The coverage helped to recast the teach-in as a "protest." Of course, the media buildup also suggested that Earth Day had momentum.[58]

Though the coverage was phenomenal, Cotton made one problematic decision. In discussions with reporters, editors, and television producers about what to cover on Earth Day, he pitched off-campus events. They were an easier sell: The media preferred spectacle. But Cotton's emphasis on community events derived as much from his own biases and aspirations as from media needs. He was bored by lectures and panel discussions. He also was keen to show that the environmental cause had mass appeal. He only partly succeeded. The middle of the day in the middle of the week was not an ideal time for adults to gather, and some of the big-city events were disappointments or even bombs. With a few exceptions, the best university teach-ins were bigger and better organized than the community celebrations. More people came to see Paul Ehrlich at the University of Minnesota, for example, than attended the rally in Chicago. By directing the media away from campuses, Cotton undersold Earth Day.[59]

The staff certainly tried to give substance to Cotton's pitch. On Earth Day, Sandoval spoke in Albuquerque at a march he helped to organize. Reid went to Minneapolis: She had worked with students there to plan a protest against General Electric. Environmental Action also organized the off-campus events in D.C.

The march in Albuquerque was a pioneering call for environmental justice. As Sandoval hoped, the demonstration attracted the attention of people outside the Chicano community. Though the *Albuquerque Journal* rarely reported on life in the barrios, the paper published a story about plans for the march on April 19. "The environmental crisis is nothing new to the Chicano population," the organizers argued. "This crisis has existed since the Chicano was forced from his farm lands into the crowded, polluted, poverty-stricken barrios. The Chicano's environment has long been one of deprivation and exploitation." In the barrios, residents endured the stench of a sewage plant. They were exposed to hazardous emissions from nearby factories. Garbage collection was erratic. The unpaved streets were dusty, and the drainage ditches were unsafe. Children lacked decent places to play. The housing was poor, with inadequate sanitary facilities. Medical care also was inadequate. To dramatize those hardships, the march would go from a city park through one of the poorest barrios to the sewage plant. The route, CBS News reported, was "seldom seen by outsiders."[60]

On April 23, the march was the lead in the *Journal*'s Earth Day coverage. More than three hundred people took part, led by a horseback rider and a mariachi band. Many marchers carried angry signs, some in English and some in Spanish. "Keep your pollution. Give us life." "Free the brown people." The speakers at the rally highlighted the tie between oppression and environmental degradation. Why were sewage plants always near the poor and powerless, one asked, and not near the owners of big houses on the ridges?[61]

The *Journal* quoted only a few lines from Sandoval's speech, but Environmental Action included an excerpt in a collection of Earth Day speeches. Sandoval argued that Chicanos could help save society. Most Americans were "afraid of their humanity because systematically they have been taught to become inhuman," he said. "They have been taught that money is God." They had no appreciation of people who were different. They also had "no understanding of what it is to love nature." They did not realize that "our father is the sun and our mother is the Earth. And that is sad, more than anything else." To regain their humanity, they needed to ponder the concept of *la raza*. "'La raza'—'the race'—goes beyond surname and goes beyond skin color," Sandoval explained. "And it doesn't address itself only to those of us who call ourselves 'Chicano.'" Everyone was oppressed by American institutions. The march through the barrio was not only a rallying of residents, but an effort to awaken the humanity of others. By shouting "Viva la raza," Sandoval said, "we command 'la raza' to live, because humanity is dying. And America—white America—has lost its ability to cry, and laugh and sing and love and live." The march expressed the willingness of Chicanos to join in making all places "human, life-supporting kinds of environments."[62]

The Minneapolis rally was one of a number of protests at

stockholder meetings in spring 1970. Despite rain and bitter cold, about four hundred people biked and walked from the university to the civic auditorium where the GE stockholders were gathered. The bikers escorted a coffin filled with appliances. At the auditorium, the group demanded that GE refuse all war contracts, lobby to change the nation's priorities, and stop producing "shoddy, wasteful, power-consuming, pollution-producing gadgets." The caravan then moved to a church next door to hold a psychedelic funeral for the appliances. After the funeral, the group proceeded to a park to plant a tree of life.[63]

Reid spoke at the church. Though the speech was her first "rap" as a protest leader, she was a rock star. "What we see here today is the beginning of a movement, it is a movement determined to make the corporate, government, and educational institutions of this country responsive to the needs of the people," she argued. "To get at the roots of the environmental crisis we face on this planet, we must begin to talk about the decision-making structure of our society. Pollution and the Vietnam war are symptoms of misplaced priorities and a warped conception of human values. To many of us it seems that individuals have lost control over their lives, that they are manipulated by a system with an inherent death wish rather than one in which enhancement of life is the primary goal. The major symbol of this death culture is the institutionalized violence perpetrated upon people and the land by corporations such as General Electric." In addition to fueling the war machine, GE stoked "our overconsumptive and 'planned obsolescence' culture." The company pushed consumers to buy "technological gadgets" that were a form of "waste," not a part of the good life. "We must be prepared to make GE contribute to a more ecologically sound world," Reid concluded. "We must begin to make some sacrifices ourselves, and those adjustments in our life-style cannot continue to be judged in terms of profit alone. GE also must begin to make some sacrifices."[64]

Washington became the responsibility of Environmental Action by default as much as design. The staff briefly considered and then rejected "a march on Washington." They did not want to draw people away from events around the country, and they were afraid that an eco-march would pale compared with the antiwar and civil-rights marches of the sixties. Instead, Garling tried to persuade D.C.-area students to organize a big off-campus event, but he struck out. The environment was not a priority at the city's two black schools. Where interest was stronger, the most active students thought that campus events would be more valuable than a media spectacle. In March, finally, a new Environmental Action staffer—Steven Haft, a veteran of John Lindsay's political campaigns in New York—took the job of organizing the D.C. celebration.[65]

Haft planned two events. Earth Day began with a march on the Interior Department—the federal agency responsible for managing public lands—to protest "the despoliation of the environment and the anti-life policies of the Nixon administration." The protest drew about 2,500 people. The rest of the day was "a celebration of life" at the Sylvan Theater near the Washington Monument. The program included a spectacular mix of music— folk, soul, new jazz, pop—headlined by Pete Seeger. The crowd reached about 10,000 by evening. As one of the musicians exclaimed, the scene was "our little Woodstock."[66]

Though the Sylvan Theater event mostly was a party, the program included five speakers: Washington minister and activist Channing Phillips, Chicago Seven defendant Rennie Davis, rebel journalist I. F. Stone, Senator Edmund Muskie, and Denis Hayes. All argued that the environmental cause could not succeed in isolation. "I'm here tonight not because we're changing issues in the middle of the stream," Phillips said, "but out of a deep conviction that racial injustice, war, urban blight, and environmental rape have a common denominator in our exploitive economic system." Davis vowed not "to be tricked into an ecology movement that diverts us from our revolutionary purposes." The system sucked, and "token changes" were not enough: "We are saying that we are going to pick up the shit in this country, but in the context of a movement to liberate ourselves." Stone warned the audience not to be conned. "The country is slipping into a widening war in southeast Asia," he said, "and we're talking about litterbugs." Earth Day couldn't succeed until Americans started to think like Earth people—"fellow travelers on a tiny planet in an infinite universe"—and until the nation had leaders "willing to make the enormous changes . . . to end the existing world system." Muskie was more moderate. But he, too, understood the theme of the event. He argued that "human resources should be conserved as well as natural resources. We ought to be talking about abuses of our fellow men."[67]

Hayes had spoken often about the values of the new movement in the three months before Earth Day. In Santa Barbara on the first anniversary of the oil spill, he critiqued the "I want it!" mind-set of American consumer culture. At the annual meeting of the National Wildlife Federation, he argued that the defense of life required "a profound change in what this country is all about," not a never-ending series of technical patches. His Earth Day speech was a summing-up.[68]

"I suspect that the politicians and businessmen who are jumping on the environmental bandwagon don't have the slightest idea what they are getting into," Hayes began. "They are talking about filters on smokestacks while we are challenging corporate irresponsibility. They are bursting with pride about plans for totally inadequate municipal sewage treatment plants; we are challenging the ethics of a society that, with only 6 percent of the world's population, accounts for more than half of the world's annual consumption of raw materials." Indeed, the United States had "a reverse Midas touch. Everything we touch turns to garbage." Of course, planned obsolescence and pollution were not the only symptoms of a failing society. "We're spending insanely large sums on military hardware instead of eliminating hunger and poverty," Hayes argued. "We still waste lives and money on a war that we should never have entered and should get out of immediately." Like the war, like injustice, the destruction of the environment could not be stopped by individual action. "You simply can't live an ecologically sound life in America." To stop the killing of the planet, Americans had to transform powerful institutions. "Things as we know them are falling apart," Hayes concluded. "People know that something is wrong." That awareness had sparked a mass movement to force drastic changes in society. The new movement valued people more than technology, more than political ideology, and more than profit. "It will be a difficult fight. Earth Day is the beginning."[69]

That literally was true for Hayes and his colleagues. They formed a new corporation, Environmental Action, so that they could go forward without the constraints of tax-exempt status. They were determined to turn the Earth Day network into a political force.

The Grassroots Organizers

Tens of thousands of people made Earth Day happen on university and college campuses, at schools, and in cities and towns. Most were essentially volunteers. They posted flyers or escorted speakers or sold "Give Earth a Chance" buttons. But thousands of people were more intimately involved. They organized Earth Day events, and their decisions defined what Earth Day would be. Many local organizers devoted three or four months to the project. During that time, Earth Day was the driving force in their lives. Because few local organizers had managed anything like Earth Day before, the process tested them both practically and intellectually. Many found the experience exhilarating, even life-changing.[70]

Graduate students in the sciences were critical to the organizing effort at many research universities. Most were excited by the challenge of using their scientific training in a popular cause. Some had protested against the Vietnam War, but the antiwar movement had never really engaged them: The environmental teach-in promised to make much better use of their energies. Relatively few of the graduate organizers already were environmental activists. The most entrepreneurial had founded campus eco-groups. At the University of Illinois, the two graduate organizers of Earth Week had started Students for Environmental ConcernS (the capital S made the acronym SECS, pronounced like "sex") in 1968. The group soon joined a fight to stop a proposed Army Corps of Engineers flood-control project on a scenic river. But the first SECS projects mostly were lighthearted. To recruit undergraduates, SECS sponsored a cleanup of a campus creek and a symbolic demolition of a junkyard car. By 1970, SECS had hundreds of members. The planning of Earth Week was by far the group's most ambitious undertaking.[71]

The undergraduate organizers of Earth Day mostly were latent environmentalists. Though they did not belong to any conservation groups, they marveled at nature or worried about environmental degradation. Many were biology majors. Some had worked summers in national parks, and organizing Earth Day seemed a logical next step. Others had grown up in smoggy cities or watched sprawl destroy places they loved. Many undergraduate organizers had read a revelatory book—*The Population Bomb* or *Silent Spring*, usually—but had not imagined that they could do anything to protect the environment until they heard about Earth Day. At Iowa State University, the undergraduate coordinators of the environmental teach-in all were students in a seminar on "Wildlife Conservation in a Changing World" who realized that their interest in environmental issues went deeper than they had thought.[72]

Earth Day also attracted many undergraduates who had

not shown any interest in the environment before. Some were campus activists who concluded that the new environmental movement was more likely to transform society than the antiwar movement. Earth Day appealed even more to idealistic students who were wary of extremism. Though they were not willing to get arrested or alienate their parents, they were keen to be involved in a cause. Who could doubt that stopping pollution was a noble mission? The respectability of the antipollution effort also inspired some student-government leaders to organize Earth Day events. As one explained, "We want to show the good side of students for a change."[73]

Professors took the lead at some schools. Some were dedicated conservationists, but most were recent converts to the cause. Though the faculty organizers came from many disciplines, scientists predominated. Biologist John Chambers at East Texas State University was typical. Though his research focused on algae, he had read a lot about population growth, pesticides, and pollution, and he had begun to fear disaster. "I guess I will be called an alarmist," he told the local newspaper a month before Earth Day. "They say we have to do something now or we're doomed. I tend to agree with them."[74]

At most universities and colleges, the planning process was ad hoc. Someone heard about Earth Day, talked about the event with friends or colleagues, and then called a public meeting for anyone interested in helping to save the world. The public meetings sometimes drew hundreds of people. The attendees became an Earth Day committee—or they formed a group with a more grandiose name. Elsewhere, established student organizations or academic departments sponsored Earth Day events. The number of campus eco-groups grew tremendously in 1969, and some of the newly formed groups made Earth Day their first big project. At some schools, the organizing effort ultimately involved several organizations.[75]

The first challenge was intellectual. Because Earth Day was a new phenomenon, organizers had no template to follow. Even the goal was not a given. Was the mission to spark discussion or inspire action? How much of Earth Day should be a spectacle? Could the teach-in be a celebration of the life-giving wonders of nature as well as a critique of environmental exploitation? Should the organizers try to tie the environmental crisis to the other great issues of the era?

The scale of Earth Day also was not a given. The simplest teach-ins involved a handful of speakers in one venue. As a rule, though, organizers planned a variety of events and activities, with many occurring simultaneously. The most complex celebrations lasted a week or more. The organizers did not start with the idea that Earth Day should be Earth Week, but as they imagined what they might do, they decided that they needed more than one day. A few organizers concluded that even a week was not enough: They put together winter lecture series to lead up to the April teach-in.[76]

At the University of Wisconsin, the Earth Week organizers decided that inclusiveness would be a major goal. If the Students for a Democratic Society and the Sportsmen's Club both wanted to participate, that was fine. "We all felt that we had to be pretty ecumenical," coordinator Tom Smith recalled. "There wasn't going to be any central control of the image. We weren't about to tell anyone what and how to worship." The Wisconsin organizers still drew some lines. They rejected protests because they did not want any risk of violence. They chose a theme—Lifestyle on Trial—to give coherence to the program. But they made space for almost everything people wanted to do, from a panel on quality of life organized by the nursing school to an "eco-pornography" exhibit of corporate advertisements.[77]

In the South, many Earth Day organizers tried to avoid anything that would cause people to dismiss the event as radical. At the University of Georgia, the teach-in coordinators—mostly graduate students in ecology—gauged the situation perfectly.

The Atlanta Constitution reported that the teach-in lacked "histrionics, dramatic burials of internal combustion engines, or lengthy diatribes against industry." The "quiet" character of the program won plaudits. The *Constitution*'s editorial page editor praised the Georgia event in a column entitled "Quiet Reform." "This was a blending of education and philosophy that sometimes reached toward religion for inspiration," he wrote. The organizers did not want teach-in participants to scream strident slogans. Instead, they encouraged thoughtful discussion. That might not sound exciting, the columnist concluded, but it was: "It will take precisely this kind of quiet contemplation and determination to maintain the good earth."[78]

The issue of tone was not just ideological. The organizers at Montana Tech wanted to avoid overblown rhetoric. Though "other programs may stress the sensational side of the environmental problem," one explained, "we as engineers are trying to present the rational approach." Their Earth Day symposium emphasized expertise. The speakers included a mining professor, a biology professor, a water-pollution specialist from the state board of health, the director of environmental engineering for the Anaconda mining company, a representative of a forest-products company, and a state fish-and-wildlife official. The only activist on the panel was a woman from the Montana Wilderness Association. "I'm in the nuts-and-bolts end of this business," the water-pollution specialist began, and that summed up the spirit of the evening: Environmental problems were serious, but they could be solved if people really worked at it.[79]

At Caltech, in contrast, the organizers concluded that a program of sober talk would have limited appeal. They paired a teach-in with a festive Ecology Faire. Students served "pollution-free food" made from organically grown ingredients. Kids could play in plywood geodesic domes. Strings of black balloons floated skyward as a playful symbol of air pollution, while brightly colored balloons on the ground suggested the joys of nature. "The Teach-In and Ecology Faire were designed around people and laughter, not numbers and fear," organizer Paul Wegener explained. "Numbers are vital to an understanding of what is to be done and how to do it, but there is a point at which they should be left behind."[80]

The decisions about the tone of the teach-ins were just the start. Every detail of the Earth Day program could become a subject of debate. What counted as an environmental issue? How much of the discussion should focus on solutions to problems? Should the program feature local speakers or outsiders? Were art and music important? Would Earth Day go beyond campus boundaries?

The treatment of industry was a big issue. To many young people in 1970, business was the enemy. Did Earth Day organizers want to stoke that fire? A few teach-ins included protests against "corporate polluters," a phrase Ralph Nader popularized at the time. But most organizers rejected demonstrations. "We were afraid that if we picketed the factories," Albion College organizer Walt Pomeroy told CBS News, "it would actually turn the community against us." Instead, some organizers presented mock awards to polluters. Industry wasn't the only target, but electric utilities, chemical plants, and mining companies were common dishonorees. At the University of New Mexico, students kicked off a "Boycott the Oil Company of Your Choice" campaign on Earth Day. Only a handful of organizers took the opposite approach: They used their bully pulpit to recognize companies that had encouraged recycling or spent considerable sums on pollution-control equipment.[81]

Organizers also had to decide how much voice to give business in teach-in discussions. Was a corporate perspective essential to any consideration of how best to protect the environment? To some organizers, the answer was yes, beyond a doubt. They tried to include representatives of industry in every panel about pollution or resource use. At other schools, organizers just gave corporate officials one session to tell their side of the story. Getting speakers from industry was not always easy in any case. Though many businesses were happy to participate, others feared that Earth Day crowds would be hostile. Only three firms provided speakers for Pittsburgh's multicollege teach-in, although the organizers would have welcomed more. "In the early days, when the teach-in was being organized, the companies didn't quite know what they were getting into," one organizer told *Industry Week*. "They didn't want to be egg-throwing targets. When they found out the type of program we were planning, it was too late."[82]

Politics was another question. Should elected officials be included? Some organizers wanted to avoid partisanship. But many others were keen to provide a forum for political debate. Some sought to force politicians to take stands on controversial questions. Others hoped to educate their elected officials. "At that time, people didn't trust politicians very much," University of Virginia organizer Alan Strahler recalled, "but we thought they needed to be made aware of the issues. We thought maybe if we reached out to them, they'd take notice."[83]

At the University of Minnesota, the teach-in committee was tugged both ways. "We wanted to keep everything nonpartisan," coordinator Karim Ahmed explained, but Senator Walter Mondale "wiggled himself into our good graces." Mondale's office called several times to ask if he could speak on Earth Day, and the committee said no. Then Mondale's staff arranged for Ahmed to meet the senator in Washington when Ahmed was at a conference nearby. "They treated me like royalty!" Ahmed recalled. "I talked with Mondale for half an hour or more, about everything under the sun. I was very impressed." At Ahmed's suggestion, the teach-in committee invited the state's congressional delegation to participate in the weeklong event. The committee organized a Friday forum where students, professors, and activists questioned the three representatives who agreed to attend. Senator Eugene McCarthy declined the invitation, but Mondale spoke at one of the main events on Earth Day.[84]

The practical demands of Earth Day organizing varied tremendously. Fund-raising is a good example. Most teach-ins required very little money, but some Earth Day organizers spent thousands of dollars, and a few had five-figure budgets. National speakers typically demanded honoraria and travel expenses. Programs and posters sometimes were big items. Many Earth Day organizers advertised in college or community newspapers. The most common source of funds was the sale of Earth Day buttons or books. School officials and student-government leaders often provided major funding. Some organizers also secured foundation grants or donations from local businesses.[85]

Though students and faculty members had considerable autonomy, some Earth Day organizers needed to assure apprehensive administrators that their events would be positive. The chancellor at the University of Tennessee summoned the teach-in coordinators to his office to address the concerns of the university police. "The chancellor asked if we planned to take over the university," coordinator Jim Harb recalled. "Ludicrous as that question was, I answered yes. A long silence! Then I broke the silence by admitting that I was kidding. The chancellor believed us, although he'd taken seriously the warnings of the security folks." At Iowa State, the faculty adviser to the Earth Week committee, David Trauger, spoke often with the university's public-relations officer. "He was keeping tabs on everything we did," Trauger said. "The administration was really concerned about things getting out of hand—not so much violence, but giving a bad image to the university. I promised him that we weren't going to embarrass the university, that we weren't going to do anything radical, that we would be responsible."[86]

At most schools, however, administrators were glad to see students excited about a constructive cause. Many university and college presidents officially endorsed teach-ins, and some spoke at Earth Day events. The administration at the University of Illinois gave the Earth Week committee $40,000. At several universities, officials allowed graduate students to use fellowships to work full-time on teach-in planning. Many schools provided office space to Earth Day organizers. Some even provided secretarial support. Officials also accommodated all kinds of special requests: They closed the heart of campus to automobile traffic, allowed students to bury a car engine in a quad, or provided a university plane to make travel easier for a prominent speaker. A few schools canceled classes on Earth Day.[87]

In K–12 schools, Earth Day in the lower grades usually did not require much planning. The celebrations mostly involved in-class activities or field trips: Kids made posters, composed poems, wrote letters to public officials, watched films, and cleaned up litter on the school grounds or at nearby parks or beaches. Junior highs often had special classes or assemblies, and teachers and school officials did what little needed to be done. In many high schools, however, more was involved. Some high-school celebrations rivaled those in colleges and universities. They lasted a week, and they involved dozens of speakers. Even one-day events in high schools often took months of planning.

The high-school events mostly were organized by students with the help of faculty advisers. Many high-school organizers loved science or the outdoors. At some schools, Earth Day appealed especially to antiestablishment students. As a Bethesda, Maryland, organizer recalled, "The degradation of the environment brought out the typical teenage angst and the '60s contempt for anyone over 30—they'd screwed everything up." But Earth Day was not just a lefty or countercultural thing. The teach-in committee at a Long Island high school included students who had participated in an Honor America march as well as anti-war activists. Student-council members planned teach-ins. For some students, Earth Day was a way to show civic spirit.[88]

The faculty advisers mostly were science teachers, but many social-science teachers also mentored teach-in organizers. Though some advisers had a keen interest in environmental issues, many did not. The social-science teachers often saw Earth Day as a way to engage students more deeply. Some already were experimenting with problem-based methods of making class more relevant. In other cases, the advisers simply were responding to student demand: Fired-up students asked them to help, and they did. In Oak Park, Illinois, biology teacher Ed Radatz became involved when sophomore Nancy Stockholm stopped him in the hall and asked what he was doing about the environment. "I said, 'Nothing,'" he recalled. "And she said we should do something." With Radatz's support, Stockholm and another student organized a weeklong environmental workshop and established a Pollution Control Center that soon won national recognition.[89]

At some schools, a few students did everything. The Earth Day effort at other schools involved crews of twenty or more. The bigger groups operated like the yearbook committee, with subcommittees responsible for speakers, exhibits, artwork, and publicity. To signify their resolve to remain active after April 22, many Earth Day organizers gave their groups names, often with classic sixties acronyms. State College, Pennsylvania, had SLOP (Student League Opposing Pollution); Schenectady, New York, had YUK (Youth Uncovering Krud); Cloquet, Minnesota, had SCARE (Students Concerned About a Ravaged Environment); and Richmond, Virginia, had SHAME (Studying and Halting the Assault on Man and the Environment).[90]

Most administrators were happy to give their blessings. That was essential. Though some high-school events were at night, the vast majority took place during the school day, so the organizers needed to ask administrators to set aside daily routines. Could some classes be canceled? Could the entire school assemble to hear a keynote speaker? The multiday events required even more disruptive adjustments to class schedules. In addition to allowing schedule changes, some administrators gave Earth Day organizers a small budget.

The high-school organizers faced many of the same challenges as their older counterparts. They debated what subjects were appropriate. They also debated the character of their Earth Day celebrations. Though some forms of protest were out of the question, for example, students still might choose to go beyond the purely educational. In Springfield, Illinois, the Earth Day assembly at one school began with a mock funeral procession for the "dead earth." After the assembly, students marched to the state capitol to present antipollution petitions to legislators.[91]

Getting speakers often took as much time as deciding what kind of event to sponsor. High-school organizers rarely asked their teachers to speak. They did not want Earth Day to seem familiar. Instead, they hoped to engage their peers in the world beyond school. That meant getting local activists, business leaders, professionals, government officials, and college professors to agree to speak. Though some organizers were go-getters, others were shy, and they had to push themselves to make pitches to adults.

The Earth Day teach-in in San Mateo, California, is a good example of the high-school organizing effort—some events were simpler, and some were more sophisticated. The San Mateo teach-in was planned by an ecology club formed in December 1969 after biology teacher Edmond Holm took his advanced-placement class to hear Paul Ehrlich speak at Stanford. By April 1970, the club had about seventy members, and twelve were especially involved with the teach-in. Most were high-achieving math or science students who saw the event as a chance to do something cool. One stalwart was a budding journalist nicknamed Captain Ecology by his colleagues on the school newspaper: His hero was Harold Gilliam, a *San Francisco Chronicle* columnist who fought to stop filling of the bay. Several of the teach-in organizers wanted to change the world. One was a cheerleader, and one later became student-body president. Four of the twelve were Asian-American. "For most of us," teach-in organizer Chris Bowman recalled, "this was our first experience with social activism."[92]

The students had a lot of help. Holm ate lunch with the teach-in committee once a week to plan the program. What would attract people who weren't interested in nature? The students abandoned some ideas because they could not find speakers. Other ideas ultimately seemed too far-out. Once the program was set, Holm met daily with the lead organizers to make sure that everything came together. "I can't overestimate the difference Mr. Holm made," coordinator Susan Obata recalled. "I thought many times that I was way over my head trying to organize this, but Mr. Holm gave us a lot of encouragement and faith we could do it." The principal also supported the effort. He agreed to end classes at 11:30 so the teach-in could last all afternoon, and he let the organizers hold a schoolwide assembly before lunch. English and art teachers allowed students to use class time to enter contests for the best eco-poems and artwork. A shop instructor helped the organizers print a teach-in program. The cafeteria served a back-to-basics Earth Day lunch.[93]

The teach-in committee decided to highlight the issue of population. That was a bit dicey, because students needed parental permission to participate in any discussion of sex. But Ehrlich's jeremiad about population growth had inspired the ecology club, and the teach-in organizers were confident that the subject would draw a crowd. The grand finale was a discussion about whether family size should be limited, with panelists from Planned Parenthood, Zero Population Growth, and United Parents Under God. Seminars on birth control and venereal disease also were part of the program.

Though the teach-in had a serious purpose, the organizers worked hard to make people smile. The price of admission was a crumpled aluminum can. The assembly speaker, a local biology professor, had earned a reputation for wit and whimsy as the host of a popular television science show: He promised to offer an ecological reinterpretation of history. Most of the seminars had clever names. The air-pollution session was titled "Does the Earth Have Bad Breath?" "Saving the Birds and the Bees" considered the issue of endangered species. The pros and cons of pesticides were the subject of "Ban the Bombing of Bugs?" "Industry Doesn't Have to Be a Dirty Word" gave a Standard Oil representative a chance to speak. The exhibits included a Noise Center and a Dirty Picture display. During breaks, students could eat algae cookies.

The rest of the program was eclectic. The assembly began with a short film about the history of San Francisco Bay, and a Save The Bay activist led a seminar on the region's future. "So You Don't Think There's a Problem?" invited skeptics to question a true believer. A water-quality official spoke about "the political facts of life." Another seminar, "Man vs. Man," was a pitch for people to overcome their differences. The school's auto-shop teacher led a workshop on tuning your car to improve gas mileage. "No one can possibly take in all that's going on," teach-in coordinator Mike Peck told the *San Mateo Times*. "We want the whole student body to be so intrigued with the variety of environmental subjects that they'll get involved with the continuing program of the ecology bunch."[94]

Though most Earth Day celebrations took place in schools and on college campuses, many people organized community events. Often the community activities were solo efforts. Churches held Earth Sunday services, libraries sponsored programs on the environment, and city councils hosted Earth Day discussions. The newspaper might list all the local celebrations in a preview of Earth Day, but the events were discrete: No one coordinated everything. In some cities and towns, however, people tried to organize community-wide celebrations. Their efforts did not always succeed. But the coordinated celebrations sometimes were impressive, and a few were spectacular.

Young professionals took the lead in organizing many community-wide events. Doctors became involved because they worried about the effects of pollution on public health. Landscape architects and urban planners hoped Earth Day might strengthen the movement to control sprawl. Lawyers and business executives volunteered because they thought that environmental problems were harming the reputation of industry. For some people, Earth Day organizing was a way to work through existential doubts: Several of the New York City coordinators were looking to get out of the "jail" of gray-flannel careers in banking and law, and Earth Day gave them a chance to try something fresh.[95]

Many well-educated housewives similarly saw Earth Day organizing as a chance to break out of their routine. Though they were not ready to seek jobs outside the home, they had skills that they didn't use raising kids and doing laundry, and Earth Day offered especially satisfying volunteer work. The work itself was exciting and challenging. The women also could justify their commitment in traditional terms: They did not want their children to inherit a polluted world.[96]

The community organizers often were boosters more than planners. They organized one or two events, but their main function was to draw attention to Earth Day. They encouraged local institutions to take part, and they publicized whatever people did. The Environmental Teach-In Coordinating Committee in Charleston, West Virginia, was purely a catalyst. The committee did not sponsor any Earth Day events. Instead, it brought together members of religious, civic, school, and social-justice groups to brainstorm about how to draw attention to the community's environmental problems. To help participants plan activities, the committee produced an "environmental inventory" of the region. The work paid off. The board of education encouraged schools to have miniature teach-ins. The Junior League decided to operate a mobile Environmental Information Center in the week before Earth Day. The brainstorming meetings sparked a series of "Protect Your Environment" panel discussions at the YWCA, several churches, and the library. Though billed as a series, the discussions had different sponsors, from the ministerial alliance to the League of Women Voters. The planning meetings also convinced the coordinating committee to incorporate as a permanent eco-action group: Citizens for Environmental Protection.[97]

The most ambitious community organizers created week-long celebrations with dozens of events. Like the organizers of the best university, college, and high-school teach-ins, they had to make many fundamental decisions about what kind of activities to sponsor. But their task was especially challenging. They did not have a campus or a school building as a physical base. They usually had to spend more time on fund-raising than student organizers. They also faced more social and political pressure. Was Earth Day elitist? Though many student organizers never asked that question, the organizers of community-wide events often discussed whether they needed to be more inclusive.

The story of Earth Week in Philadelphia illustrates many of the challenges of putting together "a major demonstration in a major city," in the words of CBS News anchor Walter Cronkite. The organizers secured a huge grant from the city's chamber of commerce, and their plans attracted national attention. They held star-studded events in the city's two showplace settings—Independence Mall and Fairmount Park—and they sponsored a host of other activities. They even published a magazine-like Earth Week program. Yet, as Cronkite concluded, their success "did not come easily."[98]

The planning began with a public meeting at the University of Pennsylvania called by a painter and a sculptor. Graduate student Austan Librach volunteered to head the effort. He formed a

steering committee of colleagues from the university's renowned program in regional planning. With the help of a faculty
member, the committee secured a $5,000 start-up grant from a
local clean-air group in December 1969. That allowed the committee to hire a project director, Edward Furia, a twenty-eight-
year-old marketing consultant who just had earned both law and
planning degrees from Penn. Furia recruited a handful of young
professionals. Many others knocked at the door. The Earth Week
committee eventually numbered thirty-three people with expertise in management, performance art, advertising, investment banking, medicine, journalism, and law.[99]

Furia and Librach shared a few basic assumptions. They
wanted Earth Week to be "a convocation, not a confrontation."
They would not demonize corporate America, though they were
keen to have business leaders acknowledge their responsibility
for environmental degradation. Instead, they sought "the support and cooperation of all groups." They wanted Earth Week to
lead to practical action, not simply demonstrations of concern,
and they took for granted that addressing the environmental
crisis would require mature judgment as well as youthful passion. They also believed that more people would participate if
Earth Week did not seem deadly serious. To set a more playful
tone, the committee's advertising expert produced a series of
hip television commercials. One had a fish complaining about
his health: "Oy, don't ask!" Another had a businessman explain-
ing why he hoped Earth Week would flop. A third showed Hog
Island, a once-pastoral community that had become so polluted
that only one man lived there. "This was brought to you by the
Earth Week Committee," the tagline said. "They feel that maybe
there's a message here."[100]

The decision to accept money from the chamber of commerce drew protests. Even some members of the Earth Week
committee opposed the decision. "They thought we were selling
out," Furia later recalled. But the partnership with the chamber

was a coup. The chamber initially planned to produce a glossy eight-page newspaper insert to counter Earth Day criticism of industry. When an anonymous caller told Furia about the insert, Furia and Librach went uninvited to the chamber's next meeting. They argued that the chamber should help solve the pollution problem, not try to whitewash it. After several more discussions, the chamber agreed to raise at least $30,000 for the Earth Week committee. Furia and Librach praised the chamber's courage. But they made clear that the Earth Week committee only would accept donations from companies that provided data about how much pollution they produced. They also promised to list non-cooperators in a Hall of Shame. To increase the pressure on the chamber's members, the Earth Week committee demanded that the city health department release confidential data about in-dustrial pollution. The city agreed to do that after Furia threat-ened to sue. The Earth Week committee still recognized the companies that voluntarily acknowledged their responsibility as polluters.[101]

The committee's effort to gain the support of sixties activists was not as successful. The antiwar radicals at the University of Pennsylvania agreed to contribute a statement on "ecology and the antiwar movement" to the Earth Week program. But black activists rebuffed the committee's overtures. They argued that their community had more pressing problems than pollution, and they discounted Earth Day as a trick to distract attention from poverty and prejudice. Still, they did not actively oppose the event. Ira Einhorn, the city's countercultural guru, posed a different challenge. Einhorn was eager to participate. Could the Earth Week organizers enlist his help without allowing him to take a leadership role? They offered him a chance to speak at the Fairmount Park event and they included one of his essays in the program, but they did not invite him to join the committee. That deal almost led to disaster. On Earth Day, Einhorn refused to leave the stage, and his antics delayed Senator Edmund Muskie's televised keynote for thirty minutes. Then Einhorn kissed Muskie on the lips![102]

Furia and Librach did not agonize about how to attract young people—the two main events offered crusading calls to action, hip philosophy, and groovy music—but the Earth Week organizers debated how best to involve established decision makers. They were especially keen to foster candid discussion about the state of the region's environment among business leaders, government officials, and academics. Because they worried that many of the people they hoped to include would be turned off by the raucous atmosphere of Earth Day, they organized a six-day "technical symposium" early in April that drew 110 panelists in ten sessions. The chamber of commerce cosponsored the symposium. Only a handful of participants were students or representatives of environmental groups. The organizing committee then hastily edited the proceedings to provide a "source book" for Earth Week attendees. The problems were urgent yet complex, the editors argued, and "ill-advised and premature action" was as likely to lead to grave harm as no action at all.[103]

Beyond the big decisions about the structure of the event, Furia and Librach were almost overwhelmed with smaller matters. Earth Week kept getting bigger and bigger. Let's arrange a tour of the unscenic landscapes of Philadelphia's industrial neighborhoods! Let's do street theater downtown at lunchtime! Let's have a booth at the garden show! Even though Furia and Librach relied on talented committee members to oversee many projects, they often worked sixteen to eighteen hours a day in a faculty lounge they commandeered at the university. The project was Furia's only obligation, but Librach still was in school. "There were people throughout the process who thought the whole thing was nuts, that it wasn't something that a graduate student should do," Librach recalled. "When I'd show up in class, professors would say, oh, how wonderful that the busy Austan Librach has deigned to join us!"[104]

That kind of commitment was common. Earth Day inspired many local organizers to drop classes, stop doing research, and neglect their families. "My kids couldn't get my attention," recalled St. Louis coordinator Dorothy Slusser. "They were disgusted that mom was so tied up with Earth Day. I was working full-time and then some." Iowa State senior Curt Freese devoted so much time to Earth Week that he was forced to postpone his graduation a term. But he had no regrets. Like many local organizers, he was convinced he was doing something special, and he enjoyed the three-month adrenaline high. "I was totally immersed," he explained later. "I remember being giddy about all the interest."[105]

3 ● Events

Earth Day was almost unfathomably big—not one event but 12,000 or 13,000. Though the events had common elements, every one was unique. Many events responded to local circumstances. The variations from place to place helped to make Earth Day a powerful force across the country.

The national media failed to do justice to the richness and variety of Earth Day events. Instead, the national overviews suggested that Earth Day was one big sixties-style demonstration—a day of symbolic gestures. In Omaha, Nebraska, so many high-school students bought gas masks to wear as a protest against air pollution that stores sold out. In Coral Gables, Florida, a twenty-five-year-old dumped a dead octopus and twenty pounds of dead fish at the power plant. In Louisville, Kentucky, 1,500 students jammed into a high-school concourse to simulate the overpopulated world of the future: "The demonstration ended in pushing, grabbing, and pinching." At Southeast Missouri State University, students buried a representation of the Earth under a pile of trash. In Ripon, Wisconsin, merchants offered to pay a penny for discarded cans, and kids collected 25,000. "Much of the day," *Time* concluded, "was given to theater and ritual." That was dead wrong.[1]

The local coverage was much better. If the national overviews were tourist snapshots from the rim of the Grand Canyon, the local reports were close-ups from the canyon floor. They typically included interviews with participants, excerpts from keynote speeches, summaries of panel discussions, and descriptions of exhibits and films. In many communities, newspapers treated Earth Day as a continuing story, not a one-day news item: They reported on both the planning and the effects of Earth Day events.

The in-depth reports made clear that Earth Day was much more than a show of support for a cause. In some places, Earth Day events changed the dynamics of local environmental politics: They were part of public debates that began before 1970 and continued after. Some Earth Day events encouraged people to imagine what a brighter future might look like, and some sought to give participants the tools they would need to reduce their environmental footprint. Other Earth Day events tried to get people with different views and backgrounds to talk with each other. In many schools, Earth Day events simply aimed to convince students of the urgency of the environmental crisis.

The variations in Earth Day events don't fit any simple pattern. The economic base and intellectual bent of the community shaped many events, but not all. Still, a detailed look at ten events can give a good sense of the many ways people celebrated Earth Day.

New York

The Earth Day organizers in New York City could have held events in Central Park, the most famous urban green space in the nation, but they had a bolder plan. They wanted New Yorkers to imagine a city without automobiles. Despite vehement protests from merchants and cabdrivers, they secured permission to close two streets in the heart of Manhattan for part of Earth Day. From noon until two, the stately stretch of Fifth Avenue from Fourteenth Street to Fifty-ninth Street was barred to automobile traffic. No cars, no taxis, no trucks, no buses. Automobiles also were barred from five blocks of Fourteenth Street from noon until midnight.[2]

New Yorkers were not alone in taking on Detroit. On Earth Day, the automobile was public enemy number one. The teach-in guide published by Friends of the Earth included a chapter titled "Warning: The Automobile Is Dangerous to Earth, Air, Fire, Water, Mind, and Body." As the symbol of environmental woes from air pollution to suburban sprawl, the automobile was the target of much of the day's guerrilla theater. Cars were put on trial, buried, and hacked to pieces. In countless communities, people refused to drive, and instead rode bicycles, walked, or even roller-skated to work and school. To encourage the use of public transportation, the Albuquerque city council voted after a spirited debate to lower the fare for city buses on Earth Day to a penny. (The dissenters argued, ironically, that the loss of revenue would be enough to add a car to the city fleet.) But the closing of Fifth Avenue was the most spectacular challenge to the automobile.[3]

Fifth Avenue became a park. By some estimates, 250,000 people rejoiced in the freedom to use the street. Some played to Earth Day sensibilities. A group of youthful demonstrators displayed dead Hudson River fish. "You're next, people!" they cried. "You're next!" Mostly, though, people just played. Near Fifty-seventh Street, the members of a small architectural firm treated the avenue like a beach or a verdant hillside. They laid a quilt on the asphalt, put a tulip in a wine bottle as a centerpiece, and picnicked in the glorious sun. A joyous crowd gathered around the picnickers and sang, "Happy Earth Day to You."[4]

Mayor John Lindsay was one of the revelers. He was a man in political motion—he had begun his career as a liberal Republican, run for reelection as an independent after the Republicans repudiated him, and soon would become a Democrat—but one constant in his politics was an aversion to ugliness. Though at first his administration was unsure how to respond to Earth Day, Lindsay soon embraced the event. He had promised to reduce air pollution, clean up the streets, and restore luster to decaying parks. He loved to walk. His slogan in his first mayoral campaign was "He is fresh and everyone else is tired," and his ads showed him, smiling and jacketless, walking a street. On Earth Day he walked down Fifth Avenue with his wife and nine-year-old son. In one photograph he was holding flowers. He spoke from the steps of the New York Public Library and again from the platform at Union Square, the hub of the day's activities. He warned that the fundamental issue was survival. "What we need," he said, "is a new technology for life." But Lindsay also rejoiced in the exuberance of the day. He had never walked with so many people in such a good mood, and he hoped that "a little bit of this will stay with us for the rest of our lives."[5]

Only a few people scoffed at the festivities. One was the pastor of a church that served a predominately black and Puerto Rican neighborhood. "While Mayor Lindsay walks the showcase streets of New York, the people of the South Bronx wallow in the same old filth and garbage," he said. "Earth Day means absolutely nothing to us—and won't mean anything until the garbage, the rats, and everything else is cleaned up."[6]

The next day, the street scene was the cover of New York's *Daily News*. "Earth Day!" the banner headline exclaimed. "Making their feelings about pollution perfectly clear, throngs take over auto-free Fifth Ave." The front page of *The New York Times* had a huge photograph of the avenue, with dozens of American flags waving above a crowd that stretched every inch of the way to Central Park. The magic of Fifth Avenue caught the imagination of the national media too. *The Washington Post* was one of the many newspapers that published a story about the "Joy in New York." Freed from automobiles, Fifth Avenue had "a festive air," the paper reported. "When the blissful respite ended at 2 p.m., even the police seemed reluctant to let the fume-belching cars and buses return." Dozens of newspapers illustrated their Earth Day stories with images of New York's most famous street. The *San Francisco Chronicle* put a before-and-after diptych on page one: "Pollution-spewing automobiles filled the avenue before noon . . . but after noon the avenue was for people only." The television networks also gave great play to the Fifth Avenue scene.[7]

The transformation of Fourteenth Street was just as stunning. The five blocks closed to traffic became a carnival, with Union Square as the main attraction. Once a parade ground for Civil War troops and a site for labor rallies, the square in 1970 was dominated—in the words of the *Daily News*—by winos and debris. On Earth Day, however, the site was clean and hip. Schoolchildren worked all morning with brooms, shovels, and rakes to remove trash. One group of girls had decorated the square with trays of geraniums and violets. Tie-dyed banners were everywhere—one depicted the Earth screaming for help—and balloons with peace and environmental slogans speckled the sky. On the stage, the microphones were wound with daisies.[8]

Two hundred booths, exhibits, and pieces of sculpture lined the street. The biggest attraction was the Pollution-Free Atmosphere, a two-hundred-foot-long, forty-foot-tall bubble that could invigorate five hundred people at a time. One booth offered bottles of Hudson River water for twenty-five cents, with the admonition that the water was unsafe to drink. At another booth, people threw darts to win plastic bags of suburban air. An actor handed out soot from incinerated garbage. A crumpled red sedan was parked on the street with a placard about New York's astounding number of abandoned cars: "57,742 Cars Removed in 1969; 21,635 Removed in 1970, As of April 21." Several works of art were made out of junk, and one included a mannequin wearing a gas mask. Many real people wore surgical masks.[9]

Kids played and protested. With their teacher pounding a tom-tom, fifteen students in Indian costumes did an "earth dance." A twelve-year-old boy led dozens of his peers in an eco-cheer. "What do we want?" "Clean air." "What do we need?" "Clean air." An eleven-year-old girl sold antipollution literature while holding a battered daisy. "If we keep things clean," she said, "people and flowers and everything will be able to go on. It's just mean what pollution does." Other kids just threw Frisbees and footballs.[10]

On the stage, music alternated with speeches. Because New York was a cultural capital, the program included a starry cast of writers, actors, and musicians. Leonard Bernstein, Melba Moore, and Pete Seeger participated. The folk singer Odetta sang "We Shall Overcome." The speakers ranged from Dustin Hoffman to Margaret Mead.[11]

The crowd was enormous. Perhaps 20,000 people jammed the square at any given time, and as many as 100,000 visited during the afternoon and evening. Some were hippies. Many wore suits. Almost everyone had a cheerfulness, *The Washington Post* reported, that "contrasted with the dire warnings they heard about the polluted environment." For a few hours, at least, the city had a human scale.[12]

One of the happiest people in the square was Marilyn Laurie, a thirtysomething mother of two who had helped to plan the day's events. Several months before, sitting in her apartment kitchen, Laurie saw a *Village Voice* ad for an Earth Day organizational meeting, felt the tug of sixties idealism, and rushed off to attend—leaving her husband to watch the kids. Though she had worried about the effect of air pollution on the health of her children, she had not thought to do anything about the issue until that moment. She had experience in advertising, and she became the press person for the Earth Day committee. The reward for all her hard work came when she stood on the stage "with universes of people in every direction." Some even had climbed lampposts and trees to get a better view. "On my left was Paul Newman," Laurie later recalled, "and on my right was John Lindsay—a pair of very blue eyes on either side of me. I remember thinking it was probably the most glamorous moment I would ever experience. It was a great coming together, a soaring celebration."[13]

Junior High in Suburbia

The most common images in media coverage of Earth Day were children picking up trash and protesting pollution. The images were symbolic. As countless orators argued, Earth Day aimed to ensure that future generations did not inherit a desolate world. If adults often seemed oblivious to the danger, kids were the great hope, since they would be most affected. But the images of children were not just symbols. The biggest group of Earth Day participants was K–12 students.

In the suburbs, especially, Earth Day was a school-centered phenomenon. Many suburbs did not have a college or university to host Earth Day events. Many also lacked large public spaces. Yet all had schools. To tell the story of Earth Day in the suburbs of New York, *Newsday* focused on the experience of fifteen-year-old Holly Berger, a ninth-grader at Jonas E. Salk Junior High in Levittown, New York.[14]

Levittown was the most famous suburb in the nation, but *Newsday*'s editors probably also picked a Levittown school because the community was politically divided. The first residents largely were veterans and their families, and most were staunch defenders of traditional values. But the community became more liberal in the 1960s. Though some residents were skeptical of the environmental cause, others were supportive: The school district left the decision about whether to celebrate Earth Day to principals and teachers.[15]

Holly had lived in New York City until sixth or seventh

grade, and she struck one of her friends as more worldly than her peers. She was part of a circle of thoughtful, bookish kids, mostly Jewish—and in 1970, that meant mostly Democrats. But as her friend later recalled, "None of us were what you'd call activists. We weren't that politically engaged or aware." *Newsday* said only that she was "pretty, bright, miniskirted and eager to enter Yale someday, 'if it's still there.'"[16]

Holly's day began with a schoolwide assembly that included a screening of an NBC documentary, *Who Killed Lake Erie?* Films were an important part of many Earth Day celebrations, and the NBC program was a popular choice. When the network aired the documentary in September 1969, many TV critics picked it as a daily or weekly "best bet." "Here's a frightening examination of what happened to once-beautiful, once-productive Lake Erie," one critic wrote. "Watch it . . . and get angry." Another critic suggested that the program was not simply an indictment of a crime but a lesson for the times: "Behind the question of pollution lies man's efforts to subdue nature rather than live with it." The film also prompted editorials and letters to the editor in many newspapers. Viewers wrote about watching with "nausea and disgust" and about feeling the same kind of horror they felt when seeing Biafran children starving to death. The broadcast also frustrated some viewers who wanted a more forceful statement about what needed to be done. "There was a vague reference to political pressure," wrote a New Hampshire League of Women Voters member, "but no suggestions as to how, where, and when."[17]

At Salk Junior High, the documentary was introduced by the director of the county planning agency, who tried to impress the students with the urgency of the crisis. "If we don't turn back pollution," he said, "the chances are excellent that none of you will reach the allotted three score and 10 years." The sight of fish suffocating to death appalled many students. For Holly, though, the most stunning image was the Cuyahoga River in Cleveland.

"Can you imagine—a river on fire," she said. But Holly quickly turned to the big question the film raised but didn't answer. The destruction of the lake had begun years ago: "Why hasn't anyone done anything about it?"[18]

At lunch, Holly struggled to get past frustration. She was persuaded that the situation was dire, but she worried that many of her peers were apathetic. "We hear that in 20 years there won't be any trees or flowers and in 45 years there may not be any people," she said, yet "a lot of kids heard about Earth Day and said, 'Oh, wow, we can get out of math class.'" With several friends, Holly debated a call for action from a high-school student who had addressed the assembly. Would sending letters to elected officials really make a difference? Was that any more effective than picking up litter, a gesture at best? "If you write to your representatives, like we were told," Holly argued, "you just get back a mimeographed letter saying, 'Thank you for your interest, we're studying the matter.' I hope tomorrow people will sit down and think about today."[19]

In English class, the teacher postponed a discussion of the novel *Mutiny on the Bounty* to let the students consider the significance of Earth Day. The discussion quickly turned to the Lake Erie film. "It scared me," one girl said, "but one day is not enough." "Well, the day is to just inform us what the problems are, first," answered another student. A third student complained: "No one seems to care what they're doing to the world." "Why?" the teacher asked. "BECAUSE THEY'RE MAKING MONEY," shouted a boy in the back of the room. "The most frightening thing," another boy said, "is the feeling the individual just can't do anything, except maybe pick up some papers."[20]

The environment also was the topic of the day in social-studies class. The teacher, Ron Zoia, was apolitical—he was a jock, he later recalled, not a radical or a hippie—but he took the opportunity to make his class relevant. He invited a representative of the county health department to speak. The official presented a slide show about the hazards of air pollution and discussed the county's efforts to address the problem. Zoia responded skeptically. "You seem to be pretty soft on industries," he said. According to *Newsday*, "Holly snorted softly to herself."[21]

In the next period, Holly watched another documentary, *Marshland Is Not Wasteland*. Released in 1962, the fourteen-minute film unwittingly showed how much had changed in the 1960s. Though the film included a few strong statements about the importance of conservation, the narration, editing, and music were typical of a natural-history essay, not a prosecutor's brief. The slow-motion opening shots suggested that the rhythms of tidal marshes were ancient mysteries. Then the film challenged the traditional view that wetlands were ugly and useless. Red, brown, and green grasses glowed in the sun. The mudflats and offshore shallows were home to crabs, oysters, shrimp, scallops—and men who had fished all their lives. The marshes also were refuges for migratory birds whose flights always had signaled the start of fall and spring. Without care, however, a marsh quickly could become a nauseating garbage dump or a graveyard for rusting cars—or a housing development. "The coming generations have a right to the things which have delighted us during our short span of years," the narrator argued. The nation soon would have to decide about "the space we want around us. We can choose—perhaps for the last time—what we are to do with our land, our water, and our wildlife."[22]

Holly was bored. "That's something most of us knew already," she said. Instead of whelks in their spiral shells and barnacles catching food with their spidery appendages, she wanted analysis. "But nobody is saying who's to blame and how it should be stopped." If anything, the film suggested that the destruction of marshes sprang from a drive basic to human nature. "As man and his housing and business needs advance over the land, marshes once avoided become a challenge to his ingenuity and his use of tools," the narrator said. "Fill or drain the marshes becomes the battle cry." That commentary hardly pointed the way ahead.[23]

The day ended with a field trip to Jones Beach. Holly and 120 classmates picked up trash and then had an hour of "beauty appreciation." Though school officials no doubt hoped the cleanup and beach walk would be a high, the trip only underlined the anxieties Holly had expressed all day. She was not content with a do-gooder activity that offended no one. She wanted to feel that people were ready to make hard decisions. Perhaps Earth Day would be a beginning, she said, expressing the hope of every participant. But then she shook her head: "I don't know."[24]

Miami

Miami was a bellwether for the environmental movement. A city of 350,000 in a fast-growing county of almost 1.3 million people, Miami was a postindustrial metropolis surrounded by natural wonders and dependent on tourists. In the months before Earth Day, the environmental cause clearly was gaining momentum there. Activists persuaded the federal government to stop construction of a jetport in the Everglades. They challenged a large residential-development proposal, and they began to draw attention to water-pollution problems in the community. Though Miami had a powerful development lobby, many members of the city's establishment saw perils in "growthmania." The editor of *The Miami News*, for example, was a transplanted New Yorker who was keen to see Miami avoid the pollution of the Northeast. By Earth Day, the movement also was attracting more upstart supporters. The shift was generational as well as ideological. In the 1960s, the city's activists largely were members of old-line conservation organizations, especially the National

Audubon Society and the Izaak Walton League. But the city's Earth Day events largely were the work of younger activists who were, in the words of one observer, "moderately militant." Many belonged to Environment! or Survive!—loosely organized groups that hoped to reform society, not just fight preservation battles.[25]

The impatience of the young activists was strikingly evident in the debut on Earth Day of Eco Commando Force '70. Before dawn, five members of the shadowy group poured bright yellow dye in eight sewage-treatment plants across the Miami region. The group included three men and two women: a landscape architect, a marine biologist, a microbiologist, a teacher, and an anthropologist. All were in their twenties or early thirties. They then returned to their base and issued their first communiqué. "The dye patches will show what happens to the sewage that is dumped into our waterways," they announced. "If the dye is not carried very far downstream from the plants, residents should be warned of possible dangerously high concentrations of pollutants due to lack of stream-flow. Dade County citizens need not worry about this attack—unless their drinking water turns yellow." *The Miami Herald* devoted only three sentences to the "bizarre" stunt, but the "lightning sorties" were the subject of a short story in *The Miami News*.[26]

The Eco Commandos struck twice more in the months after Earth Day. Before dawn on July Fourth, the Eco Commandos put eight hundred bright red warning signs on Dade County beaches:

DANGER
POLLUTED
NO FISHING
NO SWIMMING
POTENTIALLY DANGEROUS CONCENTRATIONS OF
PATHOGENIC BACTERIA HAVE BEEN FOUND AT OR

NEAR THIS LOCATION. SWIMMERS AND FISHERMEN
RISK INFECTION AND DISEASE.
DO NOT REMOVE THIS NOTICE

In a communiqué about the signs, the group encouraged an-
noyed residents to direct their anger at the true "malfeasants," the
civic leaders who refused to provide adequate sewage-treatment
facilities. "We have only done a job which the public officials
charged with protecting your welfare have refused to do," the
communiqué proclaimed. Three months later, when federal officials were meeting in Miami to consider whether the community
was doing enough to deal with water pollution, the Eco Commandos again drew attention to the sewage problem. They dumped
hundreds of bottles at the outfall of the Miami Beach sewage system two miles out in the Atlantic—a putrid place commonly called
"the Rose Bowl"—and the bottles included postcards addressed to
the governor and *The Miami News*. Though local officials argued
that the untreated sewage flowed out into the ocean, the Eco Commandos predicted that many bottles would be found alongshore.
"This drift bottle was moved by the same wind and currents that
move the raw sewage," the postcards said. "THIS IS WHERE MIAMI'S
SEWAGE GOES." Within days, seventy cards were mailed in.[27]

In addition to the first Eco Commando raid, Earth Day in
Miami included a made-for-TV mockery of the Orange Bowl
parade. The Dead Orange Parade was organized by the New
Party—a group of disenchanted supporters of Eugene McCarthy's
1968 presidential campaign—with the help of college and high-
school students. Instead of inspiring with beauty, the Dead Orange floats aimed to disgust. The grand prize went to the "most
polluted" entry. One of the twenty floats featured the Statue of
Liberty wearing a gas mask and standing on a pedestal of garbage. (In some news accounts, the gowned and crowned Liberty
was described as the parade queen.) Another float was just a toilet symbolizing "Biscayne Bay—Miami's Greatest Asset." Women

and children with protest banners walked among the floats. "You Pollute We Pay," proclaimed one girl's sign. Following the traditional Orange Bowl route, the parade wound through downtown and ended at the Dade County courthouse, where marchers danced to acid rock, read poems, and spoke against environmental degradation.[28]

Though the Dead Orange Parade made national news, the biggest draw of the day was the teach-in at the University of Miami. The auditorium was packed, and the speeches were broadcast via loudspeakers to an overflow crowd outside. The audience clapped and cheered all day. The teach-in was action oriented. In addition to professors, many activists spoke, including a pilot for Eastern Airlines. The end-of-the-day "rap up" featured the director of the state's pollution-control department, the young activist who led the campaign against the jetport, the head of the local Izaak Walton chapter, and the local expert on social movements, who argued that addressing the environmental crisis might require subversive and even revolutionary measures. "You can fight for your life—and that's what this thing is all about—in almost any way you want to," she concluded. To help people push for change, the organizers scheduled three workshops on eco-tactics. Many of the exhibits were intended to shock, especially the "People Counter," a Gerber Baby image illuminated by strobe lights that flashed blindingly every half second to mark another addition to the global population.[29]

Even officially sanctioned celebrations were far from staid. The city's Environmental Research Advisory Committee sponsored a teach-in on April 27, and the event was more like a college rally than a government meeting. Speaker after speaker exhorted the audience to pressure city officials to clean up the environment. As one concluded, "government will not do it on its own." Like the Earth Day teach-in at the university, the city event included "action clinics." The driving force behind Survive!, Phil Spitzer, gave a fiery talk. The city library also got into

the act. On Earth Day, the lobby of the main branch was dominated by a black-draped coffin holding a globe, and library employees wore masks to protest air pollution.[30]

The Earth Day spirit lasted well beyond April 22. Though the
party that sponsored the Dead Orange Parade proved ephem-
eral, the Eco Commandos became a thorn in the side of local
officials. Their exploits soon were touted nationally as examples
of a new kind of tactic—"ecotage." One of the founders of Environment!, physics graduate student Ross McCluney, turned the
best talks at the University of Miami teach-in into a handbook
for citizen activists, *The Environmental Destruction of South
Florida*. The handbook became a local bestseller. The teach-in
also inspired new organizations and activities. One housewife
and mother of three was so overwhelmed by the "People Counter" display that she read Paul Ehrlich's *The Population Bomb* and
then worked with members of her church to start a chapter of
Zero Population Growth. "I became involved in the environmental cause in a big way because of Earth Day," she later recalled.
Other activists organized eco-fairs, founded an environmental
newsletter, and formed a coalition of local eco-groups.[31]

At least in the short run, Earth Day shifted the center of environmental politics to the left. Though the antiestablishment style
of many Earth Day protesters turned off some established conservationists, other conservationists recognized that the extreme demands of the young environmentalists made their own
demands seem moderate by comparison. The Earth Day debate
also radicalized some older activists: They came away from the
teach-in resolved to do more to protect Miami's environment.[32]

The new political dynamics were exemplified in the fate of a
proposed 3,000-acre development at the southern end of Biscayne Bay. When officials first considered the proposal in January 1970, only one member of the local National Audubon
Society chapter spoke against the project, but younger activists
soon joined the opposition. The opposition intensified after

Earth Day. The crux of the dispute also changed, from beach access and mangrove preservation to sewage disposal. At the end of June, officials rejected the proposal, although the story did not end then: In 1972, the developers won approval for a drastically scaled-back project that preserved more mangroves and provided public access to the beach. Though that did not satisfy the most radical activists, older conservationists were amazed at how much had changed.[33]

Birmingham

The environmental movement was weakest in the Deep South. Sam Love, the southern organizer for Environmental Action, scraped and scraped to come up with events to boast about, while the other organizers scrambled to keep up with all the activity in their regions. But the South was not a desert for environmentalists. The region was more like a dismal swamp, slow-going but not impassable. Hundreds of communities in the South celebrated Earth Day. The southern celebrations often were simpler and more muted than those in the Northeast and the Midwest, but they still could matter. Birmingham, Alabama, is a wonderful example. The city was notorious as a place of civil-rights strife, and Alabama was a poor state, backward in many ways, yet Birmingham celebrated Right to Live Week, which culminated in a powerful Earth Day.[34]

The city's Earth Day events were organized by a recently formed group of young professionals and students, the Greater Birmingham Alliance to Stop Pollution. The group—usually called GASP—hoped especially to gain support for strong action against air pollution. Birmingham was one of the few industrial cities in Alabama, and the sky often was brown. The city was second only to Gary, Indiana, in the national rankings for worst air quality. Like Gary, Birmingham was a steel town. The city also depended on coal. U.S. Steel—South was the city's most prominent employer, and Alabama Power was the state's most powerful corporation. In 1969, the state had approved an air-pollution-control act that GASP considered "a license to pollute." GASP hoped that Right to Live Week would force the state legislature to adopt a tough antipollution law.[35]

GASP was not the first environmental organization in Birmingham. In addition to a local chapter of the National Audubon Society, Birmingham was home to the Alabama Conservancy, founded in 1967. In its first years, however, the conservancy's top priority was a campaign to establish a wilderness area in the William B. Bankhead National Forest. GASP also was not the only group concerned about the city's air quality. The local tuberculosis association long had sought to dramatize the health hazards of air pollution, with help from a committee of the county medical society. The founders of the conservancy and the head of the tuberculosis association both encouraged the GASP activists. "We were mentored," one recalled. But GASP went well beyond anything that anyone had done before.[36]

The boldness of GASP came from the two doctors who led the group, Marshall Brewer and Randy Cope. Neither were Alabama natives. They had come to Birmingham to work at the rapidly expanding university medical center, and they brought new ideas. That was critical. As a GASP member from a long-established Birmingham family explained, Alabamans grew up "knowing that dirty skies meant people were working, and clear skies meant people were out of work." But Brewer and Cope did not share the local habit of deference to industry. They argued that clean air was a right. Brewer also had a broad environmental vision. He was not just interested in wilderness preservation or public health. "We have incurred a huge debt to nature," he told *The Birmingham News*, "a debt which must be paid off if we are to survive—and the time for an accounting is drawing to a close."[37]

The Right to Live schedule was a mix of club, college, and community events. Cope kicked off the week with a talk to a women's club about the sham of the 1969 antipollution law. GASP appealed to religious leaders to devote the Sunday before Earth Day to the environmental crisis. "Our duty to protect what God has given us is of utmost importance today," Brewer said. "The advent of new technologies without equal environmental advances places us in the same situation as in Jeremiah's time, when God chastised the people for spoiling the land. Isn't it time for us to think about our future and the future of others by protecting God's precious gifts?" Several colleges held teach-ins during the week, and the speakers included a local doctor and a Catholic priest from one of the area's steel communities. For the closing activities—a morning meeting of the Downtown Action Committee and an evening rally at the Municipal Auditorium—the outside speakers all were federal officials.[38]

The closing rally was moving, especially a speech about pollution and health by Dr. A. H. Russakoff, a longtime activist. As *The Birmingham News* reported, Russakoff's activism had often sparked controversy but had won him "a wide following among young people and adults concerned about the environment." He received a standing ovation at the start of his talk, and again at the end. "I have received many accolades in my life," Russakoff told the audience, "but this is something I will remember the rest of my life."[39]

The climax of Right to Live Week came earlier on Earth Day, however, when Brewer addressed the Downtown Action Committee. The invitation list included college presidents, high-school principals, labor leaders, chamber of commerce officials, elected officials, and presidents of civic and service organizations. Several hundred people attended, and Brewer challenged them to act. "We have two choices," he said. "We can spend, pollute and be as merry as we can or we can listen to what the experts and young people all over the country are saying today. You people right here in this room have the power to make the necessary changes if you want to." To make his case, Brewer cited studies that blamed polluted air for an alarming rise of respiratory disease. He drew on the work of economist Kenneth Boulding to argue for a new kind of economic thinking. Because the earth was like the Apollo capsules, with a limited amount of air and water, industry needed to help build a conservation-oriented "spaceship economy" rather than a "devil-may-care 'cowboy economy.'" The first step was "strong, uniform legislation to control pollution so that all industries can include this in their budgets and mark it off as a cost of production and still compete effectively." To that end, Brewer called on the city's business leaders to allow the political candidates they supported "to vote their consciences" and repudiate the 1969 law, "which is not only worse than no law at all but an affront to the people of Alabama." Brewer received a "tremendous ovation." The mayor told *The Birmingham News* that GASP had made "the most aggressive assault on a problem" in decades.[40]

Of course, the applause did not lead immediately to reform. The editorial position of *The Birmingham News* made clear that many obstacles remained. The paper covered the Right to Live events in detail, and the editorial page offered qualified support for critics of the 1969 pollution law. When city officials refused to allow a GASP representative to speak at a high-school forum on pollution, the newspaper argued that people needed to "hear all views," not just U.S. Steel's argument that the 1969 measure would "get the job done if we give it a chance." During the week of Earth Day, two editorial cartoons mocked legislators for opposing sin and supporting motherhood while ducking the hard issues, including pollution. The paper also editorialized in support of a statewide effort by the Coordinating Committee for an Improved Environment to force every candidate for state office to take a stand on the pollution issue before the May primary. But on Earth Day, the editors warned against emotionalism in dealing with air pollution. "Before the issue of the environment is settled," they wrote, "the representatives of the taxpayers and wage earners will have to make some hard choices in weighing the public's interest in clean air against its interest in technological advance and industrial productivity. The choices may be very hard: What, for example, if the demand for clean air threatens a community with the loss of an industry reluctant or unable to meet pollution standards?"[41]

GASP kept at it. Three weeks after Earth Day, the group sponsored a lecture miniseries. Ralph Nader spoke at the Municipal Auditorium, and renowned ecologists Eugene Odum and Frank Golley spoke at the university. GASP members also spoke to groups in the community, especially students and women's clubs. The speakers did not shy away from working-class audiences. "I especially remember talking to garden clubs in the steel district," one GASP activist recalled. "The women were terrified about the environmental movement, because of the fear that their husbands would lose their jobs. It was hard to talk with them . . . It was obvious that this old, obsolete industry would have to downsize. Some of the women felt that an industry that had put bread and butter on the table couldn't be bad." Yet "some of the women came around." In addition to grassroots organizing in Birmingham, GASP lobbied the legislature to pass a tough antipollution law. Several women in the group used their Christmas card list as a Rolodex to recruit activists. Because eighteen-to-twenty-one-year-olds were about to gain the vote, GASP sent busloads of students to the capitol with a simple message: We are upset about pollution, and we will vote against you in the next election if you don't show that you are upset too. The lobbying worked. The 1971 legislature approved a clean-air act that remedied many of the shortcomings of the 1969 measure.[42]

Penn State

The big news at Penn State during Earth Week was not the environmental crisis. On April 15, hundreds of demonstrators marched to the administration building to demand that the university sever ties to the military, and administrators called the sheriff and the state police. The result was a violent confrontation. Twenty-nine students were arrested, and the arrests led to more turmoil. On April 20, the president of the university fled the president's house after protesters tore down a fence and threw rocks at the windows. A march the next night in support of a student strike initially attracted 2,000 people and quickly grew to 5,000. Though the strike fizzled, several thousand students protested again on April 23. The unrest at Penn State attracted national attention, along with disturbances at Stanford, Yale, and the University of Kansas.[43]

The turmoil marked Earth Week from the start. The keynote speaker at the kickoff on April 17 was a renowned conservationist, Representative John Saylor of Johnstown. In other circumstances, Saylor might have inspired his audience. Like many Pennsylvanians, he loved fishing and hunting, and he was a passionate defender of wilderness. In Congress, he led the fight for the Wilderness Act of 1964 and the Wild and Scenic Rivers Act of 1968. In the words of his biographer, he was one of the last of the great "green Republicans." But his love of nature was lost that night in his hatred of the disorder on campus.[44]

Saylor introduced himself as a veteran of many battles on behalf of the environment, with many political scars. Though the young liked to dismiss their elders, he argued, the older generation had not just made a mess. The Nixon administration was charting a new path in government. Researchers at Penn State were helping to find solutions to environmental problems. Then Saylor became more personal. "I don't know what you expected of your Earth Week kickoff speaker," he said. "If you expected him to tell you to man the barricades, burn down billboards, clog telephone lines, occupy buildings, beat up policemen, carry signs and banners, stage sit-ins or sit-downs, wear gas masks, and other childish nonsense, all in the name of conservation—

then you will be disappointed. Very frankly, there is already too much of the revolutionary motif in the student environmental movement to suit my tastes." In Saylor's view, the audience had two choices. You can take the "constructive approach" and recognize that you can protect the environment only if you collaborate with those who have the power to make decisions, including politicians, bureaucrats, and voters. Or you can take the "childish approach" and talk about revolution. The second choice was not simply immature but beyond Saylor's comprehension. How could intelligent students get "swept up in the oratorical fervor of the New Hitlerites"? Revolutionary rhetoric led nowhere. "The revolutionary underground is not dedicated to saving the environment," he said. "The price of revolution is destruction, plain and simple—not preservation, conservation, or ecological balance." To make a real contribution, young environmentalists needed to "work within the system," to develop skills and then commit to years of hard work in the cause of reform. "As I see it," Saylor concluded, "your job as students and beyond student life is to bring middle America around to the point where they, too, see the dangers facing their way of life if uncontrolled pollution is allowed to continue."[45]

Saylor seriously misjudged his audience. Despite the "riot" of April 15, Penn State was not a haven for radicals. Young Americans for Freedom were as prominent on campus as Students for a Democratic Society. For most students, however, the great issues of a college education were practical, not ideological. They hoped that college would help them succeed as farmers, engineers, social workers, or teachers. Many of the roughly 23,000 students at Penn State were the first in their families to attend college. They saw education as a privilege, not an entitlement, and they were not about to waste their opportunity. Even the most activist students generally were committed to working within the system.[46]

That certainly was true of the principal organizers of Penn State's Earth Week, Ed Beckwith and Tim Palmer. Beckwith and

Palmer became involved for different reasons, and they had different ideas about how to make Earth Week a success. But neither had any sympathy for obscenity shouters or building occupiers.

Beckwith was the president of the Inter College Council Board, the more academic of the university's two student-government organizations. He had come to Penn State intending to study electrical engineering, but he soon decided to pursue a student-designed major in science with a focus on environmental issues. He was keenly interested in current affairs, he wanted to make science accessible to nonscientists, and the environment was the most pressing scientific issue of the time. At Penn State, Beckwith worked to promote a new kind of political dialogue. With several friends, he founded a group called AID—Awareness through Investigation and Discussion—that sought "to avoid polarization between left and right. Instead of starting out with a preconceived position derived from ideology, you could study the issues and come to your own conclusion." To attract interest, AID successfully rallied students to press the university to establish a campus bookstore. For Beckwith, the bookstore was "a symbol of intellectual inquiry." Then the group planned a weeklong program of speakers and discussion called "Colloquy." The inaugural Colloquy in spring 1969 had no theme—the idea just was to get people talking outside of class— and the topics ranged widely. The week was a tremendous success. In fall 1969, AID sponsored a second Colloquy focused on a single issue, and that event became Beckwith's template.[47]

Palmer was more of a prophet than Beckwith. A landscape-architecture major with a passion for the outdoors, he became convinced at Penn State that Americans needed to develop "an ecological conscience." In fall 1969, he and a friend installed a photograph exhibit in the student union that juxtaposed beautiful and ugly landscapes, and the exhibit drew a host of comments. "We felt there was a wave of interest," Palmer recalled, "and we decided to ride the wave." Working with several friends, a few sympathetic professors, and a new city council member who had campaigned on a "save Happy Valley" platform, Palmer organized a weekly seminar on the environment in January, February, and March 1970. That organizing effort led to plans for April 22.[48]

Beckwith and Palmer worked separately, and Earth Week was a marriage of convenience. With the help of more than three hundred students, Beckwith organized events on the weekend before Earth Day, beginning with Saylor's keynote. Though the activities included film showings, exhibits, and games, the heart of Beckwith's program was a series of interdisciplinary panels on population, air quality, water resources, solid-waste disposal, land-use conflicts, transportation, and environmental health. The concluding session brought the panelists together to discuss the way forward. "I was trying to teach the university something about interdisciplinarity," Beckwith recalled. "I was only a lowly junior, but I thought that was important." Palmer's group, in contrast, put a lot of effort into convincing professors to devote their classes on Earth Day to environmental issues. About 15 percent of the faculty agreed to do that. Palmer also arranged events outside of class, both at the student union and on a downtown street adjacent to campus that was closed for the day. The April 22 events included only two discussions, one on environmental education and one on activism. The Republican, Democratic, and independent candidates for governor gave speeches at the downtown stage. In the evening, the street became a festival of folk music, drama, and film.[49]

Beckwith and Palmer sought to involve all of the university's colleges, but the College of Engineering decided to hold its own Earth Day event. The college faculty were eager to "see if some misconceptions might be cleared up," the head of aerospace engineering, Barnes McCormick, told the student newspaper. Engineers sometimes were "unjustly accused" of causing pollution.

"The technical community is as much interested in these problems as anyone else," McCormick said. "After all, we breathe the same air and listen to the same noise as everyone else." Because the college did not collaborate with the Earth Week organizers, however, the engineering dialogue about the environment conflicted with a speech by one of the gubernatorial candidates.[50]

Despite the unrest on campus, the Earth Week events were peaceful. One newly formed student group used the occasion to ticket cars for polluting the environment, but the official program did not include guerrilla theater. With the exception of the political candidates, the speakers were "home-grown talent," in Beckwith's words. Almost all were Penn State professors or students. The energy of Earth Week came from the urgency of the issues, not from conflict or celebrity.[51]

Of course, the turnout might have been bigger. On the night of April 18, the radical lawyer William Kunstler spoke at Penn State to a crowd of roughly 6,000, and no Earth Week event attracted anything like that kind of audience. As the editors of *The Daily Collegian* wrote, the protests on campus were "a very convincing argument against the theory that such pressing issues as the war in Vietnam and racism have been sidetracked by the new ecological conscience." But the opposite also was true. Though many Penn Staters were preoccupied with other issues during Earth Week, the eco-sessions still drew several thousand people. That was an achievement.[52]

Cleveland

The symbol of Crisis in the Environment Week in Cleveland was a drooping flower, and the image was apt. The Cuyahoga River was one of the most polluted waterways in the nation. Though the infamous fire of 1969 was not nearly as apocalyptic as national media accounts suggested, the Cuyahoga truly was a wasteland, with no visible life in some stretches. Lake Erie was on life support. The air in Cleveland was abysmal, especially in the steel neighborhoods.[53]

In the weeks before Earth Day, the news underscored the idea that the city faced a crisis. To prevent further pollution of Lake Erie, the state ordered a halt to sewer connections in Cleveland and thirty-three suburbs. That decision effectively barred new housing construction. After a federal report warned that fish from the lake were contaminated with mercury, the governor halted commercial fishing. The city's air-pollution-control board ordered a major employer—Republic Steel—to control emissions of red iron oxide dust. If the company did not comply, the board would shut down the polluting furnaces.[54]

Like many blue-collar cities, Cleveland struggled to deal with environmental degradation in the context of economic decline. Though the worst was yet to come, the depressing trends already were evident in 1970. The city's financial situation was becoming precarious. The population had fallen from a high of 915,000 in 1950 to 751,000. The problem went deeper than suburban flight, because the metro population stopped growing in 1970. The industrial base also had begun to rust: Employment in manufacturing peaked in 1967.

A thirty-three-year-old lawyer and urban planner in the city's development office, Laurence Aurbach, coordinated Crisis in the Environment Week. "I read about what Gaylord Nelson wanted to do," Aurbach recalled. "I thought this would be terrific, so I went to the mayor and asked him to help, and he agreed." For three months, Aurbach worked on the project almost full-time, with the help of a secretary and a steering committee.[55]

Cleveland did not yet have a powerful grassroots environmental group. The local chapter of the Sierra Club was three months old in April 1970, and another group that eventually became a force in local environmental politics did not form until after Earth Day. But the quality of the city's water and air already was a public concern. A car dealer began a billboard campaign to draw attention to the plight of Lake Erie in 1964. The League of Women Voters and the Izaak Walton League lobbied on the issue. In 1968, the city's voters approved a $100 million bond issue to improve the sewer system. Residents organized against air pollution as well. Some formed neighborhood groups, while others worked through the Air Conservation Committee of the local tuberculosis association. In 1969, a federal hearing on air-pollution standards drew a huge crowd to City Hall.[56]

The environmental cause also had the strong support of the *Cleveland Press*. Reporter Betty Klaric began to write about Lake Erie in the mid-1960s. She soon was writing about the environment full-time—she was one of the nation's first environmental journalists—and her reporting kept the pollution issue before the public. When she wrote about the lake, her stories had a signature logo: "Save Lake Erie Now." To reinforce Klaric's reporting, the *Press* sponsored a pollution conference for public officials in a downtown hotel. The paper also encouraged the disparate individuals and groups working on the environment to form a coalition, Citizens for Clean Air and Water, and the group met initially in the *Press* building. The city council honored Klaric on Earth Day. The next day, Cleveland State University students gave Klaric the Environmental Crisis award. Of course, Klaric championed Crisis in the Environment Week. "Every time we blew our noses," Aurbach said, "she wrote about it!"[57]

Because the environment already was on the agenda in Cleveland, Aurbach did not need to focus on awareness of the issue. Instead, his goal was to involve as many community institutions as he could. He talked with school officials, business and union leaders, staff at the library and cultural museums, professors, religious leaders, civic groups—"almost anyone I could think of who would be interested." Though he cared most deeply about land use and open-space preservation, he welcomed people with other concerns. "Whatever people wanted to make of Crisis in the Environment Week was fine," he said. "It was intended to be an umbrella."[58]

The planning went well, with one humiliating exception. At a ceremony in City Hall to proclaim Crisis in the Environment Week, Mayor Carl Stokes astonished everyone by questioning the new emphasis on pollution. "We're supporting this," he said, "but I am fearful that the priorities on air and water pollution . . . may be at the expense of what the priorities of this country ought to be—proper housing, adequate food and clothing." The ecology issue had more "glamour" than poverty, especially for residents of the suburbs, Stokes argued, but ensuring that children were not stunted in their physical and mental development had a greater claim to the city's discretionary funds. The mayor did not stop there. He challenged the priorities of the assembled group, which included the pastor of his church as well as several members of his staff. "How many of you," he asked, "are working for housing for the needy?" Aurbach, especially, was stung.[59]

Earlier that day, the mayor had attended a State Water Pollution Control Board meeting where many participants criticized the city, and one of the reporters at the ceremony suggested that the mayor's "snappish mood" was a response to those attacks. But Stokes was not just venting. He was one of the nation's first black mayors, and he was conflicted about the environmental cause. He knew that pollution was a serious problem. In his first campaign, he had promised to do more than his predecessor to clean up the city's air and water, and he had. But he was convinced that many inner-city residents had more pressing problems than pollution. Another black mayor, Richard Hatcher of Gary, Indiana, felt similarly divided. Both Stokes and Hatcher went back and forth, alternately supporting and denigrating efforts to protect the environment. The stunning scene at the proclamation-signing ceremony demonstrated the limits of black support for environmentalism.[60]

Aurbach was disappointed again by the failure of the first big Crisis in the Environment event, a midafternoon rally downtown on April 20. The mayor was scheduled to speak but took a long weekend instead, and the other keynoter was delayed in traffic. Few people attended anyway. The second showcase event was more successful. On Earth Day, a crowd of 1,000 marched in "a procession of death" from Cleveland State University to the spot on the Cuyahoga where city founder Moses Cleaveland landed in 1796. Leading the march, the university president apologized to Cleaveland for the desecration of the river. "I'm sorry," he said. Then a student dressed as Cleaveland arrived by boat—and turned back in disgust.[61]

The real strength of Crisis in the Environment Week was the breadth of the schedule. As Aurbach hoped, a host of community institutions signed on. The Cleveland Engineering Society sponsored an all-day conference on the environment on April 22. "A company that expects to stand up to competition in the future simply cannot pollute," a Dow Chemical official proclaimed at the keynote luncheon. The Natural Science Museum, the Garden Center, and the Health Museum held events. The city's libraries showed films, sponsored discussions, and played recordings of antipollution songs. At one church, the pastor gave a sermon entitled "Chicken Little Was Right." The Unitarian Cathedral hosted a professor from the University of Chicago Divinity School, who spoke to several hundred people about "theology and ecology." At one of Cleveland's temples, students wrote a special Crisis in the Environment service. The Air Conservation Committee set up a booth at a home-improvement show, and the League of Women Voters distributed leaflets about detergents at shopping centers. The Sierra Club organized a cleanup of a waterfront park. All of the region's colleges and universities held teach-ins. Students at the Cooper Union School of Art hung banners on the overpasses of major roads and highways. "Welcome to the 5th Dirtiest City," one said, with the drooping-flower logo as a kind of exclamation point.[62]

The school district encouraged teachers and students to participate. Officials let everyone "do their own thing," so the programs varied tremendously. Thirty students at one elementary school interviewed parents and neighbors about air pollution to prepare stories for a two-page pamphlet, which they sold for three cents. They wrote the mayor for suggestions about what to do with the $20 they earned, and he suggested donating it to the Air Conservation Committee, which they did. At another school, sixth-graders formed PYE (Protect Your Environment) and visited kindergarten and first-grade classes to preach the ecology gospel. The environmental teach-in at one high school featured politicians, industry representatives, and conservationists. The day began with a general assembly, and then the 850 students divided up to attend thirty workshops. Students at other schools performed an eco-play and offered eulogies for pure water, clean air, and open space. Social-studies teachers and students from several schools produced a radio program about solutions to environmental problems. One resource at many schools was a newsletter, *The Waste Paper*, which teachers and students from across Cleveland had begun to publish in January. Because almost every school did something, Crisis in the Environment Week truly became a community project.[63]

Small-Town Kansas

Salina, Kansas, was not the sort of place likely to make a big deal out of Earth Day. Rural Americans were less supportive of environmentalism than residents of cities and suburbs, and Salina was a community of 37,000 in the rural center of a conservative state. Though a city by Kansas standards, Salina was more like a small town than a metropolis. The city had grown by serving as a market for farm families. In the 1950s, the Catholic bishop acknowledged Salina's agricultural foundation by building a cathedral that resembled a grain elevator. The city also served the oil fields of central Kansas. But Salina was home to a talented circle of environmentalists. In addition to activities in schools, Salina had two public events on Earth Day. A group of housewives, the Salina Consumers for a Better Environment, held a workshop at the YWCA in the morning, and one of the city's two colleges sponsored a teach-in and rally in the evening.

The Consumers for a Better Environment had formed just before Earth Day. Most of the members were comfortably middle-class: Their husbands were professors, businessmen, or professionals. Several of the group's leaders were active in the League of Women Voters. The workshop aimed to encourage women to use their power as household managers to reduce pollution and conserve resources. The organizers also hoped that women would redefine the responsibilities of motherhood. As one argued, "We must be concerned, not that our children have every material convenience, but that they have air to breathe."[64]

The workshop drew seventy people. The mayor—the only man on the program—opened the gathering by pledging support for the environmental cause. Members of the group gave five-minute talks about packaging and waste, energy, pesticides and fertilizers, detergents, composting, population, and transportation. The emphasis throughout was on the need to change basic habits. "We are literally smothering in a pile of no-deposit, no-return trash," the speaker on packaging said. "In order to reverse the trend, we must be willing to inconvenience ourselves." The presentation on energy offered a weighty list of action items. "Stop buying the prestige cars which consume so much oil and gas." Drive less: Walk or ride bicycles, and work to make public transportation a possibility. In the home, resist the temptation to use electric gadgets, from can openers to toothbrushes. "Wear a sweater, instead of turning up the heat." Consumers also should lobby utilities to find nonpolluting power sources and change rate structures that favored customers who used the most electricity. To dramatize the idea of conservation, members of the group then turned off the lights and opened the curtains! Because individual action could only go so far, the morning ended with a discussion of legislation.[65]

The evening teach-in at Kansas Wesleyan began with a telephone talk by the state's senior senator, Republican James Pearson. Pearson was invited to speak at three Kansas colleges, so he spoke simultaneously to audiences at all three campuses from his desk in Washington. He tried to sound supportive, even hip, while promising nothing and dampening expectations. He called Earth Day "an act of alarm and dedication to a cause." He denied that the event was a cop-out—a refusal to solve other problems. "In a rapidly changing world," he said, "we are not allowed the luxury of meeting crises in their turn." But he predicted that progress would be difficult. "I want to warn that antipollution is not what we politicians call a 'warm puppy' issue, one which if we pass enough laws, spend enough money and have a good heart, happiness is assured and soon America will be beautiful again," he explained. "Antipollution means that someone will be hurt. Profits must be cut, comforts reduced, taxes raised, sacrifices endured. And, as in all human struggles, the powerful will fight the hardest to be hurt the least."[66]

After Pearson's address, the teach-in divided into thirteen sessions on environmental issues, from water quality to waste disposal. The speakers included the newspaper editor, the city planner, the urban-renewal director, two nuclear engineers, an oil-industry consultant, two agricultural-extension officials, a Soil Conservation Service agent, a mechanical engineer, a civil engineer, an architect, a doctor, a spokesperson for a waste-disposal company, and a representative of one of the city's biggest manufacturers. The discussions often were heated. In a session about pesticides, several people urged the audience to be wary of official assurances about the long-term safety of agricultural chemicals, but they were challenged by a man who argued that pesticides were the least dangerous of all pollutants: "I know of no one who has ever been killed by DDT," the man concluded.[67]

The evening ended with battle cries on the steps of the administration building: Pioneer Hall. Three professors rallied the crowd. The last was biologist Wes Jackson, a Kansas native from a conservative Republican family—former president Dwight D. Eisenhower was a cousin—who had become a pioneer in the field of environmental education. In fall 1969, Jackson had tried to convince his colleagues to redesign the curriculum to focus entirely on the challenge of survival. The faculty rejected that proposal but voted to establish a "survival studies" major. At the rally, Jackson suggested that Earth Day might be the turning point "between two ways of life." "It will depend on the young," he argued. Perhaps the celebration would come and go without a lasting change of thinking. "But we may find that Earth Day was the beginning of a different orientation. Man may realize that his planet is to be lived on, not exploited; that it is to be transferred to the next generation, not destroyed."[68]

In Salina, however, the dawn of the environmental age was cloudy. "Few Hear Earth Day Warnings Here," *The Salina Journal* reported on April 23. "I don't know whether to be cheered by those who came," one of the teach-in organizers told the newspaper, "or saddened by the greater number who wouldn't leave the easy chairs." Another professor was blunter. "Kansas is a terrible place to create awareness of the environmental crisis," he said. "We're living in a country club." The Associated Press report about Earth Day in Kansas supported the view that most residents were unmoved by prophecies of ecological disaster.

None of the state's elected officials joined Senator Edmund Muskie of Maine in calling for an "environmental revolution." The director of the Kansas Board of Health's air-quality office was pessimistic: "The majority of the public is not ready to accept financial responsibility for preventing pollution."[69]

The clouds did not stop Salina's activists. Consumers for a Better Environment launched a campaign to get groceries to sell milk in returnable bottles. The group also challenged plans for a new city landfill. The county owned the proposed site and was willing to donate it, but the land was within sight of one of the major entrances to the city, along the Saline River, and near a church camp. In short order, Consumers for a Better Environment secured six hundred signatures on petitions arguing that the location was problematic, and the city council agreed in June to find an alternate way to dispose of the community's garbage when the existing dump reached capacity.[70]

Despite the success of the landfill campaign, Consumers for a Better Environment was unable to build a grassroots movement in Salina. Members spoke to women's organizations during the summer and fall. The group sponsored public forums on environmental issues. But in April 1971, the group decided against holding a second Earth Day workshop. "I think we just woke up to the fact that no one would come," the group's chairwoman explained. "It sounds terrible, but that's the way we feel. People seem much more apathetic this year than last."[71]

In a different way, Wes Jackson also quit the field in 1971. He was offered a chance to direct a new environmental-studies program at California State University in Sacramento, and he accepted. In Kansas, he concluded, nothing moved. But in California, people cared about environmental issues: Things were happening. "Sacramento," he told *The Salina Journal* before he left, "may be where the precedents are going to be set for the eco-logical sanity of the planet—if there is to be any."[72]

The Central Valley of California

The most ambitious Earth Day happening in California was not a gathering of thousands but a tiny eco-fair in Newhall, a rural town about twenty miles north of Los Angeles. The festival was one stop in a six-week "survival walk" from Sacramento to L.A. organized by Berkeley's Ecology Action group. Though the walk involved only about fifty people, the organizers hoped to lead the way to a radical rejection of the nation's consumer culture.

The walk was led by thirty-two-year-old Cliff Humphrey, who had served in the army and worked for the state highway agency before seeing the light while taking a class on native Americans at San Francisco State. Humphrey founded Ecology Action with his wife and another couple in 1968. The next year, he issued "The Unanimous Declaration of Interdependence," a celebrated call for a new relationship with nature; the declaration was read at many Earth Day events. The Humphrey home became a "life house," a fount of the counterculture in Berkeley. Their home also became the Ecology Action office, staffed mostly by conscientious objectors whose volunteer work counted as their alternative to military service. A sign outside suggested that visitors walk to the house next time rather than drive. Inside, another sign offered suggestions for living less wastefully and destructively. Ecology Action organized the area's first recycling program. The group used guerrilla theater to prompt people to consider more environmentally sound ways of living. The Humphreys destroyed their car in a joyous ceremony in July 1969. Then Ecology Action sponsored Smog-Free Locomotion Day, which featured a parade headed by a coffin containing an internal-combustion engine. A third event was Unfilling the Bay Day, when activists brought money bags of mud to the offices of real-estate companies that were fighting a ban on filling San Francisco Bay. On Damn DDT Day, a group member dressed as the Grim Reaper passed out antipesticide leaflets in San Francisco's financial district.[73]

The walk was an attempt to break out of the countercultural cocoon. The route went through the Central Valley, the heart of California's agricultural empire. "People in the valley probably have much closer contact with the earth than people on the march," one of the walk organizers said. But the valley relied on a kind of agriculture—high-tech, chemical-intensive, fossil-fuel dependent—that seemed unsustainable. For society to survive, the valley's farmers, field hands, and shop owners needed to take up the environmental cause. The walkers hoped to "get together and discuss mutual problems."[74]

The group left Sacramento on March 15. The youngest walker was the Humphreys' six-year-old son; the oldest was a fifty-five-year-old businessman. Some of the participants had quit their jobs. Many were recent college graduates or dropouts, and a few came from as far away as the East Coast. "The end of the walk will not truly be an end for us," Humphrey predicted at the start, "but thousands of new beginnings." On travel days, the walkers typically covered fifteen to twenty miles, mostly on back roads. Except for the mountains near Bakersfield, the trek was flat. "After you got over the blisters," one walker said, "it was beautiful." Four retrofitted, low-polluting trucks carried supplies. Many of the walkers ate simple foods: egg-salad sandwiches, brown rice, peanut butter, honey, wheatberry bread, tea, apple juice. They picked wild asparagus, but they avoided oranges and lemons because those crops were sprayed with parathion. No one used paper plates. At night, the walkers camped in city parks or stayed at the homes of supporters. Local coordinators helped to make arrangements in many communities.[75]

Along the way, the walkers passed out literature and picked up aluminum cans—five hundred pounds in all. Humphrey gave talks at several colleges. The walkers also visited high schools, where they led discussions and showed films about the population explosion and the Santa Barbara oil spill. But the principal events of the walk were the eco-fairs. Counting a kickoff in Sacramento, the walkers organized twelve, in communities ranging from towns of 15,000 and 20,000 to Fresno, a city of 165,000.[76]

The Earth Day festival in Newhall was typical, except that more reporters were present. One walker played a guitar and sang "Welcome, Carbon Monoxide" from the musical *Hair*, and a group of third-graders responded on cue with a chorus of coughing. A troupe of puppeteers from Berkeley, the Migrant Theater, performed a show called *Ecology Punch*. A green, white, and green American flag flew above the exhibits, which addressed a number of issues: cultural aspects of the environmental crisis, population, food and the interdependence of urban and rural people, California's Water Project, and recycling, among others.[77]

The Washington Post report on the Newhall fair began with an exchange between one of the walkers and eighteen-year-old Mickey de Pompa, who was about to eat a hamburger and french fries from a Jack-in-the-Box. "By buying the stuff you bought you are increasing the demand for forests to be ripped off," said the walker, a graduate student at Brown. "You are increasing the demand for creation of chemicals which may be poisonous." De Pompa was skeptical. "O.K., so what can I do about it? I'm just a person." "You can become aware," the walker answered. The two talked for a few more minutes about the implications of American eating habits, and de Pompa still was not convinced. "I just don't see it," he said. "I don't see how one person can do anything about it." But de Pompa then went to look at the exhibits.[78]

Throughout the walk, the official response was positive. The only exception was a county supervisor who accused the walkers of cheating. They just walked the last mile into town, he said, and drove the rest of the way. The supervisor voted to deny the walkers permission to use the park at the courthouse. But no community rejected the walkers. In Modesto, the walkers were accompanied by police and sheriff's deputies, and the officers were happy to help. "It's a good crew," one said. "This is the first march I've seen in the last 10 years I can agree with," said another.[79]

The walkers received a more mixed response from passersby and residents. A group of motorcyclists threw eggs at the group, and a few motorists shouted obscenities. More often, drivers honked in support. Some stopped to give the marchers food, soft drinks, even toilet paper. In Modesto, a man donated half a pickup load of good eats. At the college campuses, Humphrey spoke to enthusiastic audiences. The school students also were receptive. The eco-fairs, however, drew relatively small crowds. But most of the people who visited were friendly and curious.[80]

The walkers reached Los Angeles at the end of April without trumpets and zithers. The initial plan was to hold a rally in the coliseum to mark the start of a new era, "the survival decade," but the required $100,000 bond was out of the question. Instead, the walkers set up their exhibits in a park off Wilshire Boulevard, where they were joined by several groups who had made shorter walks. The walkers spoke modestly about what they had accomplished. "We planted a seed in most towns," one said. The wrap-up stories in the media focused on what the walkers had learned, not what they had tried to teach. "I could never go back to living like I was before—wasteful consumer living," a walker from suburban New York concluded.[81]

For Humphrey, the walk also was a catalyst. Not long after the walk ended, he and his family moved to Modesto "to develop a model of environmental sanity." Humphrey was encouraged by Lester Corn, a leader of Students for a Better Environment at Modesto Junior College who had quit school to join the walk. But Humphrey already was thinking about leaving Berkeley. The Bay Area was too big to transform. He thought the valley might be better, and the response to the walk in Modesto—a city of 60,000—was encouraging.[82]

The Humphreys lived in a tent in Corn's backyard for several months. By the end of July, Cliff had begun to build the Modesto chapter of Ecology Action. He led a community workshop titled "The Ecology Perspective" on July 22. On July 30 he met with city officials to discuss his hopes. The city's planning director warned that Humphrey likely would face skepticism and apathy. Ecology Action might be a flash in the pan. The institute's vision, he said, "may be out of step with community goals." Humphrey answered that Ecology Action was "trying to avoid conflicts." We hope to "excite everyone with the image of what this country could be," and then let people discover for themselves how best to make change. "We need to transcend polarizations in the country and retool our life style so it does not depreciate the health of others," he said. "Everybody must participate."[83]

The first Ecology Action project in Modesto was a recycling program. In 1970, recycling was novel, and Humphrey hoped that the simple task of sorting garbage would make people more environmentally conscious. He already had had success with recycling in Berkeley, where the weekly drop-off day became a hip country fair, but the challenge would be greater in Modesto. "If we can make recycling work here," Humphrey said, "it will work anywhere." As the city planner predicted, a lot of residents saw the project as a weird landing from planet Berkeley. But Humphrey quickly made converts. "He can talk to anyone," *Look* reported. "He doesn't come on messiah-like, ranting and raving 'J'accuse.'" By April 1971, a year after Earth Day, Ecology Action had a modest office in a shopping center, next to a credit union, a beauty salon, and a convenience store. The supporters of the recycling program included the wives of the city's doctors, the YMCA, the Unitarian church, the Boy Scouts, and the owners of several bars and gas stations. "We're way past the doomsday thing," Humphrey said. "We're starting to build something."[84]

Alaska

Earth Day in Fairbanks, Alaska, came at a pivotal point in the destiny of the state. In the words of writer John McPhee, Alaska at the time was "a handful of people clinging to a subcontinent." With a sublime expanse of over 350 million acres, the state had a population of only 300,000. The Fairbanks metropolitan area, the state's second largest, was home to just 45,000 people. Yet a new gold rush seemed about to begin. In 1968, oil was discovered on the state's northern slope, and a consortium of oil companies proposed a trans-Alaska pipeline to carry the black gold to market. Because the pipeline required a permit from the federal government, the project soon became a public issue. Environmentalists in Alaska and elsewhere worried that the pipeline would do grave damage. On April 13, 1970, the Wilderness Society, Friends of the Earth, and the Environmental Defense Fund won a court order requiring a detailed environmental-impact assessment before the government could approve the first stage of the project. The week after Earth Day, a delegation of state political and business leaders traveled to Washington to try to expedite the permit process.[85]

In Fairbanks, especially, the pipeline was a hot topic. Fairbanks was the only city along the proposed eight-hundred-mile route. Once a mining town, Fairbanks had become dependent on the military, and civic leaders were keen to diversify the economy. Many residents still had the boomer spirit of the early mining days. Yet Fairbanks also was home to the Alaska Conservation Society, the state's foremost advocate for wilderness preservation.

At the University of Alaska, opinion about the pipeline was divided from the first. The president, William Wood, was adamantly prodevelopment. (He even had favored a plan a decade earlier to use nuclear bombs to create a harbor in northern Alaska.) He also welcomed the chance for university researchers to work on pipeline-related projects. Yet a number of faculty members had doubts about the pipeline, and the conductor of the university symphony headed the local chapter of the Sierra Club. The grounds outside the University Museum symbolized the divide on campus. In fall 1969, the pipeline consortium put a forty-foot section of pipe on display there, and the pipe immediately became a protest site. The first piece of graffiti simply said "Sell Out." Other protest slogans played on the pipeline acronym: TAPS. "Toward a polluted state" was one. Another mourned the death of arctic ecology.[86]

The organizers of the environmental teach-in at the university knew that the pipeline would be a pressing issue. Though pollution was center stage at most Earth Day events, oil dominated the program in Fairbanks. After a primer on April 21 on the principles of ecology, a series of talks on Earth Day dealt with specific environmental issues, including oil development. A federal geologist critiqued the design of the pipeline, while oil officials spoke about the industry's efforts to protect the environment. Other speakers addressed the impact of oil on wildlife and water quality. The evening program on Earth Day featured addresses by U.S. Secretary of the Interior Walter Hickel, who would make the decision about the pipeline permit, and Stanford University environmentalist Donald Aitken. On April 23, the concluding session of the teach-in was a roundtable on oil in the arctic.[87]

Even before the opening session, the teach-in drew fire. In a letter to the *Fairbanks Daily News-Miner* published on April 18, miner and developer Joe Vogler charged that Earth Day was part of a communist plot. Ecology was the latest weapon in a diabolical campaign to destroy "the initiative which developed our farms, our mines, our oil fields, our industries." Though some environmentalists complained that Americans consumed more than half of the earth's resources despite accounting for only 6 percent of the world's population, Vogler trumpeted that statistic as a measure of the greatness of the American system. He urged "every unemployed person in Fairbanks" to attend the teach-in "and learn who are their real enemies and how those enemies are accomplishing their purpose."[88]

The chamber of commerce and the *Daily News-Miner* also tried to shape perceptions of the teach-in, but their take was more positive. They sought to make eco-sentiment into a hand-maiden of economic growth. The chamber endorsed Earth Day in a small display ad published on April 22. "The future economic stability of Alaska is closely tied to the development of the mineral resources of our Arctic regions," the ad proclaimed. "That this development occurs in accordance with sound environmental practices is a goal shared equally by the business community and the sponsors of Earth Day." The newspaper made a similar argument on April 21. The teach-in organizers were not radicals or preservationists, the editor argued, but students with a mature understanding of the need to develop land and utilize resources. The head of the organizing committee was a marketing major! In the words of the committee, the intent of the teach-in was to provide "an exploration of issues, not a protest; an awakening of concern, not a final prophesy of doom; and a search for praiseworthy accomplishments as much as a condemnation of offenses against the environment." Because Alaska was still a place of blue skies, pure water, and abundant wildlife, the editor concluded, all Alaskans could share the hope of avoiding the mistakes of older states.[89]

In truth, the boosters and the young environmentalists were not all of like mind, but the teach-in organizers tried to make the event acceptable to a wide audience. Only one talk addressed the divisive issue of preservation. The program did not include a representative of the Alaska Conservation Society. The most forceful speakers were professors from the lower forty-eight— Aitken and Joseph Sax, a pioneer in the field of environmental law—so the teach-in did not challenge the booster belief that the strongest support for environmentalism came from outsiders.[90]

The turnout was excellent. Though the university enrollment was only 1,800, most of the sessions attracted several hundred people. The crowd at the evening program on Earth Day was nearly 1,000. The addresses that night by Aitken and Hickel were worth hearing.[91]

Aitken made the biggest impression on the students. A founding director of Friends of the Earth, he was cast in the role of eco-prophet, and he did not disappoint. He argued that the pipeline was the first great modern survival decision. Because technology was advancing faster than the ability of science to predict the environmental consequences, everyone needed to slow down. "Making wild guesses and plunging blindly ahead" was folly. The pipeline project proved that. The initial plan called for the pipe to be buried—a design that inevitably would have led to breaks. The environmentalists who raised questions about the project were heroes, Aitken argued, not meddlers and obstructionists. Without their intervention, the industry and the people of the state would have suffered a billion-dollar calamity.[92]

Hickel made national news. He announced that he would issue a permit for the pipeline once the legal and scientific questions were resolved. He had served as governor of Alaska before his appointment as secretary of the interior, and he knew that many Alaskans were counting on the pipeline to provide jobs and profits. But his speech was not just a reassuring wave to a home-state crowd. In his confirmation hearings, he was savaged for saying that he was against "conservation for conservation's sake," and he saw the pipeline issue as a chance to demonstrate his philosophy of proper planning. "This will be the largest private construction project ever undertaken," Hickel said, "and I am determined that it will be a showcase to prove that enlightened development and wise conservation practices can go hand-in-hand." Though convinced that the pipeline could be built "with complete safety," Hickel made clear that the design would have to be modified. Before issuing the permit, the Department of the Interior would examine all relevant ecological factors, including the migratory patterns of wildlife. Hickel promised—guaranteed, in fact—"that we will not approve any design based on the old and faulty concept of 'Build Now, Repair Later.' "[93]

Outside Alaska, the response to Hickel's address mostly was critical. *Sports Illustrated* published a laudatory account of Hickel's trip, but the Associated Press story about the speech focused on the shock of environmentalists. "I think it was inappropriate," a Sierra Club spokesperson said. *The New York Times* editorialized against Hickel's "premature" decision. His speech, the editors wrote, "introduced an ominously sour note into the Earth Day observances." In Fairbanks, however, the worst criticism was that Hickel mainly offered glittering generalities. "The speech was blah," one student said. "But there were good signs among the platitudes." The *Daily News-Miner* was thrilled: Now Alaskans knew that the pipeline would go forward, the editor wrote, and they could thank Hickel for ensuring that the project would be sound.[94]

The commentary on the teach-in as a whole was positive. In a letter to the *Daily News-Miner*, a geology professor wrote that the discussions were constructive and "quite lacking in preservation emotionalism." Other commentators judged the teach-in balanced and thought-provoking. "We're proud of our U students," the newspaper editor proclaimed. The teach-in was an outstanding example "of concerned but responsible students presenting both sides of a perplexing problem."[95]

The good feelings did not last, however. After Earth Day, environmentalists in Alaska and elsewhere became bolder in attacking the pipeline, and the boosters hit back. In 1971, university president Wood blasted pipeline opponents as "anti-God, anti-man and anti-mind." His comments were seconded by the mayor of Fairbanks. The boosters were willing to acknowledge the importance of environmental concerns—but only as long as everyone accepted the imperative of development.[96]

The Today *Show*

Television celebrated Earth Day too.

National Educational Television—the precursor of PBS—saw Earth Day as a chance to make a statement about the quality of public broadcasting. The network broadcast only in the late afternoon and evening, and NET devoted all of its airtime on April 22 to Earth Day programming. That was unprecedented. Even *Sesame Street* and *Mister Rogers' Neighborhood* were about the environment. To promote the special programming, NET affiliates took out newspaper ads promising "the most extensive public television presentation in history." Because Americans were protesting and celebrating across the nation, the ad in *The New York Times* proclaimed, "That's where NET cameras will be—all over America—to bring you 6½ hours of Earth Day events, plus the latest developments in everyone's battle to save our decaying environment." In addition to live reports and interviews, the day's highlights would include performances by Pete Seeger, Judy Collins, and members of the Philadelphia cast of *Hair*.[97]

The three commercial networks broadcast Earth Day programs throughout the week. The network programmers no doubt considered the subject to be hot, but the decision to air Earth Day specials also resulted from a peculiarity of the television industry. Earth Day happened to fall in the middle of a "black week"—a time with no ratings—so the networks did not have to worry about audience share. That meant they could afford to broadcast more documentaries and special reports, which helped to satisfy federal regulations about public-interest programming. On NBC, the *Today* show focused on the environment for the entire week of April 20–24. NBC also aired a two-hour Earth Day report on the twenty-second. ABC broadcast three prime-time environmental specials during the week. The first focused on the teach-in at the University of Michigan, the second was called *Earth Day—S.O.S. for Survival*, and the third profiled defenders of the environment. In addition, ABC devoted its Sunday *Issues and Answers* program to Earth Day on April 12 and 19. CBS joined the crowd with *Earth Day—A Question of Survival.* Many network affiliates broadcast multipart series of their own. So did a number of regional networks.[98]

The *Today* show's made-for-TV teach-in was by far the most ambitious undertaking. The show was on every morning from 7:00 until 9:00, so the special broadcasts totaled ten hours. In the eighteen years since the show's debut in 1952, *Today* had never made that kind of commitment. The text of the broadcasts then appeared as a paperback edited by Frank Herbert, author of the science-fiction classic *Dune.*[99]

Host Hugh Downs introduced the week's theme, "New World or No World," in words intended to make viewers put down their toast and orange juice:

> Our Mother Earth is rotting with the residue of our good life. Our oceans are dying, our air is poisoned. This is not science fiction. And it is not the future; it is happening now and we have to make a decision now.
>
> Do we have the will to turn our way of life upside down?—because that is what it is going to take. To make personal, corporate, and national sacrifices in order to keep this earth alive? Or do we go on breeding, demanding more and more power, more of everything until we suffocate or die of plague or famine? Probably within the next century, perhaps within the next couple of decades?

Downs paused. "Now if these ideas disturb your breakfast," he continued, "I'm sorry. They are not original ideas. We wish they were. We wish we had thought of this a year ago, or ten years ago. We didn't. We are jumping on the bandwagon a little late in the game. But we have made a decision for the new world, and we hope you will too."[100]

Especially at the beginning of the week, the show provided evidence of the severity of the nation's environmental problems. On Monday, for example, a *Today* reporter led a tour of the Houston Ship Canal—"one big cesspool." The first guest on Tuesday was a photographer who documented pollution for the U.S. Public Health Service. Some of his images showed the corrosive effects of acidic emissions from power plants and steel mills. Another image caught a Los Angeles child enveloped by smog.[101]

But the mainstay of the week was discussion, not show-and-tell. The guests included an impressive array of scientists, social commentators, business leaders, government officials, and activists. Paul Ehrlich spoke about population, and Barry Commoner was part of a roundtable with executives from an oil company and an electric utility. Ralph Nader argued that pollution was a form of violence. Anthropologist Margaret Mead, environmental planner Ian McHarg, and biologist René Dubos discussed the cultural dimensions of the environmental crisis. The discussions of politics featured prominent environmentalists from both parties, including former secretary of the interior Stewart Udall, Senator Edmund Muskie, and federal Council on Environmental Quality chair Russell Train. Though the show did not have a representative of labor, the publisher of *Urban West* magazine lamented that the environmental movement was slighting the woes of the ghettos, where residents often lived next to polluting factories and could not count on basic sanitary services.

Despite the quality of the guests, the *Today* broadcasts were no substitute for a serious course of reading. The show's format did not allow extended back-and-forth. Each day was divided into segments of thirty minutes, including commercial breaks, and almost all of the guests only appeared in one segment. After the first program, one critic complained about the interruptions and the lack of depth. "The material presented wasn't earth-shaking—it was reiterated that something had better be done before it's too late—all very reasonable," the critic wrote. "Still it was better than nothing." That judgment was too harsh. The discussions seldom were mere fluff or bluster, and often were thought-provoking.[102]

One of the best segments was the roundtable about the root causes of environmental degradation with Mead, McHarg, Dubos, and Episcopal cleric Don Shaw, a former director of Planned Parenthood. McHarg argued that the critical problem lay in "the attitudes of Western man to nature." Mead gently challenged the view that the problem was wholly Western. "No society," she said, "has ever yet been able to handle the temptations of technology to mastery, to waste, to exuberance, to exploration and exploitation." But Mead's recommendation was cultural, like McHarg's: We needed a new view of the world, as something finite and fragile. Shaw similarly argued for "a new ethic." But he suggested that a deep change in thinking would not come easily. "We creatures are not very happy about being creatures," he said. "We like to pretend to be more than we are. And we must learn to return to our creature-ness."[103]

In another provocative segment, Downs asked three economists whether environmental protection required a no-growth economy. No one answered yes. But the three guests had different ways of understanding the issue. The chief economist at the U.S. Chamber of Commerce argued that the economy could continue to grow by making better use of resources and by shifting to less resource-intensive and less pollution-producing endeavors, especially services. E. J. Mishan, author of *The Costs of Economic Growth*, sought to shift the discussion toward the question of goals. In his view, growth had become a god, worshipped uncritically. Liberal economist Robert Lekachman argued that the standard measures of growth were "exaggerations." The harmful effects of economic activity were treated as positives, not negatives. If cigarette production increased, the gross national product went up—and then the GNP went up again when more people were treated for lung cancer. The environmental crisis was evidence that the minuses were growing faster than the pluses, Lekachman concluded, but the continued growth of GNP hid that truth.[104]

Though the guests often disagreed, the week produced few explosions. Even those who might have attacked the popular new cause took pains to seem sympathetic. The publisher of the conservative *National Review*, for example, argued that a lot of people were "riding their hobby horses on the pollution issue," especially those who "just like to get mad at industry"—but he also said that he hoped the concern about pollution would not become a fad, because the problem was serious.[105]

The *Today* producers worked hard to promote concord. The choice of guests from the business world makes that clear. Two of the three participants from finance and industry had conservationist credentials. (If one of the automakers had accepted an invitation to participate, the split would have been two and two.) The representative of Wall Street, Dan Lufkin, was on the national Earth Day advisory board. Charles Luce, the head of New York's electric utility, had worked at the Department of the Interior under Stewart Udall. In a question-and-answer session with a group of students on the Friday program, Luce encouraged one questioner to go to work for the power company and "bore from within," and Downs underscored the point: Luce was doing that himself, working for change as an insider.[106]

Downs was the voice of consensus. He hoped that the environmental issue would not fracture the nation as the civil-rights and antiwar movements had. Throughout the week, he emphasized the shared positions of the guests, not their disagreements. His closing comments were in that spirit: "Survival is everyone's business, from Main Street to Pennsylvania Avenue, and only together as a people, as a nation, as a unified planet can we finally answer the question New World or No World."[107]

THE GAYLORD NELSON NEWSLETTER

Washington, D.C.

May 1970

Earth Day - 1970

Mass Movement Begins

In New York City, thousands of persons thronged in the warm Spring sunshine, and the world-famous Fifth Avenue belonged to the people.

For a few hours, a small portion of the great city banned motor vehicles, and people promenaded on a proud boulevard usually congested with buses, taxies and cars. It was April 22--Earth Day in New York--and it was a holiday. Assistant Chief Inspector Arthur Morgan, who was in charge of the police on the scene, observed:

"Everyone's Beautiful"

"Everyone's beautiful. Just look at them. We're actually enjoying it."

In Madison, Wis., Earth Day was observed at sunrise over Lake Mendota with a Sanskrit invocation and a reading of the last chapter of the Book of Genesis with an apology to God for man's assaults on the landscape.

Earth Day observers in Milwaukee nominated the toad, the praying mantis and the ladybug as substitutes for DDT.

Thousands Marched

In Greensboro, N.C., in Atlanta, Ga., and in Miami, Fla., thousands marched in demonstrations for a clean environment. The Governor of Maine called for the Earth Day commitment to be "a truly lasting one," and the mighty Chicago Tribune observed incredulously that, after demonstrations on the city's broad new Civic Center Plaza, "there was no post-rally litter remaining to be cleaned up."

A new movement had begun, and uncounted millions--students, laborers, farmers, housewives, politicians, professional people, liberals and conservatives--who might have found it difficult to find common agreement on any other subject, were gathering together in a massive educational effort to talk about survival and the quality of survival in a world they all share.

In the little more than seven months after Sen. Gaylord Nelson suggested the idea of national teach-ins to discuss the crisis of the environment, the movement grew rapidly through March and April. On Earth Day, it was estimated that 2,000 college campuses, 2,000 community groups and 10,000 elementary and secondary schools were holding events.

In some places it was as the poet exclaimed while watching a rally of 30,000 in Philadelphia's Fairmount Park, an "educational picnic;" in others it was the serious business of government.

Special Legislation

During April, the state legislature of Massachusetts and the House of Representatives in Pennsylvania set aside time for important addresses on the environment and the introduction and passage of legislation aimed at protecting, preserving and restoring the environment.

Scientists, ecologists, environmentalists, educators and political leaders warned darkly before massive gatherings and small meetings that time was running out for the world and that all men had a responsibility to themselves and to leave a legacy of life for their children.

500 Invitations

Senator Nelson, who received nearly 500 invitations to speak at Earth Day observances, described the national teach-ins as "dramatic and successful" in their educational value, but warned that Earth Day must become the beginning of a "hard-fought political movement at all levels of government to insure that the spirit of the day is carried forth into actions to save, preserve and restore the environment for all living things."

The former Wisconsin governor's 18-stop speaking tour took him from coast to coast during April. He spoke in 10 states and the District of Columbia.

Nelson speaks at a multi-university teach-in on the eve of Earth Day at Milwaukee Area Technical College.

On September 20, 1969, Wisconsin senator Gaylord Nelson vowed to organize a nationwide environmental teach-in in spring 1970. His call to action succeeded far beyond his hopes. Millions of people participated in thousands of events. For the first time, the environmental cause seemed to be a "mass movement," as the headline in the May issue of Nelson's newsletter proclaimed. (Wisconsin Historical Society, Image ID 57066)

April 22.
Earth Day.

A disease has infected our country. It has brought smog to Yosemite, dumped garbage in the Hudson, sprayed DDT in our food, and left our cities in decay. Its carrier is man.

The weak are already dying. Trees by the Pacific. Fish in our streams and lakes. Birds and crops and sheep. And people.

On April 22 we start to reclaim the environment we have wrecked.

April 22 is the Environmental Teach-In, a day of environmental action.

Hundreds of communities and campuses across the country are already committed.

It is a phenomenon that grows as you read this.

Earth Day is a commitment to make life better, not just bigger and faster; To provide real rather than rhetorical solutions.

It is a day to re-examine the ethic of individual progress at mankind's expense.

It is a day to challenge the corporate and governmental leaders who promise change, but who short change the necessary programs.

It is a day for looking beyond tomorrow. April 22 seeks a future worth living.

April 22 seeks a future.

National Staff: Denis Hayes, Coordinator; Linda Billings, Stephen Cotton, Andrew Garling, Bryce Hamilton, Sam Love, Barbara Reid, Arturo Sandoval, Philip Taubman

We are working seven days a week to help communities plan for April 22. We have come from Stanford, Harvard, Bucknell, Iowa, Missouri, New Mexico, Michigan and other campuses.

We are a non-profit, tax exempt, educational organization. Our job is to help groups and individuals to organize environmental programs to educate their communities.

Earth Day is being planned and organized at the local level. In each community people are deciding for themselves the issues upon which to focus, and the activities which are most appropriate.

We can help, but the initiative must come from each community. We have heard from hundreds of campuses and local communities in all fifty states. Dozens of conservation groups have offered to help. So have the scores of new-breed environmental organizations that are springing up every day.

A national day of environmental education was first proposed by Senator Gaylord Nelson. Later he and Congressman Paul McCloskey suggested April 22. The coordination has been passed on to us, and the idea now has a momentum of its own.

All this takes money. Money to pay our rent, our phones, our mailings, brochures, staff, advertisements.

No list of famous names accompanies this ad to support our plea, though many offered without our asking.

Big names don't save the environment. People do.

Help make April 22 burgeon.

For you. For us. For our children.

The Environmental Teach-In, Inc.
Room 200
2000 P Street, N. W.
Washington, D. C. 20036
I enclose $10, $20, $50_____dollars (tax deductible)
How can I help my community?
Name
Address

Environmental

Action: April 22

Vol. 1, No. 3   March 3, 1970

Environmental Action April 22

Courtesy the Washington (D.C.) Star

OPPOSITE: Gaylord Nelson allowed other people to take ownership of the event, and that decision had profound consequences. Nelson did not even insist on keeping the original name. The young activists he hired to help coordinate the "environmental teach-in" thought that phrase sounded too academic. They asked the advertising guru Julian Koenig to propose alternatives, and "Earth Day" was one of Koenig's suggestions. The teach-in staff used the new name for the first time in this full-page advertisement in *The New York Times* on January 18, 1970.

ABOVE: Gaylord Nelson hired a handful of young activists to help coordinate the teach-in, and they gave the event a hip and activist image. They called themselves Environmental Action. Their newsletter promoted the idea that Earth Day was building a powerful new movement. The newsletter circulated to thousands of Earth Day organizing groups, and after Earth Day, Environmental Action used that network of local activists to lobby for national environmental legislation. (Wisconsin Historical Society, Image ID 80854)

EARTH DAY APRIL 22

ENVIRONMENTAL TEACH IN
ORGANIZATIONAL MEETING

MON. JAN. 26   7 PM

FINE ARTS B-3

ALL INTERESTED INVITED

The great strength of Earth Day was the grassroots organizing effort. Tens of thousands of people organized Earth Day events. Because the local organizing effort was empowering, the involvement of so many organizers ensured that Earth Day left a lasting legacy. The organizers of Earth Week in Philadelphia recruited volunteers with this simple poster. (Photograph courtesy of Austan Librach)

Making their feelings about pollution perfectly clear, throngs take over auto-free Fifth Ave. You're looking north from 42d St.
Stories start on page 3; other pictures in the centerfold

The Earth Day organizers in New York City wanted people to imagine a city without automobiles. Despite protests from merchants and cabdrivers, they secured permission to close a stretch of Fifth Avenue to vehicular traffic for part of Earth Day. From noon until two, the avenue became a park. The next day, photographs of the city's car-free celebration appeared on the front page of many newspapers, including New York's *Daily News*. (Daily News Archive/Getty Images)

The national media portrayed Earth Day as a sixties-style demonstration, but Earth Day was much more than a show of support for a cause. Earth Day was an unprecedented debate about "the environmental crisis." Tens of thousands of people gave speeches, participated in panels, or led discussions. Most had never spoken about environmental issues before. The speakers in these photographs were part of Earth Day teach-ins at the University of North Carolina at Chapel Hill (*top*) and the University of California, Irvine (*bottom*). (Top photograph courtesy of The State Archives of North Carolina; bottom photograph courtesy of Steve Owen)

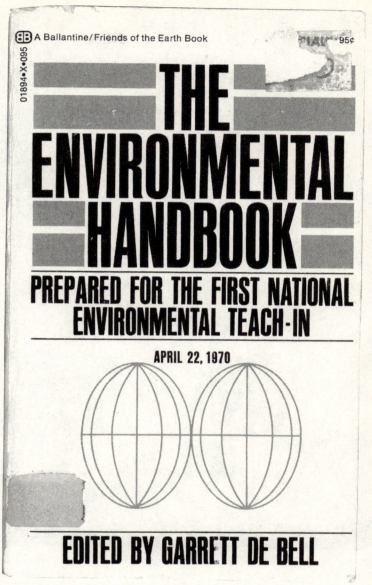

A Ballantine/Friends of the Earth Book

95¢

01894•X•095

THE ENVIRONMENTAL HANDBOOK

PREPARED FOR THE FIRST NATIONAL ENVIRONMENTAL TEACH-IN

APRIL 22, 1970

EDITED BY GARRETT DE BELL

Eco-publishing was one of the institutional legacies of Earth Day. In addition to analyses of every aspect of the environmental crisis, publishers brought out guides to ecological living and readers for environmental-studies courses. Many were mass-market paperbacks. *The Environmental Handbook*—a Ballantine paperback original rushed into print in January 1970 as a guide for teach-in organizers and participants—quickly sold more than a million copies.

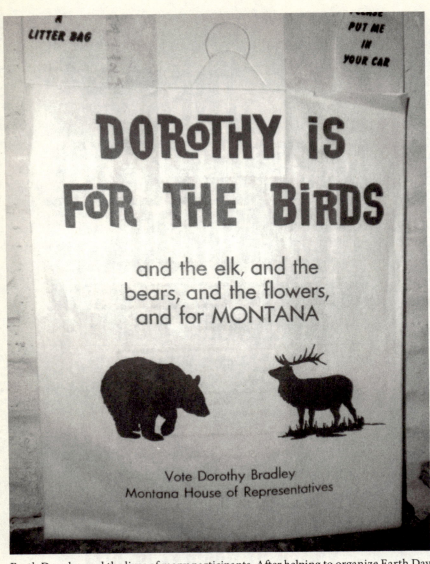

A LITTER BAG

PLEASE PUT ME IN YOUR CAR

DOROTHY iS FOR THE BiRDS

and the elk, and the bears, and the flowers, and for MONTANA

Vote Dorothy Bradley
Montana House of Representatives

Earth Day changed the lives of many participants. After helping to organize Earth Day events in Bozeman, Montana, Dorothy Bradley decided to run for state representative. She was just twenty-three, and she had never before thought about a political career. She saw her campaign as a way to sustain the spirit of Earth Day. She promoted her candidacy by giving away litterbags that people could hang in their cars: One side of the litterbag had this witty pitch, and the other side offered suggestions about how to protect the environment. Bradley won—and served eight terms in the legislature. (Photograph courtesy of Dorothy Bradley)

4 ● Speakers

The heart of Earth Day was public speaking. Tens of thousands of people gave addresses, rallied crowds, participated in panels, lectured, or led discussions. Some even read poetry. Though the exact number of speakers is unknowable, a conservative estimate is 35,000.[1]

The involvement of so many speakers was a stunning achievement. Earth Day radically increased the number of participants in public discussion of environmental issues. In 1970 the nation had few renowned experts in the field. Yet Earth Day proved that many more people had something to say about the environmental crisis.

Professors were the largest group of speakers. From anthropologists to zoologists, faculty members sought to bring their expertise to bear on the questions of the day. Some offered big-picture addresses, and some took part in interdisciplinary panels. At large state universities, where the Earth Day programs typically included fifty to one hundred speakers, most professors spoke about specific issues, from nuclear power to population growth. At smaller institutions, faculty members were more likely to offer overviews: "Philosophical Aspects of the Environmental Crisis," "The Economics of Pollution," "Art and the Environment."[2]

Students spoke too. In some high schools and junior highs, students addressed all-school assemblies or led workshops. Graduate students spoke at many universities, and undergraduates were part of hundreds of programs. At the University of Wisconsin–La Crosse, undergraduates gave almost all of the speeches. Their topics included "The Affluent Society Is Not So Rich," "Population: The Real Pollution," "The Military vs. the Environment," "Don't Turn a Deaf Ear to Noise Pollution," "America Lying in Waste," and "Practical Ecology." Many of the undergraduate speakers were activists in campus eco-action groups. Others held offices in student government or represented student interest groups. At historically black Grambling College, the Earth Day program was a kind of honor roll: Faculty advisers gave speaking assignments to the top majors in biology, business, chemistry, economics, education, geography, history, home economics, physics, and sociology.[3]

Bureaucrats probably were second to professors in the ranks of Earth Day speakers. Though the Environmental Protection Agency did not yet exist, the federal government had many agencies that dealt with environmental issues, and the Department of the Interior alone provided more than 1,000 speakers. Employees of state public-health, resource-conservation, and pollution-control agencies also were very active. So were local planning and sanitation officials. Some of the government speakers were defensive: They expected people to ask why their agencies were not doing more to protect the environment. Others welcomed the many new supporters of their cause.[4]

Politicians often were headliners. Congress took the day off so that members could speak around the country, and roughly two-thirds did. Several governors gave major Earth Day addresses. Thousands of state legislators and local officials also spoke. Many were part of panels on government and the environment. Others took the opportunity to tout specific measures, from mass transit to abortion rights. For some political hopefuls, Earth Day was a campaign event. In a speech at Georgia State University, gubernatorial candidate Jimmy Carter suggested that Americans might need to reconsider the goal of "growth for growth's sake."[5]

Local activists or representatives of national conservation groups were part of most Earth Day programs. The leader of a campaign against a proposed BASF chemical plant on the coast of South Carolina was the main attraction at Furman College. A Kentucky anti-strip-mining activist spoke at UCLA. In Pittsburgh, every willing member of the Western Pennsylvania Conservancy was booked. In contrast to the professors, bureaucrats, and politicians, the activists often were women. Hazel Henderson, the founder of New York City's Citizens for Clean Air, spoke in Indiana. Marge Levee of Stamp Out Smog and Harriet Miller of Get Oil Out spoke in California.[6]

Architects, doctors, engineers, and other professionals were among the speakers. Though only a handful of Fortune 500 executives addressed Earth Day crowds, many local business leaders offered their perspective. So did some union members. Religious leaders gave sermons as well as speeches. Artists, writers, musicians, and celebrities spoke. Members of the League of Women Voters and the Jaycees participated. The roster of speakers also included countercultural gurus, community organizers, and civil-rights leaders.

In national overviews of Earth Day, a few journalists mocked all the talk. The oratory, one wrote, was "as thick as smog at rush hour." Another concluded that "Earth Day drew the kind of nearly unanimous blather usually given only to the flag—or to motherhood, before motherhood ran afoul of the population explosion." But the critiques were glib exaggerations. Earth Day was not a patriotic celebration, a sentimental holiday, or a rally against cruelty to animals, where the arguments all were predictable. Though some speakers simply expressed opposition to pollution, their bland denunciations were not the rule.[7]

Indeed, many Earth Day speakers addressed difficult and potentially divisive issues. The root cause of the environmental crisis was an especially contentious question. Earth Day speakers blamed the exploitive character of capitalism, the unprecedented complexity of modern technology, the hostility to nature in the Judeo-Christian tradition, the explosive growth of human population, the wastefulness of a newly affluent society, and the shortsightedness of human nature. The other basic questions on Earth Day also were open to debate. Was environmental degradation largely an issue of quality of life, or was the danger dire? Could we end pollution by passing legislation or investing in new technologies, or would we need to change our fundamental values? What were the most effective ways to force government and business leaders to do more to protect the environment?[8]

The experience of speaking on Earth Day often was transformative. Some Earth Day speakers had never before talked publicly about environmental issues. As they considered what they wanted to say, they concluded that the stakes were higher than they had realized. Veteran speakers also were stretched by the occasion. Their Earth Day audience often was the biggest and most diverse they had ever addressed. They had to go beyond their expertise—to consider new issues and articulate new ideas. Many felt compelled to adopt a new tone. Some spoke more intimately, while others found a more prophetic voice.

Because so many kinds of people spoke about so many subjects, no sample of Earth Day speeches can be truly representative. But the breadth of the discussion is evident in the stories of seven speakers: ecologist LaMont Cole, Southern Baptist minister John Claypool, economist Kenneth Boulding, population activist Stephanie Mills, lawyer Victor Yannacone, Hudson River defender Richie Garrett, and Montana governor Forrest Anderson. In different ways, all seven contributed to an unprecedented debate about environmental issues.

Science Nonfiction

"Are we doomed?" That stark question came up again and again on Earth Day. Was man an endangered species? Would we drown in our wastes or choke on our own effluent? Were we poisoning ourselves? The questions about the human prospect were not solely scientific, but science seemed the starting point in seeking answers, and almost every Earth Day event featured talks by scientists.

Ecologist LaMont Cole spoke at Kearney State College in Nebraska, and that was a coup for the school. Cole was one of the few eco-celebrities in 1970. He was not a superstar—he was not in the same league as Paul Ehrlich or Barry Commoner—but he was in demand as a speaker.[9]

Cole's celebrity was not a matter of charisma. "He is a small, nervous man who considers the environment raw data, to be measured and tested, analyzed in the laboratory and reported on," a *Playboy* editor wrote after Cole spoke to 8,000 people at the Northwestern University environmental teach-out in January 1970. "The size and chaos of the crowd seemed awesome to him . . . That made him more nervous and he spoke quickly, glancing up and down from his notes, never establishing eye contact with his audience or trying for any dramatic effect. He just passed his information on to them—quickly, so he could get out. When the audience interrupted to applaud, he became even more disconcerted, as if to ask how the hell anyone could applaud *facts*."[10]

Though not a dynamic speaker, Cole had a compelling point of view. He saw the world headed for disaster, and he felt a duty to sound the alarm. His willingness to speak to lay audiences about controversial issues set him apart from most scientists.

Cole also had outstanding academic credentials. He was a professor and department head at Cornell. From 1961 to 1963, he served on the editorial board of *Ecology*, the leading journal in the field. He was president of the Ecological Society of America in 1968, and the American Institute of Biological Sciences in 1969. He made his name as a zoologist with mathematical studies of population dynamics.[11]

In the late 1950s, Cole began to worry that humans might destroy the earth's life-support systems. In a 1958 article on "the ecosphere" in *Scientific American*, he expressed anxieties about nuclear fallout and global population growth. Like many ecologists, however, he did not begin to think hard about the public responsibilities of the discipline until the publication of *Silent Spring*. By 1964 he was urging his peers to leave "their sheltered retreats" and "lend their specialized fund of knowledge to the attack on important public problems."[12]

Cole's first general alarm came in a 1966 article in *Saturday Review*. "Recently man's influence on the environment has become so ubiquitous that a careless calculation might destroy or drastically alter the entire pattern of life on earth," he argued. The nitrogen cycle exemplified the peril. Life depended on the bacteria that maintained the nitrogen cycle, yet we never considered whether those microbes would be harmed by our latest chemical inventions, from DDT to detergents. The same was true for many other essential natural systems. "Nobody knows for certain how vulnerable to human blunders some of these systems may be," Cole concluded. "A species that presumes to dominate the earth and to name itself *Homo sapiens*, the wise one, can hardly take pride in remaining ignorant of the needs for its own survival."[13]

Really, how dumb *were* we? The more Cole thought about our ecological ignorance, the more dire the situation seemed. Could the world be saved? In December 1967, Cole addressed that question at the annual meeting of the American Association for the Advancement of Science, and his AAAS talk turned out to be a preview of many of the arguments he made on Earth Day.[14]

In our quest for what we called "a better way of life," Cole argued, we were "destroying the natural environment that is essential to any human life at all." We were ruining the land, polluting the air and water, and altering the planet's "biological, geological, and chemical cycles." Though seldom discussed, the last set of threats was the most severe. The prospect of climate change was one of Cole's examples. Our unprecedented combustion of fossil fuels was increasing the amount of carbon dioxide in the atmosphere, he explained, and the resulting "greenhouse effect" was likely to alter "climates in ways that are still highly controversial in the scientific community but that everyone agrees are undesirable." Cole also warned about the risks of nuclear technology. One by-product of fusion reactors—tritium, a radioactive form of hydrogen—"would become a constituent of water" and therefore "would contaminate all environments and living things." Other contaminants threatened the oxygen and nitrogen cycles. Was a breakdown imminent? No one knew. But that was Cole's point: We were gambling without knowing the odds. "Surely," he concluded, "man's influence on his earth is now so predominant, so all-pervasive, that he must stop trusting to luck that his products and schemes will not upset any of the indispensable biogeochemical cycles."[15]

The AAAS talk made Cole a public figure. *The New York Times Magazine* published a version of the talk. *Newsweek* reported on Cole's warnings. Cole received invitations to speak around the country. He even attained a humbling cachet: His speeches often generated short wire-service stories that newspapers used as filler. The headlines were blunt. "Says Man Is Tampering Too Much with Nature" was one. In the lead-up to Earth Day, Cole was quoted in almost every report on the new prophets of doom. *Time* called him "a charter member of the doomsday school of ecologists." Walter Cronkite launched a periodic feature on the CBS Evening News that considered Cole's question: Can the world be saved? Cronkite interviewed Cole, and that interview led to another wire-service filler: "Suicide Possible, Ecologist Says."[16]

Speaking on Earth Day, Cole began by putting the environmental crisis in historical context. People had been degrading the environment "at least since Neolithic man began using fire as a tool," he said, but the scale of pollution increased profoundly with the Industrial Revolution. From coal to petroleum, fossil fuels had quickened the pace of our transformation of nature. The years since World War II brought a blitzkrieg of potentially devastating innovations. "Now I know to many of you World War II seems a long time ago," Cole said. "It doesn't seem very long to me. Think just in this period since World War II of some of the entirely new classes of materials we've asked our environment to cope with—plastics, antibiotics, radionuclides, synthetic pesticides, and detergents."[17]

The threat from new chemicals was especially grave. We already had created 500,000 chemicals, Cole explained, and we added 5,000 more to the environment every year. The use of so many new substances led again and again to new forms of pollution. Even scientists constantly were surprised. "Just last summer," Cole said, "I became aware of a new class of compound, the polychlorinated biphenyls, or PCBs for short." PCBs were widely used in industry, from plastics to rubber, and they turned out to be important pollutants. Like DDT, they became more concentrated at each step in the food chain, so that predators stored more of the substance than their prey. Like DDT, PCBs had spread throughout the world. Penguins in Antarctica had PCBs in their flesh. Yet no one knew how much PCBs were produced, because even the most basic information about chemical use is "shrouded in industrial secrecy. So it's hard to tell what we will discover next as a new environmental pollutant."

The proliferation of new technologies was not the only cause of environmental problems. The explosive increase of human population was like a cancer, Cole said, and we had to stop the cells from multiplying. Cole also decried "the Chamber of Commerce syndrome"—the drive to "keep everything expanding." But he warned against the simplistic urge to blame everything on the profit motive. The growth mentality dominated government as well as private enterprise. In the United States, the Army Corps of Engineers, the Bureau of Reclamation, the Agriculture Department, and the Atomic Energy Commission were among the agencies most responsible for environmental deterioration.

But Cole did not linger on the social, economic, and political roots of the environmental crisis. He was most concerned to illustrate the dangers of messing with nature. We were conducting experiment after experiment without any thought to the risks. So far, he argued, we'd had "a run of dumb luck." But we could not count on that luck to continue. Sooner or later our stupidity would catch up to us, unless we began to think ecologically. And we had to become smarter right away, because some disruptions of natural processes might be irremediable before we saw obvious warning signs.

To dramatize that argument, Cole offered a series of disaster scenarios. Even some sympathetic commentators wondered if the doomsday speculations were more akin to science fiction than responsible analysis. But Cole was convinced that a range of eco-catastrophes was possible.[18]

The fate of oxygen was Cole's favorite example. "Our atmosphere itself is a biological product," he said, and we were unwittingly threatening the very air we breathed. Most of the atmosphere is nitrogen and oxygen, and both are there because living things keep putting them there. With oxygen, one critical source was "the microscopic, free-floating green plants in the oceans which we call the marine phytoplankton." But now we were polluting the oceans, which were the ultimate sink for all the chemicals we'd invented. "If by any chance one of these half million chemicals . . . should turn out to be a deadly poison for the marine phytoplankton," Cole concluded, "our atmosphere would start running out of oxygen." Was that inconceivable? Not at all: A case study of Long Island Sound had shown that DDT in low concentrations could harm phytoplankton.

Cole tried to end on a more upbeat note. That was not easy, because his speech offered little grounds for optimism. He was a scientist, not an activist. He described what might happen if present trends continued, but he did not say what could counter or reverse the trend lines. Instead, he ended with a secular prayer. "I hope," he said, "that before it is too late, if it isn't already, all peoples will insist in unison upon the theme that many schools have adopted for this Earth Day: Give Earth a chance."

The Theology of Ecology

"'Two years ago I am not even sure I had heard the word 'ecology,'" the Reverend John Claypool told members of Louisville's Crescent Hill Baptist Church, "and I certainly did not realize the gigantic proportion of the problems this word stands for. Since then, however, we have all been inundated about what may happen very shortly to this planet Earth; and whether we like it or not, we have to make some kind of response to all of this."[19]

Like Claypool, most religious leaders in 1970 were novices in the environmental order. Before Earth Day, few theologians tried to articulate a Christian environmental ethic. But interest in "the theology of ecology" had begun to grow in 1967, after historian Lynn White Jr. argued in a shocking article in *Science* that the environmental crisis had religious roots. According to White, the Christian triumph over paganism had destroyed a powerful check on exploitation of nature—the sense that natural objects had spirits, like people. The sharp division in Christian thought between the human and nonhuman encouraged the scientific drive to master nature. So did "the Christian axiom that nature has no reason for existence save to serve man." The environmental crisis would continue to worsen, White concluded, "until we find a new religion, or rethink our old one." White's critique provoked a heated debate. Could the Bible be read more positively? The first important books about religion and ecology appeared in 1970.[20]

Earth Day inspired more reflection about the environment in religious circles. In early 1970, newspaper religion writers reported a growing theological interest in environmental questions. Religious publications explored the ecological crisis. The National Council of Churches encouraged church leaders to devote the Sunday before Earth Day to the environment. Hundreds, perhaps thousands, did just that.[21]

Claypool was one of the few Southern Baptist leaders to preach regularly about public issues. He took charge of Crescent Hill in 1960 at the age of twenty-nine, and he argued in one of his first sermons that religious institutions were in danger of becoming irrelevant. Would the church engage with the great questions of the day? At first, that meant addressing the issue of race. Claypool also spoke about poverty. At the end of the 1960s, he questioned the U.S. involvement in Vietnam. In one sermon he compared the nation to the prodigal son. His sermons often divided the congregation, but most members appreciated his social ministry.[22]

Claypool approached the environmental issue in the same way he approached civil rights and Vietnam. He looked to the Bible as a resource, he read widely, and he drew on his experience. The result was a sermon that joined religious and psychological insight.[23]

Claypool began with a parable about a farmer and tenant in his native state of Tennessee. To provide the tenant and his family with a place to live, the farmer wired a building for electricity. He also installed a cistern and indoor plumbing. The tenant brought a bunch of relatives as well as his large family, and they quickly destroyed the place. The plumbing stopped working because the tenant's family used up the water in the cistern. Then the family overloaded the electrical system with too many appliances, and the house burned down. Claypool still remembered the farmer's angry lament: "This was a decent place to live—a workable set-up—and look what they have gone and done." The moral was clear. The tenant's family had viewed the plumbing and wiring "as so much 'stuff' to be treated any way they pleased." Americans had approached nature with the same arrogance, Claypool said, "and this is why the whole thing is starting to collapse around us." Now we needed to acknowledge that we could not make unlimited demands on the earth. We had to control our population, and we had to respect the natural systems that supported us.

For Claypool, the beginning of ecological wisdom lay in Genesis. He did not mention the controversy over the injunction to subdue the earth. He simply offered his reading of the creation story. God was "a joyful Creator," and everything fit together masterfully in God's creation. Humans could not survive without oxygen, for example, "and we inhale this from the atmosphere and exhale carbon dioxide. However, many forms of plant life need carbon dioxide to live, and they inhale it and exhale oxygen." The cycling of oxygen and carbon dioxide exemplified "the fantastic balance built into the way God put it all together," Claypool said, "and Genesis indicates that man's place was to be a knowing partner in this finely balanced process. He was called on to name the animals; that is, to understand their structures and penetrate the mystery of their lives, and then to collaborate with them in a reciprocity that flowed back and forth. Man was part of the animals' and plants' support system, just as they were part of his, and so life was to be."

Unfortunately, Claypool continued, Genesis also tells that man refused to collaborate with nature. Instead, man became an "arrogant manipulator." As a result, "all of creation was thrown out of kilter." The dangers of that disharmony had only grown. Now we were at an "ecological impasse," and we were imperiling our very survival. We were paving over oxygen-producing plants, poisoning our life-giving rivers and oceans, and so much more.

What could we do to prevent disaster? The standard answer was a call for education: "Get out the facts." That was fine as far as it went—we needed more "heralds of truth like Rachel Carson"—but education was not enough. The issue was not simply ignorance. "There is a darkness deeper down in us than not knowing," Claypool argued. "It is the darkness of not wanting to be, of not wanting to live, or not wanting to grapple with existence as it is given to us in freedom and responsibility."

Again, the Bible could help. Claypool recalled the question Jesus asked the lame man in Bethesda: "Do you want to be healed?" The man had lain helpless by the pool for thirty-eight years, and Jesus knew that sickness can become a habit: "To be sick is to be exempt from responsibility and complex decision-making." Was the man willing to change his routines, to accept the challenges of health? That question also could be asked of well-to-do Americans. Our relationship to the environment was unhealthy. Were we willing to be healed? That would require "admitting openly and honestly that there is a problem and that we are sick and are partly at fault." Because "our capacities for denial and evasion" are vast, that admission would require courage. Then we would need "a willingness to become involved in the cure and not expect it to be done for us without any cost or effort." The cure would be painful. Though some people hoped for a quick technological fix, Claypool argued, that was a kind of childishness. Instead, people had to be mature enough to recognize "that because we are the ones who are sick and have made ourselves sick, we must be involved painfully in any cure."

That meant changing lifestyles. "The Good Life—however vaguely it may be defined—has most of us securely in its clutches," Claypool said, "and this glut of affluence is one of the main culprits of our environment." Every year we produced billions of disposable cans and bottles. We poured billions of tons of pollution into the air. In every way, the average American did far more damage to nature than the average Indian peasant.

"These are the apocalyptic facts," Claypool continued, "and Jesus' question is the real issue: 'Do we want to be healed?' Which means, are we willing to undergo the radical alteration of life style that will be called for if the balance of man and air and earth and water is to be restored? Nothing less than this will really touch the depths of the problem. Yet nothing could be harder than to get people to change what they have grown accustomed to having and spending and consuming."

Claypool paused. "I must admit that I fluctuate between pessimism and optimism on this point," he said. That kind of confession had become a hallmark of his preaching. Unlike many Southern Baptist ministers, Claypool acknowledged doubts. Instead of standing above his congregation, he spoke modestly, from his own flawed experience.

Thinking about his sermon, Claypool felt compelled to ask what changes he himself had made since he learned of the ecological crisis. "We have changed soap powder, take shorter showers and try to buy lead-free gas," he said, "but I still have two eight-cylinder cars, have done nothing to work for mass transit systems, still buy plastic milk cartons, and have yet to write that first public official in either support or disagreement. If I am to do my part in the healing, one hundred times more radicality than I have shown thus far is going to be called for. And while a few are doing more, I do not see many people aroused, and thus my pessimism."

But then Claypool looked again at the Bible and felt the stir of optimism. "I realize that God is on the side of health and wholeness and is at work for good in all this as he always has been," he said. "This does not mean he is going to do everything for us so that without any pain or effort what is crooked will come straight . . . But it does mean that we are not alone in our efforts. The promise of God applies to ecology; if we will confess our sin, he will do something in faithfulness and justice to forgive us our sins and cleanse us from all unrighteousness. If we will just be sons of God with all the responsibility and freedom that implies, things could be different."

That meant there was hope, Claypool concluded, although our salvation was not guaranteed. The dignity of humanity was that we had to decide whether we wanted to be healed. We had to decide whether we wanted to live or die. The biblical teaching pointed the way. In Deuteronomy, Moses is depicted "standing before Israel for the last time and saying: 'I call heaven and earth to witness this day, that I have set before you life and death, the blessing and the curse. Therefore choose life.' This remains the challenge to every generation, and to us. Well?"

The Spaceship Economy

Was economic growth incompatible with environmental protection? The boldest answers to that question came from University of Colorado professor Kenneth Boulding. Though many others spoke in technical terms about the relationship between economics and ecology, Boulding offered a striking metaphor that became part of the common language of environmentalists. He also sketched a conceptual tool that might help hasten a greener future.

By Earth Day standards, Boulding was an elder statesman. He had earned his Ph.D. in the 1930s, and he just had finished a term as president of the American Economics Association. But he was not a typical economist. Though he could do equations, he saw himself as a social philosopher. He had written about the economics of peace. He also had started a center for the study of conflict resolution. He was keenly interested in systems theory, and he was drawn to ecology as a science grounded in the analysis of systems. He was not afraid to preach, especially about the fate of humanity. Yet Boulding never was solemn. He had effervescent curiosity, and he relished life. He even wrote doggerel.[24]

Boulding first addressed environmental issues in 1964 in a book titled *The Meaning of the Twentieth Century*. The world was in the midst of a transition from agricultural to industrial civilization, he wrote, and that transition was one of the great experiments in human history. If the experiment succeeded, the result would be unprecedented comfort and creativity. But the experiment might fail, with dismal and even catastrophic results. One potential trap was war, especially nuclear war. Another was uncontrolled population growth. And a third was resource exhaustion. Because the transition to industrial civilization literally was fueled by energy sources that would not last forever, one of the critical unanswered questions was whether we could create a stable, high-technology society based on renewable resources. The answer might simply be no, Boulding cautioned. Even if the answer was yes, he argued, no one knew whether we could create the new economy before we ran out of fossil fuels. The margin for error might be great, or it might not. The prudent course now was to devote ourselves to building the knowledge we'd need, rather than to wasteful consumption.[25]

Boulding revisited the great transition in a talk published in 1966, "The Economics of the Coming Spaceship Earth." For much of history, he argued, people could imagine that they lived "on a virtually illimitable plane. There was almost always somewhere beyond the known limits of human habitation." People had powerful images of frontiers—places they might go "when things got too difficult, either by reason of the deterioration of the natural environment or a deterioration of the social structure." In recent centuries, however, people had begun to appreciate that the world was a globe. But the meaning of that fact still had not sunk in. "Even now," Boulding wrote, "we are very far from having made the moral, political, and psychological adjustments which are implied in this transition from the illimitable plane to the closed sphere."[26]

Economists especially had failed to consider the significance of the shift from the "open" world of the past to the "closed" world of the future. To drive home the profound differences between the economies of the two worlds, Boulding suggested the metaphoric terms that would become commonplace. "For the sake of picturesqueness," he wrote, "I am tempted to call the open economy the 'cowboy economy,' the cowboy being symbolic of the illimitable plains and also associated with reckless, exploitive, romantic, and violent behavior, which is characteristic of open societies. The closed economy of the future might similarly be called the 'spaceman' economy, in which the earth has become a single spaceship, without unlimited reservoirs of anything, either for extraction or for pollution, and in which, therefore, man must find his place in a cyclical ecological system."[27]

So what? Boulding acknowledged that many readers might not care about the future. If the day of reckoning was a long way off, why not "eat, drink, spend, extract and pollute, and be as merry as we can, and let posterity worry about the spaceship earth?" That argument had particular appeal to economists, who were trained to discount the future. Income today was more valuable than income down the road. At some point, future income had a discounted value of zero. Future expenditures were discounted similarly. From a traditional economic point of view, considering the distant future made no sense.[28]

Boulding countered with two arguments. Our lives only have meaning when we are part of a community, and the most meaningful community extends across time as well as space. We are most fulfilled when we connect the past to the future. For society, too, a tie to the future was critical to "morale, legitimacy, and 'nerve.'" Without a compelling image of tomorrow, a society "soon falls apart."[29]

Boulding also argued that the day of reckoning was not as distant as people might imagine. "The shadow of the future spaceship . . . is already falling over our spendthrift merriment," he wrote. We were not yet facing shortages of vital natural resources, but we were beginning to face limits on repositories for pollution. "Los Angeles has run out of air. Lake Erie has become a cesspool, the oceans are getting full of lead and DDT, and the atmosphere may become man's major problem in another generation, at the rate at which we are filling it up with gunk."[30]

Of course, many people already were working to reduce pollution. Even economists were beginning to explore the issues of externalities and public goods. But Boulding warned against becoming preoccupied with immediate problems. A long-term perspective was necessary, even in the short term: If we appreciated the deep crisis that faced humanity down the road, we likely would do more to deal with the deterioration of the environment today.

Boulding's ideas attracted some attention in the 1960s, but the response was nothing like what happened in early 1970, when "The Economics of the Coming Spaceship Earth" got a second wind. An excerpt from the essay was included in *The Environmental Handbook*, the bestselling paperback guide to Earth Day. The metaphor of the cowboy and spaceship economies suddenly became popular. Boulding became a sought-after eco-speaker. In March and April, he spoke at environmental teach-ins in Ann Arbor, Pittsburgh, Philadelphia, Denver, and Madison, among other cities.[31]

Boulding seized the opportunity to say something new. Reflecting on what economists might do to smooth the shift to the spaceship economy, he focused on the way we measured economic progress. "The Gross National Product is one of the great inventions of the twentieth century," he argued, "probably almost as significant as the automobile and not quite so significant as TV."[32]

That was hyperbole, to make audiences perk up. But Boulding was serious about the importance of "social inventions." Social inventions can change the world as much as technological breakthroughs. Yet because social inventions often occur "softly and imperceptibly," they rarely are acknowledged. "Who for instance invented the handshake?" Boulding asked. "How did we change from a society in which almost every man went armed to a society in which we have achieved almost complete personal disarmament, and in which human relations are governed by conventions of politeness, by disarming methods of communication, and by largely nonviolent techniques of conflict?"[33]

The concept of GNP was developed in the 1930s, Boulding explained, and the invention had profound consequences. In some ways, the ability to quantify the performance of the economy was a godsend. GNP certainly helped policymakers to stop economic downturns from becoming shattering depressions. But GNP also was pernicious—something to "view with alarm"—because GNP was a misleading measure of progress.[34]

The most obvious problem was that GNP counted many bad things as good. If a company polluted a lake, whatever we spent to clean up the lake increased the GNP. A true measure of economic performance would count pollution as a debit, not a credit. Boulding also saw a deeper problem. In a spaceship economy, he argued, "the idea of GNP simply falls apart."[35]

The spaceship economy would depend on recycling, but GNP exalted the opposite. GNP measured throughput—input becoming output. That was a linear process, not a loop. The process began with useful material and ended with effluent and garbage. GNP did not account for the depletion of natural capital. GNP also did not account for the accumulation of waste. GNP only measured the intermediate steps in the process—production and consumption. As a result, GNP hid the worm at the core of the apple of development. "Economic development is the process by which the evil day is brought closer when everything will be gone," Boulding argued. "It will result in final catastrophe unless we treat this interval in the history of man as an opportunity to make the transition to the spaceship earth."[36]

Boulding readily acknowledged that GNP was not the only reason why people failed to appreciate the challenge ahead. Since the eighteenth century, the economy had grown tremendously. The wealth created since World War II was so extraordinary that the future seemed to promise "absolutely secure and effortless abundance." But exponential growth could not continue forever. Though the cowboy era would not end in the lifetime of anyone in the audience, the new day would come sooner or later. Possibly in one hundred years—and certainly in a few centuries. "I am sure it will be no longer than 500 years off," Boulding said, "and that is not a tremendously long period of historical time."[37]

The construction of a spaceship economy would require a replacement for GNP. Without a true measure of economic success, we would continue to misdirect our energies. Boulding predicted—presciently—that a "perfect measure of which way is up" would be hard to devise. But we had to make the effort. "In the next hundred years," he said, "we will very much need social inventions for the discouragement of bads and the encouragement of goods." The sooner we started, the better.[38]

Motherhood

Stephanie Mills gave three speeches on Earth Day. Though just twenty-one, Mills already was a popular prophet of population control, and population was second only to pollution on the Earth Day agenda. But Mills did not speak only about the threat of overpopulation. Population was the glue that held together reflections on Western attitudes toward death, affluence, and women's rights.

For Mills, the road to Earth Day began with a drug-enhanced

"armchair wilderness epiphany." She was a student at Mills College, a women's school in Oakland, and she was visiting her boyfriend in Berkeley. Waiting for him to finish an architecture project, Mills got high on pot and picked up *The Place No One Knew: Glen Canyon on the Colorado*, the Sierra Club coffee-table book about a scenic wonder flooded by a dam. Mills had grown up in a suburb of Phoenix—the antiwilderness, she later wrote, where "outside" meant the "irrigated backyard, the irrigated city park, and the air-conditioned mall." Though she loved to drive, she never explored the desert. But at her boyfriend's apartment, stoned, "hungry for a vision," she was overwhelmed by the lost canyon. "Eliot Porter's astonishing photographs were the only remaining sight to be had of a place of pristine and unimaginable beauty," she recalled. "A place that no air-breathing creature would ever again be able to inhabit or see. The sanctuary depicted by those photographs of water-streaked grottoes was a haunting contrast to the social violence and ugliness outside the walls of that south-campus apartment. It felt like a clear invitation to make common cause with the planet."[39]

Mills organized a campus symposium on the environment. She began to read the classic American nature writers. She had not studied much biology—her major was contemporary thought—so she rushed to become environmentally literate. In the spring of 1969, a few months before graduating, Mills found her muse: Paul Ehrlich.[40]

Mills was one of many young people turned on by Ehrlich. Though the population issue worried people of all ages, the baby boomers were Ehrlich's biggest audience. To the boomers, the population explosion was not a far-off abstraction. The boomers were born in crowded maternity wards. They went to schools struggling to deal with exploding enrollment. In many elementary schools, the auditorium could not hold all the students. Many high schools divided the students into shifts. Then many boomers went to universities so big that the students feared becoming numbers. Looking for after-school and summer jobs as teenagers, the boomers faced a glutted market. They also found crowds when they went to pools and parks.[41]

Mills began to fear a future with no solitude, no space for creativity, no peace of mind. "Everything is too crowded even now," she thought. Mills also began to fear that all the Glen Canyons in the world were doomed. The half-conscious unease she felt growing up in Phoenix suddenly seemed a portent. In a world with more and more people, sprawl was inevitable. "Beauty is vanishing right and left," she wrote a few months after reading Ehrlich. "It is no longer a comfort to see untouched places near the city, since it is virtually certain that someday those places will be 'developed.' It is hard not to see natural places and feel an impending sense of loss."[42]

Mills decided to preach about the population explosion in her valedictory speech at commencement in June 1969. "Traditionally, commencement exercises are the occasion for fatuous comments on the future of the graduates present," she began. "This future is generally painted in glowing terms . . . My depressing comment on that rosy future, that infinite future, is that it is a hoax. Our days as a race on this planet are, at the moment, numbered, and the reason for our finite, unrosy future is that we are breeding ourselves out of existence." That was startling— and her listeners' surprise soon turned to shock when Mills announced her post-graduation plans. She was a liberal-arts major, with few job prospects. She foresaw that "it would be easier for me to leave this ivory tower to earn a living as a cocktail waitress than to earn a living as a crusader, of sorts, for human survival. If I had enough time, I'd try to get rich, become a philanthropist, and endow a foundation." But she wanted to do something right away. What, then? "I am terribly saddened by the fact that the most humane thing for me to do is to have no children at all," she said. "I have asked myself what kind of world my children would grow up in. And the answer was, 'Not very pretty, not very clean.

Sad, in fact.' Because, you see, if the population continues to grow, the facilities to accommodate that population must grow, too. Thus we have more highways and fewer trees, more electricity and fewer undammed rivers, more cities and less clean air. Mankind has spread across the face of the earth like a great unthinking, unfeeling cancer. We have horribly disfigured this planet, ungrateful and shortsighted animals that we are. Our frontier spirit involved no reverence for any forms of life other than our own, and now we are even threatening ourselves with the ultimate disrespect of suicide."[43]

The speech caused a sensation. The vow not to have children was one of the quotes of the week in many Sunday newspapers. *The New York Times* reported that Mills had made "perhaps the most anguished statement" by any college graduate that year. Mills was deluged with requests for interviews. In the week after commencement, Mills College received one hundred calls a day from parents and alumna who had heard about the speech.[44]

Commentators heatedly debated Mills's decision. Many were bewildered or saddened. Was the environmental crisis really so extreme that a smart, pretty girl felt compelled to take such drastic action? To some observers, Mills epitomized the waywardness of modern youth. She lacked faith. How could she assume that God's world was incapable of supporting His highest creation? Though Mills did not attack the idea of motherhood, many critics interpreted her speech as a denunciation, not a reluctant renunciation. By rejecting motherhood, they argued, Mills was selfishly shirking a kind of civic duty. Yet many women applauded the feminist subtext of her decision: Mills was asserting that motherhood was a choice, not a biological destiny. Other commentators considered Mills a hero for sacrificing so much to help save the planet.[45]

Mills instantly became the environmental voice of her generation. *Rolling Stone* founder Jann Wenner hired her to edit a new monthly magazine, *Earth Times*, that debuted in April 1970.

In the ten months from her graduation to Earth Day, Mills gave almost eighty speeches. She made headlines again when she became the first woman to preach from the pulpit at San Francisco's Grace Cathedral. She was profiled in *Look* and honored by *Mademoiselle*. A *Washington Post* columnist touted Mills as a symbol of the radicalizing power of the environmental crisis. She was quoted in Earth Day preview stories, and she appeared on two network television specials. Mills was welcomed into the countercultural scene in San Francisco, and she helped Gary Snyder write a widely circulated ecological manifesto, "Four Changes," that explored population, pollution, consumption, and consciousness. Mills also was sought out by establishment conservationists. Population activist John D. Rockefeller III flew her to New York to discuss how to involve young people in the cause. Celebrity activist Arthur Godfrey and *Saturday Review* editor Norman Cousins arranged to meet her. Former secretary of the interior Stewart Udall invited Mills to speak to a class he was teaching at Yale. Planned Parenthood hired her as a regional organizer and made her a member of the organization's national advisory group. David Brower asked her to serve on the board of directors of Friends of the Earth.[46]

The frenzy of fame was overwhelming. "I was in way over my head," Mills wrote later. But Mills managed to find time to develop her thoughts. The more she considered the population explosion, the more complex the issue seemed. Her speeches became more philosophical and more political.[47]

Mills questioned deep-rooted attitudes about life and death. Why was taking the Pill so much more controversial than taking antibiotics? Both interfered with the natural order. Because the Western tradition sanctified human life, we saw procreation as a blessing. "Be fruitful and multiply," the Bible commanded. Yet we refused to accept death as part of life. "Death is finiteness, and Western man rejects finiteness," Mills argued. "We long for a limitless supply of everything: air, water, food, wilderness, time." The result of our "misguided aspirations" was a potentially suicidal imbalance between birthrates and death rates. To save ourselves, we needed to accept a world of limits. We could not seek at all costs to conquer death without also trying to control population.[48]

Mills deepened her critique of the psychological costs of population growth. "We crowd ourselves in, and we become alienated," she argued. "We lose total contact with the forces that shape our lives." The loss of a sense of the real warped our conception of "quality of life." Because we had little opportunity to enjoy the pleasures of true individuality and community, we became obsessed with the acquisition of material goods. Yet that acquisitiveness produced more sprawl, more pollution, and more demand for finite resources.[49]

Indeed, Americans were "the pigs of the world." We consumed more resources and produced more waste than anyone else. Mills pressed her audiences to tally the environmental costs of their affluence. "As you go through your daily routine, ask yourself where it all came from," she urged. "Where did the power come from? Where did the water come from? Where did the paper come from? What was destroyed in the process of getting it, whatever *it* may be?" That knowledge was the beginning of responsibility.[50]

In the months before Earth Day, Mills made her feminism more explicit. To reduce birth rates, we needed to build a society "where many different ways of coping with our sexuality coexist happily. Thus, you men can be bachelors without being condemned. Thus, we women can remain unmarried without humiliation. Thus, we can marry and have no children. All these possibilities need to be accepted. Obviously this attitude implies a change in the role of women." The issue was political as well as cultural. Women needed rights! "You cannot go to a woman who has nothing else to do in her life but raise children and command her to forgo children," Mills argued. Women would not be happy with smaller families without "at least an equal crack at the jobs men hold down."[51]

Mills also began to talk about electoral politics. That was a big turnabout. In college, she thought that public life was mostly riots and tear gas, and her vow not to have children was an expression of her mistrust of the political system: She had confidence only in decisions she could make herself. In her first speeches, she called for a revolution in consciousness. But she soon concluded that political reform was essential too. When she became editor of *Earth Times*, she promised to cover politics, because politicians would decide the future "for better or worse." She was more emphatic on Earth Day. She attacked the Nixon administration's environmental agenda, and she urged her audience to "dump" the president. "We must become the government," she proclaimed. "Revolution is very convenient but power is the only way to get change. Learn all you can—then turn the situation around from inside. Otherwise we are witless zealots."[52]

Like many young activists, Mills saw the environmental crisis as a struggle of Life against Death, and she often ended her speeches with a call to celebrate. "It takes more than lockjawed resolution to save a world for all creatures," she said. "It takes love and joy. There can be no survival without passion. Passion for humanity, love of the earth, joy of existence, and hope for the future." On Earth Day, Mills closed with a simpler plea: "Put joy back on earth."[53]

Sue the Bastards

What was the best way to stop corporations and government agencies from despoiling the environment? Because so many Earth Day programs were action oriented, that question came up again and again. Victor Yannacone, one of the pioneers of environmental law, offered a blunt answer: "Sue the bastards."

For most environmentalists in 1970, litigation still was a last resort, not a first recourse. But the field of environmental law was booming. The Conservation Foundation held the first environmental-law symposium in September 1969. Three months later, *The New York Times* reported that a majority of law schools were offering courses on the subject, up from just a handful a year or two before. The first environmental-law journal appeared early in 1970, and the first handbooks in the field soon followed. The Natural Resources Defense Council was established in March 1970. On Earth Day, several teach-ins included panels on environmental law.[54]

Yannacone had done more than anyone to build the field. He was a tireless proselytizer. Whenever he had a chance, he made his case for the efficacy of environmental law to conservationists, trial lawyers, and students. He also was a bold and brilliant litigator, and his cases attracted considerable attention.

Yannacone identified with underdogs and outsiders. Unlike the stereotypical conservationist, he was not a member of the WASP elite. He looked like a young Vince Lombardi, and he once dreamed of becoming a football coach. He did not have an Ivy League education. He liked to tell audiences that he was the worst student at Brooklyn Law School, which was not one of the nation's best. He grew up wary of concentrated wealth and power. His father used to rail against a statue of a robber baron in New York City—"a pretty poor example to youth," he argued—and eventually persuaded Mayor Fiorello La Guardia to take the statue down. Yannacone practiced law with his father in a small town on Long Island, not at a big firm, and they worked mostly on workmen's compensation and personal-injury cases. Yannacone also had experience in civil-rights and labor disputes. He did not wear stylish suits.[55]

Yannacone saw the courts as protectors of the unprotected. He venerated Thomas à Becket, Thomas More, and other martyrs who had given their lives over the centuries to ensure the rule of law. Because the legal system was a check on wanton use of power, the law was the great hope of all who cared for human rights. At a time of environmental crisis, the law also could be the champion of the earth. "Every bit of progressive social legislation of the last 50 years has come about only after litigation," Yannacone told the Conservation Foundation conference on environmental law. "It's the highest use of the courtroom—even when we lose—to focus public attention and disseminate information about intolerable conditions."[56]

Litigation also allowed environmentalists to seize the initiative. For Yannacone, that was crucial. Conservationists traditionally had allowed the despoilers to define the terms of battle. Because they fought from defensive positions, they rarely struck with great force. Though conservationists had won some skirmishes and even a few major engagements, they had no strategy for winning the war. In contrast, litigation took the fight to the enemy. In the courts, environmentalists could hope to win decisive victories.

Yannacone already had demonstrated the power of environmental litigation in a series of legal challenges to the use of DDT. The first came in 1966, when Yannacone was thirty. His wife, Carol, had become convinced that DDT was killing fish in a Long Island lake that she had come to love as a child. At her urging, Yannacone sued to stop county officials from using DDT to control mosquitoes. The Yannacone suit was not the first against DDT. In the late 1950s, a group of Long Islanders had argued in an unsuccessful personal-injury suit that DDT spraying endangered their health. Yannacone's class-action suit was more ambitious. He sought to protect all residents—present and future—from the hazards of DDT. The judge concluded that only the state legislature could ban the pesticide, but the suit persuaded the county to use alternative methods of mosquito control. Yannacone and several other people involved in the case formed the Environmental Defense Fund, the first organization to use the power of lawsuits to secure environmental rights. EDF sued to halt pesticide use in Michigan and Wisconsin, and the litigation led to bans in both states. Yannacone then raised the bar. In October 1969, he sued the major manufacturers of DDT for $30 billion in damages to the environment.[57]

Yannacone's ambition was even more evident in a suit filed in 1968 against the Hoerner Waldorf pulp mill in Missoula, Montana. The mill was responsible for almost all the air pollution in the Missoula region, and the suit sought to force the company to install pollution-control technology. "The people of the valley live at the bottom of a veritable sewer of bad air," Yannacone argued. "It affects human health, reduces ecological values and destroys the amenities of civilized life—the ability to breathe deeply and to appreciate the many delicate odors of nature. You can't smell the flowers in Missoula, Montana!" For Yannacone, however, the issue was not simply the quality of life in one city. He saw the case as a chance to determine "whether the right to breathe clean air is a constitutionally protected right."[58]

Though environmental law was too new to have a standard MO, Yannacone's approach was a radical departure from the first celebrated case in the field, *Scenic Hudson Preservation Conference v. Federal Power Commission*. The Scenic Hudson plaintiffs sued to attain a traditional goal: They sought to stop a proposed development. They argued that the FPC had acted improperly in granting a permit for a power plant on the river, and they won two precedent-setting procedural victories. The judge agreed that conservationists had the right to intervene even though they did not have a direct economic stake in the permit decision. The judge also ruled that the FPC had to consider the environmental impact of the power plant, especially the effect on the natural beauty of the Hudson.[59]

Yannacone was not content to use new legal weapons to fight classic preservation versus development battles. He also was not interested in winning procedural victories: He did not sue to get a seat at the table, or to force policymakers to consider the environmental impact of proposed developments. He sought to change the way corporations and government agencies operated. He argued that Americans had a right to a healthy environment. His models were the legal battles to destroy racial segregation and secure workers the right to organize.

As a litigator, Yannacone was fearless. He knew that his opponents were more powerful, but he was confident that right could beat might. He did not fret over the lack of precedents for his arguments. If he could get a hearing, he believed, the facts would compel judges to make new law. "He was combative, energetic, imaginative, and irreverent," recalled one colleague. "He had enough chutzpah that he easily would have brought a class action suit against the Deity for unconstitutionally . . . inflicting upon us all a too generous measure of the ennui of life."[60]

That sort of brashness troubled some conservationists. David Brower suggested that the Environmental Defense Fund needed "some people who are older and stuffier." At the Conservation Foundation conference on environmental law, several pioneers in the field warned against premature, overly ambitious efforts to establish environmental rights. Even the Environmental Defense Fund directors ultimately became concerned about Yannacone's agenda, and the organization severed ties with Yannacone at the end of 1969.[61]

But Yannacone won many converts. By 1970, many Americans were ready to take a more confrontational approach to environmental problems, and Yannacone's call to sue the bastards perfectly expressed the new militance. He became a popular speaker, especially on college campuses. He was the subject of admiring profiles. "All He Wants Is To Save The World," *Sports Illustrated* proclaimed in 1969.[62]

On Earth Day, Yannacone began by making the case for class-action suits. Lobbying for new laws might work, but the legislative process was ponderous, and the danger to the environment often was immediate and irreparable. Appealing to government agencies for new regulations might help, but the established bureaucracies had narrow mandates and lacked ecological expertise. The Federal Power Commission, for example, was established to consider the economics of electricity, not the environmental consequences of power generation. Though environmentalists had begun to sue polluters for damages, that sort of lawsuit was inherently limited. The economic harm to the plaintiffs was only a part of the social loss from environmental degradation. The awards in suits against polluters were also trivial: They became a cost of doing business—"a license to pollute"—not a deterrent. But class-action suits offered a chance to address the critical issues decisively and expeditiously.[63]

Though government could be as destructive as private enterprise, Yannacone focused on the need to discipline corporate polluters. "The time has come to housebreak industry," he said. "The time has come to establish, once and for all time, as a fundamental principle of American justice, that industry owes the American people the cleanest air and the cleanest water that the existing state of the art in pollution control can secure."

To secure that principle, environmental groups needed skillful, passionate, and courageous advocates. "Great industries will never lack for advocates!" Yannacone proclaimed. "Government will never lack for advocates! Political organizations will never lack for advocates, and the established institutions of the political-industrial-military-power-structure, in their rape of our human and natural resources and their prostitution of the legal profession, need no more advocates." He paused, before the trumpet blast: "PEOPLE need advocates! PEOPLE need champions!"

Would young Americans respond to that need? Yannacone understood that many college students had become skeptical about the system, and he made a special pitch to disaffected idealists. Though marching in the streets seemed the only recourse, litigation was a better antidote to desperation and alienation. The catharsis of demonstrating was short-lived. At best, the shouts and signs won a few seconds of television time. But a lawsuit had real power. "Industry and government can ignore your protests," Yannacone argued, "and certainly they can repress your demonstrations. But no one in industry or government ignores that scrap of legal cap that begins: YOU ARE HEREBY SUMMONED TO ANSWER THE ALLEGATIONS OF THE COMPLAINT ANNEXED HERETO WITHIN TWENTY DAYS OR JUDGMENT WILL BE TAKEN AGAINST YOU FOR THE RELIEF DEMANDED."

That led to another populist crescendo. Riffing on Woody Guthrie, Yannacone called on Earth Day celebrants to reclaim their birthright:

This land does not belong to General Motors, Ford, or Chrysler; this land does not belong to Consolidated Edison, or any other private-investor owned utility; this land does not belong to Penn-Central, B&O, C&O, Union Pacific, Southern Pacific, or any other railroad; this land does not belong to American Airlines, United Airlines, TWA, or any other common carrier; this land does not belong to Minnesota Mining & Manufacturing Company, Minneapolis Honeywell, IBM, Xerox, Eastman Kodak, Polaroid, or any other company marketing technological marvels; this land does not belong to International Paper Company, Scott Paper, Boise Cascade, Weyerhaeuser, Crown Zellerbach, or any other paper products company; this land does not belong to United States Steel, Bethlehem Steel, Inland Steel, Crucible Steel, or any other steel company; this land does not belong to Anaconda, Kennecott, Alcoa, or any other nonferrous metal company; this land does not belong to any soulless corporation!

This land does not belong to the ICC, FPC, FCC, AEC,

TVA, FDA, USDA, BLM, Forest Service, Fish and Wildlife Service, or any other federal or state alphabet agency!

This land does not belong to the president of the United States, the Congress of the United States, the governor of any state, or the legislatures of the fifty states. This land belongs to its people. This land belongs to you and this land belongs to me.

Yannacone could have ended there. Instead, he made one more pitch for action. "Don't just sit there like lambs waiting for the slaughter, or canaries waiting to see if the mine shaft is really safe," he said. "Don't just sit around talking about the environmental crisis, or worse yet, just listening to others talk about it. Don't just sit there and bitch. Sue somebody!"

The Power of Place

Like all the activists who spoke on Earth Day, Richie Garrett hoped to show that ordinary people could make a difference. But his story was more compelling than most, because he came from unusually humble stock. His parents grew up in one of the poor Irish neighborhoods of New York City. His father was a manual laborer, and his mother was a maid. They moved during the Depression to a working-class town north of the city, Crotonville, where almost everyone built their own houses. Richie, born in 1935, was the fifth child in a family already struggling to make ends meet. After high school, he served in the Marine Corps Reserve and worked as a bridge builder. In 1962, Garrett succeeded his father as superintendent of a Catholic cemetery. Despite the administrative title, his work was mostly digging graves.[64]

From early boyhood, however, Garrett was a river rat. His neighborhood overlooked the Croton, a tributary of the Hudson, and he could walk down to the riverbank on a stairway made from railroad ties. In a town without parks or playgrounds, where no one had the money for fancy vacations, the river was the one respite. "Our Monte Carlo," Garrett liked to say. "Our Riviera." Families had picnics there. In the summer, the boys turned a fifty-pound snapping turtle into a carnival or rodeo ride, with a wire bridle that held the turtle's mouth shut. Garrett often spent summer afternoons watching girls sun on the rocks. He sometimes celebrated daybreak by building a bonfire on the bank before fishing for stripers. He caught bait for men who fished for a living. In high school, he and a buddy began to build a fleet that eventually numbered six rowboats and two outboards, and the two fished the Hudson as well as the Croton. For Garrett, being on the river was peace. The fish, the current, the wind—the river gave a sense that all was right.[65]

Except that, by the mid-1960s, all was not right on the river. When Garrett went to the founding meeting of the Hudson River Fishermen's Association in 1966, several people told stories about fish kills. Everyone recounted insults to their beloved river. Garrett told about the waste paint flushed from the Tarrytown Chevy plant into a stream that fed the Hudson. He told about detergent foam along the banks of the Croton, because Crotonville had no sewer system and people sent washing-machine rinse down to the river through a drain and culvert. He also told about the pipe that discharged oil from a Penn Central Railroad maintenance shop into Croton Bay, where he fished for bass. The bass always had the taste of diesel, he said, no matter how much he scrubbed the fish.[66]

The meeting was hosted by a *Sports Illustrated* writer, Robert Boyle, and most of the inaugural members of the association were professionals, including an oceanographer, a law professor, an entomologist, and an airline pilot. Garrett went to the meeting with his longtime fishing buddy, Augie Berg, who worked as a prison guard at Sing Sing. The group soon made Garrett president. He knew the river intimately, he was passionate yet composed, and he gave the lie to the charge that only the effete cared about preservation. Garrett attracted many more working-class members, from mill workers to roofers. He arranged for the association to meet at the American Legion post.[67]

On Earth Day, Garrett spoke at Union Square in New York City. He often had addressed high-school classes and outdoor clubs, but the crowd in the square would be far bigger and more diverse than any he had faced before. What did he want to say? The association had fought the Penn Central railroad, Governor Nelson Rockefeller, and the Consolidated Edison electric company, and he definitely would describe those fights. But could he say something more personal? Working with Boyle, Garrett wrote draft after draft. He still was not sure about a few passages as he drove into Manhattan the morning of April 22.[68]

"God bless you all for being here today," Garrett began. "My name is Richie Garrett, and I am president of the Hudson River Fishermen's Association. The association includes all sorts of members—writers, marine scientists, housewives, interested kids, commercial fishermen, and people who give a damn. I happen to be a cemetery superintendent in Ossining, and I'm told I was elected [president] because I'm the last guy to let anyone down."[69]

The joke fell flat. No matter: The lack of laughter just underscored the point Garrett wanted to make next. His life had not gone exactly the way he'd hoped, but he had no regrets. He had felt "completely fulfilled" since he joined the fight to save the Hudson. "The Hudson is my life," he said. "I'm not involved in fighting the dope problem or the crime problem. There's only so much of me to go around. But the way I figure it, clean water and clean air—a clean earth—is the most important issue of all. If you don't have a clean earth, there's no point in doing anything else. You might as well open up all the prisons and let everybody out so we can all choke to death together."

Garrett then made a pitch for unity. Boyle had advised him

not to mention the nation's divisions, but Garrett was adamant: Healing the environment was the first step in binding the wounds of society. "Our country has its problems," he said. "Black versus white, hawk versus dove—you name it, we got it. But unless we can get in tune with the world again, put ourselves in touch with nature, nothing will ever be solved. Black or white, hawk or dove, we'll all drown in garbage up to our eyeballs."

Garrett had confidence that the environment could be restored. "You can do the job," he said. "In fact, I know damn well you can. The fact that I'm up here speaking to all of you shows that a persistent voice can be heard. If anyone had told me five years ago, or even last year, that I'd be speaking here like this in Manhattan, I'd tell them they were out of their mind. Now that I'm here, let me tell you how to go about it to be effective. To start, do what you think you can do, and be honest. Sure, I want to save the world, but I've picked out a small marvelous piece of it to save, the Hudson River Valley, from the Adirondacks to New York Harbor. That's no small job, because every rotten thing that is being done to the country today is being done to the Hudson, times ten."

For four years, Garrett said, the Hudson River Fishermen's Association had pressed federal officials to enforce a little-known 1888 law that barred dumping in the Hudson. The law allowed citizens who reported violations to receive half of any fines, so the association distributed 10,000 "Bag-a-Polluter" postcards. The postcards were prepaid and addressed to Garrett. In addition to many postcards, Garrett received dozens of telephone calls about river pollution. The callers often worked for the polluters. The Penn Central was target number one. Garrett, Boyle, and other members of the association wrote letters, made phone calls, and visited government offices to protest the railroad's oil dumping. Garrett took a Federal Water Pollution Control Administration official to see the discharge pipe. The official was disgusted but did nothing. Other agencies also refused to act.

Finally, with help from the association, U.S. Representative Richard Ottinger sued the railroad and won.[70]

Against long odds, the Hudson River Fishermen's Association helped to defeat a proposed expressway along the river's east bank. Rockefeller rushed the authorization of the project through the state assembly without debate. But the project required federal approval, and the association rallied defenders of the river to protest the harm the expressway would do to shellfish breeding grounds. Garrett testified before a House subcommittee. (He was too modest to recall his testimony, which made a powerful impression. The expressway was "jobbed from start to finish," he said. "People who love the Hudson were supposed to take the count. I say no. Anything that Congress can do to stop New York from killing resources of the Hudson estuary will be like the Seventh Cavalry riding to the rescue on Saturday afternoon in the Victoria Theater in Ossining.") The expressway opponents also went to court to stop the project, and their lawsuit succeeded. For Garrett, the lesson was clear: "You can whip Albany and shove the decisions right down their bumbling bureaucratic throats."[71]

The association also joined the opposition to the proposed power plant that inspired the Scenic Hudson case. Though the crux of the dispute was the value of scenery, the effect of the project on the Hudson ecosystem also became a contentious issue. The association fought unsuccessfully for the right to participate in a study of the project's impact on fish—and then argued that the study was biased. The future of the project still was unresolved in 1970.[72]

In every fight, the association had allies. Garrett saluted Ottinger as a stalwart in Congress. But a few good friends were not enough—not in this fight. "You have to get involved," he concluded. "It's necessary that YOU get involved. One organization can't do it alone. Call your Congressman. Call your Senator. You can't wait until tomorrow. Today is the day we start. You're not just saving the river. You're saving your own lives."

Garrett joined the old and the new. Like so many preservationists before him, he spoke to the power of place. But he was not simply carrying on a tradition of defending rivers, mountains, canyons, shorelines, bays, marshes, forests, and deserts. He offered the hope that the environmental cause might bridge class divides. Would the new movement fulfill that potential?

The Politics of the Possible

Some politicians were keen to speak on Earth Day, and some spoke with reluctance. Governor Forrest Anderson of Montana was more eager than not. He did not have a deep passion for the land, but he recognized that the environment was becoming a more potent issue. He took the opportunity to make a major statement of his governing philosophy.

Anderson was a middle-of-the-road Democrat in a politically divided state. Montanans often elected liberal Democrats to the U.S. Senate, but they were more conservative in state races. Republicans ran the legislature. Anderson was the first Democratic governor in almost a generation. He defeated the incumbent in 1968 largely because he opposed a state sales tax.[73]

On environmental issues, Anderson was more a follower than a leader. He knew that most Montanans loved the outdoors. As a candidate for governor, he promised to protect the state's air and water, but environmental protection was not one of his priorities. His major goals were restructuring state government and promoting economic development. In his first year in office, he had gotten on the bad side of the state's most ardent environmentalists because he supported the Anaconda mining company in a dispute about the future of a relatively unspoiled area of western Montana. On Earth Day, he wanted to explain why he could not do everything that his eco-critics expected. He also hoped to convince the majority of Montanans that he would work dutifully to satisfy new environmental demands—especially if the state's citizens continued to demonstrate that they really cared.[74]

The Earth Day crowd at the University of Montana in Missoula was the most skeptical and hostile that Anderson could have faced. The *Missoulian* had begun to crusade against pollution, and the university was a haven for environmental activists. The student newspaper editorialized that inviting Anderson to speak on Earth Day was like inviting Adolf Hitler to a bar mitzvah.[75]

Anderson began with a lecturette from Poli Sci 101. As governor, he could not listen only to "the loudest or the most persistent" voices. He was obliged to consider all sides of an issue. He could not crusade for a cause "unless that cause is supported by the public." Unlike a private citizen, he did not have "the privilege of being adamant or even stubborn." He was "not free to make strictly philosophical decisions." Instead, he had to think practically about "the needs of the people." Politics was "the art of the possible—and compromise, adjustment and understanding make politics possible."[76]

With those caveats, Anderson endorsed the new environmental movement. "I agree with the philosophy of Earth Day," he said. "This is a noble cause. It is a crucial cause. And those who have gathered for Earth Day observances all across the country must keep this cause alive."

Anderson then listed the grievous ways Americans were abusing the environment. His list was generic, with no mention of conditions in Montana; any national leader could have offered the same indictment. "The skies are hung with an acrid shroud," he said. Oil spills smeared the coasts, and concrete covered once fertile and beautiful land. "Strip mining desolates forests and prairies"—that issue soon would hit home, when a coal boom began in Montana. "Our rivers have been turned into continental sewage systems. Pesticides infect both human and wildlife."

Anderson paused. "People have finally realized that this is unacceptable."

Though a middle-of-the-roader, Anderson borrowed the rhetoric of liberal Democrats. He argued that the nation needed to emphasize "quality over quantity." He quoted Adlai Stevenson's lament about the imbalance between public and private goods. While we enjoyed bigger cars and brighter kitchens, our shared environment became more polluted, more crowded, more ugly, more worn-out.

Anderson called for a cultural revolution. Most of the nation's environmental problems were "the result of well-established, almost sacred attitudes in our society," he argued. "For years, Americans have been proud of the nation's high standard of living, soaring gross national product, amazing technological developments and ever-expanding affluence and increasing population. Materialism has been established as a national religion." But our "voracious consumer economy" was destroying the environment. "If pollution is to be ultimately controlled, consumer demands on industry and resources must be reduced and the population explosion must be stopped. People will have to become willing to accept less powerful cars, fewer appliances and gadgets and smaller families. We will have to come to believe that material progress is not social progress. This will require deep and personal attitudinal changes by all Americans."

That was an applause line. Unlike many politicians who called for an environmental revolution, however, Anderson immediately looked down from the stars to the ground of the practical. Was a revolution in attitudes really possible? "Not tomorrow," he answered, "not for many tomorrows."

Because cultural change would not come immediately, "government, industry and technology must carry the fight." Anderson expected that government would rise to the challenge. "The people want the environment protected," he said. "And politicians, who intend to remain in office, do what the people want." Anderson also hoped that industry would develop the "conscience" to control pollution. To some Earth Day speakers, that was a forlorn hope, but Anderson did not try to make the case for corporate social responsibility. He was much more interested in technology. Though he had little power to influence technological development, the subject gave him another chance to define his anti-extremism.

"Technology made this nation what it is," Anderson said. "It is responsible for both our affluence and the environmental crisis. From this time forward, we need a balance between technology and the environment. We cannot escape the past. We cannot solve the environmental crisis by abandoning our machines and technology. We must use technology to meet the legitimate needs of the people, and at the same time to control the effect and quality of our lives. Technology is ingenious . . . I believe that the technological tools we need to protect and reclaim the environment are available in our society." All that was lacking "is the priority and motivation," Anderson concluded, and the environmental movement "will create the priority and establish the motivation."

The issue of priorities allowed Anderson to attack Washington. The nation had spent $35 billion on the space program, he said, and only $4 billion on environmental control. "We continue to ridiculously bankroll the Defense Department in a dangerous arms race. We continue to throw good money after bad all over the world." Indeed, environmental technology offered more hope for real security than nuclear technology. With new priorities, technology would be free to follow a higher calling, protecting the environment and enhancing the quality of life.

Like many Democrats, Anderson took pains to argue that the environmental crisis could not be addressed in isolation. "Ecology is not restricted to considerations of air and water pollution and degradation of the landscape," he argued. "It is the science of the total environment. Watts is as much an environmental question as the Santa Barbara Channel. Malnutrition is as much an environmental question as Los Angeles smog." In Montana, the destitution of Indians on reservations was as much an environmental question as the fate of wilderness. That meant the state's citizens had to worry about the "pollution of the spirit that occurs when a man does not have a job, or cannot get an education, or is inadequately housed and fed, or is the subject of discrimination." Though the nation's leaders had tried to address those concerns in the sixties, the problems still were serious. "Is the protection of the environment so important that we must ignore unemployment, poverty and discrimination?" Anderson asked. "I do not believe so. We must take up the new cause, while continuing to fight for the old causes."[77]

Without a stronger economy, however, Montana could not hope for much. The state had the third highest unemployment rate in the nation. Per capita income was far below the U.S. average. Because college graduates had few career opportunities in Montana, the state suffered from a high rate of out-migration. Because the economy was not growing, government continually was forced to raise taxes. "We must have jobs for the people and an expanded tax base to allow government to provide the services people require," Anderson argued. "We cannot do this by closing the state off to development. Montana cannot be a wilderness—and it will not be a wasteland."

That promise was the heart of Anderson's message. Unlike his critics, he did not believe that conservation and development were "mutually exclusive." He vowed to make progress in solving both environmental and economic problems.

Anderson ended by offering a ten-point environmental program. He did not request any new funds, and he did not propose legislation. The most specific item was an annual report on the state of the environment. Anderson supported "programs of environmental education to convince people that preservation of the environment is essential" and expanded environmental research at the state's universities. The items that dealt with the most pressing problems all were vague. Anderson called for "definition of industry's responsibility to the environment," "consideration of long-term effects of industrial development," and "establishment of better land management policies." He also called for "a legislative program to write new laws to correct existing environmental problems and to provide protection for future contingencies."

Anderson's speech won praise from political commentators. The state's most reliably Democratic newspaper—*The Montana Standard*—called the speech "courageous, candid and realistic." Conservative newspapers also were impressed. The *Billings Gazette* printed the complete text. The speech mostly dealt in generalities, the paper editorialized, but the governor voiced the ideals of most Montanans. The Helena *Independent Record* agreed: "The governor's approach is a moderate one, and one which should find acceptance with most everyone except the radical environmentalists . . . and the radicals on the other side—those who think they have a God-given right to pollute." Even the *Missoulian* responded favorably. Though the true measure of the speech would be future actions, the paper argued, Anderson at least committed himself to environmental improvement. "He said things his listeners did not expect to hear and said them well."[78]

Despite the conditional support of the *Missoulian*, Anderson did not win over the state's environmentalists. But he stayed true to his word: As the new cause gained strength in Montana, he made environmental protection a higher priority. In his 1971 State of the State address, the environment was one of the three issues he discussed; the other two were efficiency in government and economic development, his original priorities. His environmental proposals were more concrete than in 1970. He asked for money to build sewers, urged passage of water-pollution and mining-reclamation legislation, and called for staff increases at environmental agencies. The state's voters were willing to go further. In 1972, Montanans adopted a new state constitution that required the government to maintain "a clean and healthy environment" for "present and future generations." The next legislature passed several measures to make those words a reality. In Montana, as Anderson predicted on Earth Day, the environmental cause was not a fad.[79]

5 ● The New Eco-Infrastructure

Earth Day accomplished far more than Gaylord Nelson ever dreamed. The prospectus for the national environmental teach-in called for 40 events, yet Nelson's call to action ultimately inspired more than 12,000. Millions of people took part.

As Nelson hoped, the nation's political leaders took notice. Congress adjourned on April 22 to allow members to speak at Earth Day events. Legislators in Massachusetts and Michigan approved measures to guarantee "environmental rights." The governors of New Jersey and New York established state environmental-protection departments, and the governor of Maryland signed twenty-one environmental laws and resolutions.[1]

But the legacies of Earth Day went beyond politics. Earth Day led to a tremendous increase in grassroots activism. According to a survey by the federal Council on Environmental Quality, the number of local environmental organizations nearly doubled from 1968 to 1973. The new groups lobbied in state capitols, organized recycling programs, and established "ecology centers." Earth Day also inspired institutional change. Environmental education took root. News editors assigned reporters to environmental beats. Because publishers saw that millions of Americans cared about the environment, Earth Day set off an eco-book boom, and environment sections became common in bookstores.[2]

The impact of Earth Day often was direct and tangible. In many communities, the Earth Day organizing effort became the seed of a new organization. The organizers of New York City's celebration formed the Environmental Action Coalition, for example, and Albion College organizer Walt Pomeroy founded the Michigan Student Environmental Confederation. Several Earth Day organizers wrote books, including the national teach-in coordinators hired by Nelson, who produced a collection of Earth Day speeches and a "Tool Kit" for activists. Earth Day organizers created ecology centers and environmental-studies programs. At some newspapers, the reporters who covered Earth Day became full-time environmental writers.[3]

The post–Earth Day eco-infrastructure gave the environmental movement staying power. After the passions of Earth Day cooled, the first generation of environmental lobbyists ensured that politicians still felt pressure to protect the environment. The reporters on the environmental beat kept the subject on the public agenda. The eco-books encouraged readers to think more deeply about what they could do to save the earth. In environmental-studies courses and programs, students continued to learn about environmental issues. The ecology centers helped to sustain community activism.

National Politics

Before 1970, environmentalists had limited ability to shape the nation's politics. None of the old conservation groups endorsed candidates for elected office. Though the conservation movement had political allies, conservationists rarely were able to pressure lawmakers in any concerted way. The Sierra Club, the National Audubon Society, the National Wildlife Federation, and the Wilderness Society sometimes arranged testimony at legislative hearings. They urged members to call or write to their elected officials. But none of the major conservation groups had full-time lobbyists. They all relied on charitable contributions, and federal law restricted lobbying by tax-exempt organizations. Though some conservationists tested the limits of the lobbying restriction, most took no chances.[4]

Earth Day enabled environmentalists to build a powerful political operation. In 1970, two new groups, Friends of the Earth and Environmental Action, broke with the past by actively engaging in electoral politics. The two groups also became cornerstones of a new professional lobbying effort in the nation's capitol.

Friends of the Earth was formed in 1969 by David Brower. Brower just had been fired by the Sierra Club, in part because his militant campaigns against federal dam projects had led the IRS to suspend the club's tax-exempt status, and he resolved that his new organization would pursue his agenda with no holds barred. Friends of the Earth would not be tax-exempt, he explained, "because it will concentrate on legislative and political action." Brower promised that the new organization would have at least one lobbyist in Washington. He also promised that a subsidiary group, the League of Conservation Voters, would support pro-environment candidates in campaigns at all levels of government.[5]

If not for Earth Day, Friends of the Earth might have remained a lone wolf breaking from the pack. But the young activists hired by Gaylord Nelson to help coordinate the teach-in resolved to keep fighting for change. When they established Environmental Action, they rejected the restrictions of tax-exempt status. Though that decision meant they had to scrape for funds, they recognized that their Earth Day experience gave them two critical resources. Their Rolodex included several thousand groups, and they knew they could mobilize that network of local activists to push for new laws and campaign for more committed leaders. Because Earth Day was such a success, Environmental Action also had tremendous credibility with the national media, which gave considerable attention to the group's legislative and electoral campaigns.[6]

Especially in 1970, the electoral work of the two groups was symbolic as well as practical. The League of Conservation Voters and Environmental Action actively helped about thirty candidates. But they also sought to send a message to politicians that the environment mattered, and that voters would hold elected officials accountable for their action or inaction on environmental issues.

The League of Conservation Voters was the great project of Marion Edey, a recent graduate in political science from a wealthy family. Essentially a new type of political action committee, the league endorsed candidates in twenty congressional, gubernatorial, and state legislative races in 1970, and it raised money to contribute to their campaigns. In a few cases, the league sought to remove officials with egregious records on environmental issues. But most of the league's endorsees had a demonstrated commitment to the cause: Some were challengers, and some were incumbents in potentially close races. The league's contributions totaled only $45,000, which was not a lot of money even in 1970. But a $2,500 contribution might make a difference, especially in campaigns for the U.S. House of Representatives, because many House candidates spent only about $50,000.[7]

Friends of the Earth also put together an electoral handbook published in paperback by Ballantine Books in October 1970. In addition to chapters on the major environmental issues, *The Voter's Guide to Environmental Politics* included a pioneering analysis by the League of Conservation Voters of the environmental voting records of every member of the U.S. House of Representatives. The analysis was based on ten votes from 1961 to 1970 on measures to clean up pollution, limit logging in national forests, support mass transit, protect wetlands and wilderness areas, stop federal subsidies for the supersonic transport, and more. Because most politicians now claimed to support the environment, editor Garrett De Bell argued, the voting-record analysis was critical: "Only when the American voters can distinguish self-serving rhetoric from real commitment to reform will environmental quality improve."[8]

Environmental Action took a different approach. Like a sheriff posting "Wanted" handbills, the group targeted twelve congressional incumbents for defeat: "The Dirty Dozen," they dubbed them. The decision to focus entirely on defeating incumbents appealed to a broad and growing movement to elect "a more responsive Congress," free from the ossification of the seniority system. The targeting strategy also invited the media to see the Dirty Dozen campaign as a measure of the strength of the new movement. Incumbents were expected to win—but if they lost, the media would have to explain why. When Environmental Action announced the campaign at the start of September, the Associated Press predicted that the fate of the twelve would become "the first organized test of 'environment' as a political issue." Denis Hayes seconded that. "I would hate to see the environment sink or swim on the basis of these elections," he said, "but I hope they will indicate how the public feels."[9]

Because Environmental Action hoped that the Dirty Dozen campaign would demonstrate the power of the environmental cause, the selection process was multifaceted. The targets had to have poor records on several issues, not just the environment, and their opponents had to offer promise of doing much better. With the aid of information provided by members of its network, Environmental Action weighed the political dynamic of potential target races. Did the challengers have a chance? Once the twelve were picked, Environmental Action used its network to mobilize environmentalists in each district. Though the group did not make financial contributions to the challengers, it provided summaries of the incumbents' voting records, and it offered help in writing speeches and issue papers about the environment. Environmental Action also publicized the twelve races.[10]

In at least one Dirty Dozen race, the spotlight alone made a difference. Though the incumbent, Republican William Ayres, had represented Akron, Ohio, in the House for twenty years, Environmental Action thought he might be vulnerable because the district had a large Democratic majority. His challenger, John Seiberling, already had the support of local environmentalists: He had fought to preserve a scenic river, and he had made an issue of sprawl as a member of the regional planning commission. But Seiberling otherwise had little political experience. He also was unabashedly against the Vietnam War, which earned him some passionate support but cost him in blue-collar neighborhoods. In August, *The New York Times* reported that his campaign appeared "underfinanced and poorly organized." But after Environmental Action targeted Ayres, Seiberling was able to attract an experienced political operative as a full-time campaign coordinator. That proved critical. Ayres tried to make Environmental Action a campaign issue: The group only supported "candidates sympathetic to campus rioters, do-gooders, and ultra-liberal causes," he argued, and he predicted that the district's factory workers would not listen to "a bunch of long haired, hippie kids." On Election Day, however, Seiberling held his own with working-class voters, and he did much better than previous Democrats in affluent areas, where many voters appreciated his stalwart environmental record. He won easily.[11]

The national media was quick to recognize that the League of Conservation Voters and Environmental Action were doing something unprecedented. In a front-page story, *The New York Times* reported in September that the environment had emerged as "a new and possibly portentous fixture of the political landscape." Environmental issues were playing a role in campaigns in more than half of the states. In part, the new focus on the environment dated to Earth Day, "when the potentialities of the ballot box were urged on discontented citizens." But the *Times* also credited the politicking of the two new eco-action groups.[12]

The election results confirmed that environmentalists had become an electoral force. The League of Conservation Voters batted 16 for 20. Seven of the Dirty Dozen lost—one by only 100 votes. The most notable win came in Maryland, where both the league and Environmental Action worked to defeat a thirteen-term Democratic representative, George Fallon, the chair of the powerful House Public Works Committee and the most ardent congressional supporter of highway building. *The New York Times* acknowledged the victories in an editorial as well as a news story. As the editors wrote, "A new ingredient, and a good one, has been added to American election campaigns—the candidate's record on improving the environment."[13]

The 1970 campaign was just the beginning. In 1972, environmentalists received most of the credit for the primary defeat of Representative Wayne Aspinall of Colorado, a twelve-term incumbent. As the longtime chair of the House Interior Committee, Aspinall staunchly supported development of the West's natural resources, and conservationists considered him their most powerful foe. The League of Conservation Voters contributed $15,000 to his opponent, who spent only $41,000. Environmental Action named Aspinall one of the Dirty Dozen, and he was one of four Dirty Dozen targets to lose in 1972. In 1974, for the first time, Environmental Action sent several staff members into the field to work on Dirty Dozen races, and eight of the twelve were defeated. The League of Conservation Voters had similar success. In the early 1970s, the league also expanded its voter's guide, which became a bible for local activists.[14]

Like the new electoral work, the new lobbying effort was striking. In 1969, the conservation movement had just two lobbyists, and both worked for groups formed in 1954 to oppose a proposed dam in Dinosaur National Monument. The two groups continued to lobby on wilderness issues, but neither directly represented a grassroots membership. In 1970, eleven environmental lobbyists joined the Washington crowd: four from Friends of the Earth, three from Environmental Action, and four from Zero Population Growth. The difference was not just in numbers: The new lobbyists worked on issues that conservationists seldom or never had addressed.[15]

At first, the environmental lobbyists struggled to gain respect. As one Capitol Hill veteran observed, they did not know what unmarked office doors to walk in. They were very young. They did not fit the image of the Washington insider. They worked "in cramped office spaces on a shoestring budget" and relied on "their wits and energy," *The New York Times* reported in 1971. But the new lobbyists soon proved that they knew the issues—and they knew how to marshal public support for their positions.[16]

By the end of 1970, indeed, the new lobbyists already had made their mark in two major battles. They helped to stop development of the supersonic transport. They also strengthened the Clean Air Act.

The SST was the cutting edge of progress in the most technologically advanced sector of the economy. Because the Europeans and the Soviets were developing supersonic planes, the SST became a matter of national prestige. Would we cede the clouds to foreigners? In the mid-1960s, the plane always had strong support in Congress. But in 1970, after the House again approved funds to subsidize development of a prototype, the Senate did a 180-degree turn. The year before, the Senate had supported SST funding by a comfortable margin. In December 1970, however, eighteen of the pro-SST senators changed their votes, and three other senators who had not voted in 1969 but had voiced support for the SST also joined the majority. The final blow came early in 1971, when the House joined the Senate in halting the project.[17]

Though a number of ad-hoc groups had fought the SST since the late 1960s, the tide only began to turn when Friends of the Earth entered the fray. Friends of the Earth used several of Brower's classic Sierra Club tactics, including purchase of a full-page ad in *The New York Times* and publication of a battle book. The organization's young activists also fought in the trenches. Legislative director George Alderson led a diverse Coalition Against the SST that included labor, consumer, and taxpayer groups. Environmental Action also was a key member of the coalition.[18]

The diversity of the coalition reflected a broadening of the indictment of the SST. The plane's critics initially focused on the danger of sonic booms. But noise was not the only argument against the plane. The coalition publicized the opinion of many leading economists that the SST never would be commercially viable. At a time of tightening government budgets, the coalition argued that the SST was at best a low public priority and at worst a waste of tax dollars. In the words of one critic, the plane was a "boomdoggle"! The coalition also put new emphasis on the possibility that the SST might do untold harm to the upper atmosphere. The water vapor created by the SST might change the climate. The SST also might destroy the ozone that protected against cancer-causing solar radiation.[19]

The coalition also made the SST a litmus test of commitment to environmental protection in the 1970 election. With the help of the League of Conservation Voters, the challengers in two Senate races pressed pro-SST incumbents to promise to vote against further funding. That worked in Vermont. Though the league-endorsed candidate lost, Republican Winston Prouty switched from an SST supporter to an opponent. Many other senators also concluded that the SST had become one of the few issues that might sway votes. In Iowa, a November poll showed that 63 percent of the state's voters opposed the SST, while only 8 percent were in favor. Iowa Republican Jack Miller—though not up for reelection until 1972—got the message: He voted no.[20]

To some commentators, the defeat of the SST bespoke a fundamental shift of values. Evidently Americans no longer took for granted that technological development was unquestionably good. Other commentators focused instead on tactical errors by the plane's proponents. But almost everyone concluded that the vote demonstrated the new political muscle of the environmental movement. The SST had the backing of the Nixon administration, some of the most powerful members of Congress, the aerospace industry, and several big unions—yet the opposition won.[21]

Spectacular as the SST defeat was, the issue was a variation on a familiar conservationist theme: Conservationists had succeeded before in stopping development projects. The work of environmentalists on the Clean Air Act truly was a new song. The act was a regulatory measure of unprecedented scope, and the environmental lobbyists sought to shape the bill's provisions. They wanted to build a better bill, not to knock a bad idea down.

Environmental Action took the lead. The group put together a Clean Air Coalition that included the auto and steel unions, among others. One old political hand called the coalition "unique in the field of conservation." With the help of Ralph Nader's air-pollution expert, John Esposito, Environmental Action also released a "plan for clean air by 1975," and the 1970 Clean Air Act ultimately included most of the plan's provisions.[22]

The success did not come easily. In the House, the environmental lobby was caught off guard in June when the leadership rushed a weak air-pollution measure to a vote. The bill allowed industry to argue that antipollution measures were not "economically feasible," increased the red tape before the government could ban lead in gasoline, and did not require car manufacturers to prove the long-term effectiveness of emission-control devices. The bill also provided little money for research or regulatory enforcement. Yet the measure passed without debate, and with only one dissenting vote. "Environmentalists have muffed their first big legislative test since Earth Day spot-lighted them on the side of the angels," columnist Stewart Udall concluded. "If they want to get results from now on, they'll have to swap their halos for a lot more political savvy."[23]

Environmental Action soon found a way to get a seat at the table. In the Senate, Edmund Muskie's Public Works committee had charge of the air-pollution bill, and Environmental Action warned that corporate lobbyists were camping out in the com-mittee's offices. In late August, the group learned that the committee's staff was meeting with auto-industry officials, and Barbara Reid showed up. She asked to be allowed to sit in, and she pressed the staff to hold a similar session the next day with the Clean Air Coalition. The staff agreed, and the meetings be-came national news. Environmentalists had broken the corpo-rate monopoly on access to the capitol's smoke-filled rooms. When the head of General Motors asks if industry representa-tives can have a session with committee staff, Reid told the As-sociated Press, "They're going to get it. Now we can have a chance for the same thing."[24]

In the final push for the legislation, coalition members skill-fully used an insider/outsider strategy. They lined up congressio-nal sponsors for their plan. They developed a working relationship with Muskie's staff director, Leon Billings, who understood that the most radical elements of the coalition plan allowed him to pitch tough provisions as compromises. At the same time, the coalition mobilized citizens and local officials to demand a strong bill. The grassroots effort especially sought to pressure Muskie: He was expected to run for president in 1972, and his claim to leadership on environmental issues would be critical to his chances. But Environmental Action and other coalition members also marshaled letters, phone calls, and office visits to many other senators and representatives. The Senate overwhelm-ingly approved a much stronger measure than the House, and the House then accepted the Senate version.[25]

The Clean Air Act was just the beginning. In the early 1970s, environmental lobbyists were instrumental in shaping congressional action on a number of issues, from the 1972 Clean Water Act to the redirection of highway funds for mass transit in 1973. By the mid-1970s, environmentalists in suits had become a fixture in Washington.[26]

The E Beat

For the news media, 1970 was the great environmental awakening.

Before 1970, environmental issues were "conservation" issues, and they were not sexy. Even after the Johnson administration defined air and water pollution as top priorities of "the new conservation" in the mid-1960s, the subject did not excite most journalists. Robert Cahn was typical. He resisted when his editors at *The Christian Science Monitor* assigned him to do a major series on the tribulations of the national parks in 1968. In fact, the editors were prescient, and the series changed Cahn's life. He won a Pulitzer Prize; he was appointed in 1970 to serve on the new White House Council on Environmental Quality; and he then returned to the *Monitor* to cover the environment. But Cahn initially saw the parks assignment as a dead end: He wanted to cover urban unrest instead.[27]

When *The New York Times* made Los Angeles bureau chief Gladwin Hill the paper's first environmental reporter early in 1969, Hill had only a handful of compatriots. The two national wire services—Associated Press and United Press International—did not have environmental writers. Neither did the three television networks. *Time* and *Saturday Review* debuted environment sections in 1969, but otherwise the newsweeklies and the general-interest magazines did not treat the environment as a continuing story. Because the environment was not yet a beat, the media missed many important stories. The first congressional debates over the National Environmental Policy Act received almost no coverage, even though NEPA ultimately had far-reaching consequences.[28]

In 1970, however, many news editors got religion. Especially in the print media, environmental coverage in 1970 was unprecedented. *Time, Newsweek*, and *U.S. News & World Report* published twice as many environmental stories in 1970 as in 1969—and their 1970 output matched the total for the five years from 1964 through 1968. Studies of *The New York Times*, the *Chicago Tribune*, and the *San Francisco Chronicle* found a similar surge.[29]

Of course, 1970 was full of environmental news. President Nixon argued in his State of the Union address in January that the environment would become a major concern of the 1970s. Earth Day was both a dramatic event and a compelling pretext for background stories on the nation's environmental woes. The federal government and several states created powerful agencies to protect the environment. The Clean Air Act passed. Hundreds of environmental groups formed across the country.

But the boom in environmental coverage was not simply a response to events. Many media executives decided in 1970 that their organizations needed to cover the environment as a matter of routine—day to day, week to week, month to month. Dozens of journalists became full-time environmental writers. Many more devoted at least half their time to the new beat.[30]

Though every form of news media devoted more attention to environmental issues after Earth Day, newspapers led the way. The newspaper industry still had tremendous resources in 1970. Most cities had two dailies, which often competed vigorously. The biggest papers had the staff and the space to compete with the television networks and the newsweeklies. Even small papers could provide in-depth coverage of many subjects.

In August 1970, the trade magazine *Editor & Publisher* reported that one hundred newspapers had assigned staff members to the "ecology beat." *The New York Times* and the *Chicago Tribune* were the largest. Several other papers on the list also had daily circulations in the hundreds of thousands, including the *St. Louis Globe-Democrat, The Houston Post,* and *The Milwaukee Journal.* But the new beat was not just a big-city phenomenon. The Fremont (CA) *Argus* (daily circulation 8,413), the Morgantown (WV) *Dominion-News* (10,114), and the Doylestown (PA) *Daily Intelligencer* (15,548) had environmental writers. So did the *Tucson Daily Citizen* (52,455), *The Palm Beach Post* (55,658) and the Albany (NY) *Knickerbocker News* (71,349). The beat took hold most firmly in California and in states around the Great Lakes, but every part of the nation was represented.[31]

Newspapers boasted about their environmental writers. The *Chicago Sun-Times* showcased its new two-man "Ecology Team" in an eight-page special section on the Sunday before Earth Day. The *Chicago Tribune* countered with a full-page Earth Day advertisement touting the paper's crusade for a cleaner environment. The heart of the ad was a giant drawing of a gunk-soaked eagle on the lake, under a smoke-filled sky. "The Chicago Tribune wants you to stop breathing the second dirtiest air of any city in the United States," the text proclaimed. "That's why we turned Tribune reporters and photographers loose to intensify our reporting of pollution problems. That's also why we appointed specialist Casey Bukro as Chicago's first full-time environment editor."[32]

Smaller papers were just as proud of their coverage of the beat. In Long Beach, California, the jointly published *Independent* (morning) and *Press-Telegram* (evening) ran display ads for months in 1970 to make sure readers knew about their new ecology editor, Gil Bailey. One ad—illustrated with two oil-soaked birds on a beach—had the stark headline "ECOLOGY." "It's the big thing, now," the ad proclaimed, "but will people stay concerned? Because it's one of the most important problems this country and the world faces, we want our readers to be informed about it—and stay informed. That's why we have Gil Bailey." Every Sunday, the front-page list of highlights on the combined Long Beach *Independent and Press-Telegram* directed readers to Bailey's weekly column, "Down to Earth." The two papers also gave the star treatment to Bailey's first special report, a seven-part series on smog in the Los Angeles Basin: "Don't (cough) miss it!"[33]

The beat continued to grow after 1970. By 1972, the *Los Angeles Times* had three full-time environmental writers. The *1973 Editor & Publisher International Year Book* listed almost twenty papers that had added environmental writers since 1971, including the New Orleans *Times-Picayune*, the Ann Arbor (MI) *News*, the Newark *Star-Ledger*, the *Seattle Post-Intelligencer*, the *Wilmington* (DE) *News*, the Moscow (ID) *Idahonian*, the *Honolulu Star-Bulletin*, the *Jefferson County* (MO) *Press-Times*, the *Roanoke* (VA) *Times/World News*, and the Rock Springs (WY) *Daily Rocket-Miner.*[34]

The institutionalization of environmental reporting was not inevitable. The environment was the only cause of the time that became a common beat. In 1970, few newspapers had a race-relations writer despite the growing power of the civil-rights movement in the early 1960s. The same was true with feminism: Though the women's liberation protests at the end of the 1960s drew attention, few newspapers established a gender beat.[35]

Newspaper editors gave many explanations for expanded environmental coverage. The most common was the simplest: The subject keenly interested many readers—and potentially touched everyone. Because newspapers were especially eager to reach young people, the eco-activism of students was another reason to publish more environment stories. For some editors, the environment promised to be a rousing crusade, and they wanted to carry swords. Many other editors concluded that the subject was sexier than they had thought. Though protecting the environment might unite people who were on opposite sides of other issues, the new cause undoubtedly would provoke conflict, with winners and losers. The effort to reduce pollution would affect the economy, and the environment would become a topic of political debate. Earth Day underscored many of those arguments. The huge turnout, the impressive organizing effort by new grassroots eco-action groups, the eagerness of politicians to speak at Earth Day events—all suggested that the environmental beat would attract attention.[36]

Often, editors were prodded to establish the beat. Readers wrote to ask why papers were not doing more to help citizens address a potentially catastrophic issue. Members of newly formed or newly energized environmental groups met with editors to point out the stories they were missing. Reporters also pitched the beat to their bosses. At many papers, editors readily accepted the idea. Others needed to be won over. The managing editor of the *Kingsport* (TN) *Times-News* was skeptical when reporter Mary Kiss asked to focus on the environment. "He said that's a fad," Kiss recalled. "But he was open-minded, he was willing to try new things, and he let me do it." In industrial Kingsport, Kiss soon found an abundance of front-page stories.[37]

The first environmental writers had diverse backgrounds. A few had done special projects on environmental issues in the 1960s. Some were science writers, and some wrote about hunting and fishing. Others covered suburban communities struggling to deal with the problems of sprawl, from sanitation to land-use planning. Paul Hayes of *The Milwaukee Journal* wrote about transportation policy. But most of the pioneers started from scratch. They typically were general-assignment reporters on the city or state desk, although some covered business. At a time when gender still limited opportunities in the newsroom, the new beat also allowed some women to escape the confines of the society, fashion, and home sections.[38]

The environmental writers produced a prodigious number

of multipart projects. For most, a series on a big issue was a rite of passage. William Montgomery of the *Albuquerque Journal* analyzed how a slew of mega-sized power plants would affect the air, water, and land of the Southwest. Several environmental reporters did projects on smog. Jo-Ann Albers of *The Cincinnati Enquirer* produced a seven-part survey of the state of the city's environment. But the special projects never were the heart of the new beat. Newspapers had done occasional projects on environmental issues before—the challenge was to make the environment a regular story.[39]

At some newspapers, the new beat focused on politics. But most environmental writers defined their job more broadly. They might write one day about a high-school class collecting recyclables and another day about a speech by a visiting environmental guru. Some wrote about the economics of pollution or about how consumers could reduce their environmental impact. The beat writers often used a variety of reportorial modes. They boated down polluted rivers for you-are-there stories, investigated how companies disposed of waste, profiled local environmentalists, and analyzed looming controversies.

The biggest change came in the coverage of industrial pollution. Business reporters shied away from stories about the environment: If they drew attention to pollution, they might sour their relationship with their sources. But many of the new environmental writers named names. In September 1970, Richard Krantz of the *St. Louis Globe-Democrat* analyzed the records of the area's forty biggest air polluters. How much had they spent on pollution control? Were they on track to comply with a new clean-air law? Robert Frederiksen of the *Providence Journal* and *The* (Providence) *Evening Bulletin* identified 153 industries that dumped waste into Rhode Island's waterways in a prizewinning 1971 series entitled "Our Dirty Water." Though some of Frederiksen's material came from applications for discharge permits, the newspaper sued to gain access to the records of more than 3,000 state pollution investigations. Frederiksen then sought comments from all 153 companies.[40]

The institutionalization of environmental reporting also led to more detailed coverage of policymaking. In addition to stories about the nitty-gritty of legislation, the new beat writers wrote regularly about the work of antipollution agencies. They covered public hearings. They took for granted that simply recognizing the seriousness of a problem was not enough. Did deeds match rhetoric? How were the provisions of new laws turned into administrative rules? Was enforcement effective? Though the new beat reporters relied on government officials for much of their material, public agencies faced more scrutiny than before: Environmental writers gave activists a platform for criticizing the laxness of antipollution efforts.

At many papers, the environmental beat included a weekly column. The eco-columns typically ran on Sundays, the biggest circulation day of the week. They had catchy names: "Keep It Clean," "What on Earth," "Environs in the Fire," "Quality in Living," "The Earth and You," "Eco-Logue," "Life Line," "Your Environment," "Down to Earth." Though a few columns appeared on the opinion page, most ran in feature sections, and some were part of a page devoted to environmental issues.[41]

The eco-columns were signs of the complexity of the issue, not just the importance of the subject. Because the environment touched every aspect of life, the beat did not fit within the traditional divisions of the newsroom. A column allowed environmental writers to transcend those divisions: They could write about lifestyles, business, science, pop culture, or politics, as they pleased.

Though many of the new columnists treated their weekly space as a venue for more wide-ranging reporting, some relished the opportunity to take stands. Mary Walton of *The Charleston* (WV) *Gazette* was especially bold. In one of her first columns, in

August 1970, Walton called out her employer as a polluter. Discarded newspaper accounted for 100 to 125 tons of solid waste a week in the county, yet the *Gazette* had made no effort to encourage recycling. Why not? Walton asked the publisher. "We've got to be forced to do something—like everybody else," he told her. In another column, Walton sought out the homes of the city's industrial titans to see how many lived in polluted neighborhoods. Not many. Most lived in the hills, high above the "burning fumes and horrid smells," the grime and grit, that plagued most Charleston families. The chairman of the State Air Pollution Control Commission also had a home at elevation 1,070 feet. "All this is not to say that there's anything wrong with living away from the pollution," Walton wrote. She herself had moved up from the valley, where she often saw the sun for only three hours a day. "But I have heard these managers and their emissaries on countless occasions talk apologetically about pollution. What they say is that it's going to take a long time to do anything." Of course, that was easy to say from the pristine heights. "I suggest," Walton concluded, that if the plant managers and air-pollution officials all lived in the polluted lowlands, "they might find ways to clean up the air a little bit sooner." [42]

Walton's columns sparked comment. "The company people—as you might expect—were not very friendly," Walton recalled. "But I had a pretty big following among readers." People often called Walton with tips about stories. Readers also praised her columns in letters to the editor. "If it takes sarcasm and people like Mary Walton to wake up people to the seriousness of the pollution problem," one reader wrote, "then I say give us more Mary Waltons. I am 65 years old and don't worry about myself but I have three grandchildren and I really worry about them and the future." [43]

The reaction to Walton's work was typical of the response to the beat across the country. Though some people complained that reports about pollution might hurt the local economy, many readers were glad that somebody finally was paying attention to the smog that kept their kids from playing outdoors or the stench that ruined their favorite creek or the soot that dirtied their clean clothes on the line. Often, the beat became a topic of discussion in the community: Many environmental writers received invitations to appear on local television and radio shows.[44]

The beat ultimately affected coverage in papers that did not have environmental writers. Editors felt pressure to assign more environmental stories. They also published more environmental stories from outside sources. In-state newspapers often shared stories through the wire services, so a report by the environmental writer at the *Wisconsin State Journal* might appear in *The Sheboygan Press* or the *Fond du Lac Commonwealth Reporter*.[45]

At the national level, the Associated Press soon recognized that the environment had become a more compelling subject. Before Earth Day, a reporter in the AP's Washington bureau, Stan Benjamin, covered the Department of the Interior, the federal agency responsible for parks, fish and wildlife, and water quality, but Benjamin also covered other agencies. The Department of the Interior assignment gradually evolved into a full-time environmental beat. Benjamin expanded his coverage of federal policymaking. He then began to report on developments outside Washington. In a four-part 1972 series on "the cost of cleaning up," for example, he explored the impact of new anti-pollution regulations on companies and communities across the country. The series appeared in dozens of papers.[46]

Benjamin had good company. After Earth Day, former secretary of the interior Stewart Udall began a syndicated twice-a-week environmental column that soon appeared in forty papers. *The New York Times* news service allowed Gladwin Hill's reports to reach readers across the country. Because *Newsweek* had a feature service, newspapers also could publish stories by the magazine's first environmental writer, James Bishop Jr., who took up the beat early in 1971.[47]

Hill's work was especially important. He truly was a national reporter, not a Washington correspondent, and his stories offered rich insight into the successes and failures of the new environmental movement. Were corporate managers serious about reducing pollution? Were environmental issues becoming more salient in elections? How much influence did industry have on state enforcement of environmental regulations? What communities might be models of environmental initiative? What environmental problems just were emerging? Many of Hill's stories allowed readers to compare local conditions with national trends. Hill's work also helped set the agenda for other environmental writers.[48]

Hill stayed on the beat for more than a decade. When he retired at the end of 1979, he looked back at what had changed since he began to write full-time about the environment. "In answer to the question 'What became of the enthusiasms of Earth Day, 1970?' the past decade brought an impressive answer," he wrote. "Those enthusiasms have been 'institutionalized' in legislation, regulation, litigation, political dynamics and new personal values, and woven into the fabric of national life." Hill was perhaps too modest to add that Earth Day also had changed the media.[49]

Education

Earth Day made environmental education a hot topic. Everywhere, speakers argued that saving the planet required new ways of thinking. Though Earth Day was a huge educational project, many Americans concluded that much more needed to be done. Environmental education had to become a priority.

Even Richard Nixon acknowledged the need. In a message to Congress in August 1970, the president argued that the nation's schools were on the front lines of the battle to protect the environment. Colleges and universities needed to train "environmental managers" to reduce pollution and ensure wise use of land. "It is also vital that our entire society develop a new understanding and a new awareness of man's relation to his environment—what might be called 'environmental literacy,'" Nixon concluded. "This will require the development and teaching of environmental concepts at every point in the educational process."[50]

At the college level, environmental education already had some momentum before Earth Day. The first issue of *The Journal of Environmental Education* appeared in fall 1969. By then, professors at several schools were pushing to establish interdisciplinary environmental majors. The new University of Wisconsin campus in Green Bay won acclaim in fall 1969 as the first university in the nation to focus on solving environmental problems. Several other experimental eco-colleges were in the planning stage, from the College of the Atlantic in Maine to the Huxley College of Environmental Studies at Western Washington State University. *The New York Times* and the Associated Press reported at the end of 1969 that the environment was becoming the rage on college campuses. At the University of Oregon, a new course entitled "Can Man Survive?" attracted nearly 2,000 students—roughly an eighth of all undergraduates—in January 1970.[51]

After Earth Day, the energy devoted to environmental education increased by an order of magnitude. Earth Day emboldened those who already were committed to the cause and convinced many others that the subject was timely. "Man and Environment" surveys became common. Dozens of colleges and universities created environmental-studies majors or minors. Many schools established graduate programs in environmental policy, education, journalism, design, or management. At one university, the number of ecology courses jumped 443 percent from 1966 to 1976.[52]

The spread of environmental education at junior colleges

shows the depth of the trend. In the 1960s, two-year schools grew tremendously by offering a combination of general-education and vocational courses to part-time students. Only a handful had a course about the environment. But a 1971 survey found that 25 percent of the nation's community colleges added at least one course in environmental studies in the year after Earth Day, and another 17 percent planned to do so in 1971–72.[53]

The most ambitious community-college initiative was a television course produced by Miami-Dade Junior College for national distribution. "Man and Environment" included thirty half-hour television shows, a textbook published by Prentice-Hall, a study guide to help teachers integrate the shows and the text, and assignments that could be mailed or handed in. When Miami-Dade debuted the course early in 1972, students could discuss the material on a radio call-in show. The course was designed to be a yearlong introduction to the scientific, philosophical, social, political, and economic aspects of environmental problems. But the materials could be customized to suit any course length. Miami-Dade spent over $1 million to develop the course. The planning began in May 1970 and involved officials from more than twenty community colleges as well as national experts in environmental education.[54]

"Man and Environment" was a huge success. Roughly one hundred colleges and universities offered the course in the mid-1970s. Many supplemented the course with local programming. In Arkansas, the state educational television network followed each broadcast with a discussion by a panel of public officials. In Vermont, the university's new environmental-studies program produced a companion series on the state's major environmental issues. The "Man and Environment" series also attracted hundreds of thousands of not-for-credit viewers on public-television stations across the country. Because "Man and Environment" was the first nationally distributed telecourse, the effort also received a lot of news coverage and scholarly analysis.[55]

The biggest change at four-year schools was the rise of environmental-studies programs. At some schools, Earth Day enabled boosters to break down barriers. At other schools, Earth Day convinced administrators to hire program builders in the field.

Indiana University illustrated the new dynamic. A small group of professors began to lobby for the creation of an environmental-studies program in 1965. One member of the group, political scientist Lynton Caldwell, soon developed a national reputation: He called for schools to put more emphasis on the environment in a widely cited 1966 essay, he helped draft the National Environmental Policy Act of 1969, and he summarized his ideas about how society should respond to the environmental challenge in a book published in January 1970. But the environmental-studies proposal did not attain "critical mass" (in the words of the program's first director) until after Earth Day. In July 1970, a faculty committee finally endorsed the idea, and the program debuted in fall 1971.[56]

Though many environmental-studies programs had to make do with limited budgets, some enjoyed strong backing. In the summer of 1970, San Jose State in California hired Stanford physicist and Friends of the Earth director Donald Aitken to establish a department of environmental studies. Several universities conducted national searches for founding directors of environmental-studies programs in 1971 and 1972. In each case, other hires followed.[57]

Several of the pioneer program builders drew on experience as Earth Day organizers. Herman Sievering is a good example. As a Ph.D. student at the University of Illinois, Sievering worked with students and faculty from many disciplines to put together the Earth Day program. The organizing effort required him to see problems whole. That was a valuable skill in a wide-ranging interdisciplinary field. After he earned his degree in 1972, he became one of the first professors in the environmen-

tal college at Governor's State University, a new experimental
school in Illinois. He also was commissioned by the Illinois
board of higher education to assess the potential for environmental studies at all of the state's public universities.[58]

The environmental-studies programs had many personali-
ties. Though all joined faculty from several disciplines, the mix
differed from school to school. The mission also was not a given.
Was the goal simply to make students environmentally literate?
Should the coursework be purely academic, or should the curriculum encourage activism? Some programs stressed science,
while others emphasized policy. Morehead State University in
Kentucky expected students to pursue careers in the new environmental professions. The University of California, Santa Barbara, in contrast, aimed to educate "generalists." Sacramento
State offered several applied courses—the principles of environmental law, the science of environmental-impact assessment,
even the techniques of organic gardening—but the foundational
course was "Towards an Ecological Ethic." "We didn't want to
just train people to mop up pollution," founding director Wes
Jackson later explained. "I always liked to say that the planet can
go down the tubes with wind generators and solar collectors all
in place. That was a statement that the problems aren't just
technical, they're about values."[59]

The new programs quickly became big draws. The social
ecology program at the University of California, Irvine, began in
January 1970 with just one faculty member and 20 students. By
the fall of 1974, the faculty had grown to 27, and the program
had 750 majors. That round number was no accident: The program had a cap—and a huge waiting list. The few pre-1970 initiatives also took off after Earth Day. Ohio State's school of natural
resources opened in 1968–69 with 179 majors, and the number
grew to 200 the next year. But in 1970–71, enrollment jumped 50
percent. By 1976–77, the school had more than 1,200 majors.[60]

The environmental-studies programs did not just compete

with older majors. They also competed with each other. After Earth Day, some college students transferred to be where the eco-action was. Earth Day also inspired thousands of high-school kids, and many decided that they wanted to devote their college careers to environmental issues. Where would they go?

The Earth Day generation was especially critical to the success of the experimental eco-colleges. In different ways, all offered the opportunity to live and breathe environmental studies. The tiny College of the Atlantic was the most radical. Everyone worked toward one degree, a B.A. in human ecology. The required curriculum included courses on ecology and on human effects on natural systems as well as several interdisciplinary, problem-oriented workshops. The inaugural workshops in 1972–73 focused on the relationship of humans and whales, the controversy over offshore oil development, and the future of the Maine coast. The electives addressed environmental issues from the perspectives of literature, art, politics, law, anthropology, and genetics. At other schools, students designed degrees around a problem, with concentrations of relevant courses rather than traditional majors.[61]

The University of Wisconsin–Green Bay probably benefited the most from the Earth Day effect. The first students almost all were in-state, but that soon changed. The editor of *Harper's* touted Green Bay as "Survival U," while *Newsweek* dubbed the school "Ecology U." *Seventeen* praised Green Bay as one of the nation's most innovative colleges. The publicity attracted a tremendous number of transfer students. The buzz also drew committed high-schoolers from across the country. "I was an Earth Day activist," a student from Albuquerque later recalled. "When I started in 1971, I found a large group of out-of-state 'Eco-Freaks.' I felt as though I found my own people."[62]

In K–12 schools, the environmental-education initiatives of the early 1970s did not have the flash of Survival U. Even the most forward-looking public-school administrators could not dream of establishing new eco-schools. As a result, the development of environmental education in the schools rarely made national headlines. But the story still was noteworthy. Teachers and administrators basically started from scratch. Though some schools had a science course that focused on nature study or resource conservation, the K–12 curriculum did not seek to prepare students to deal with environmental problems.

The simplest way to respond to the demand for more environmental literacy was to add a unit to a basic science or social-science class—or to add a standard elective course in one of those areas. Despite the difficulty of bridging the divide between the major subject areas, however, many teachers and administrators concluded that environmental education could not simply be a new part of the science or social-science curriculum. Some schools introduced interdisciplinary courses that forced students to try to solve real-world environmental problems. Other schools encouraged teachers in every department to make the environment a topic in their classes.

The action-oriented programs benefited from the trendiness of the "open classroom" ideal. They took students into the community to assess air and water quality, establish recycling programs, create nature trails, or study the effects of noise pollution. Participants in Iowa's Project SCATE (Students Concerned About Tomorrow's Environment) worked with science and social-studies teachers on issue reports that they discussed with state legislators. In southeastern Pennsylvania, biology students at two high schools assessed the likely effects of urbanization on a rural watershed. They studied water quality, soil composition, and drainage patterns—and they concluded that much of the area was ill suited to development. After the students reported their findings to the township planning committee, the county commissioners revised the zoning ordinance. "They were really glad that we had studied the problem because no one else had," one student recalled. "We were giving them new information." That study was part of a five-county initiative that became a national model: Project KARE (Knowledgeable Action to Restore Our Environment).[63]

The environment-across-the-curriculum idea first attracted attention in two New York counties. In 1971, administrators established Project ECOS to demonstrate that environmental education was not "some separate exotic category of learning." Soon students of French read articles about pollution, land use, and energy consumption from French newspapers. English students discussed the way people related to the environment in science fiction. Social-studies students compared water use in Egypt and the United States to consider differences in the two societies. Math students analyzed traffic patterns on town streets: Could they reduce air pollution and gasoline consumption by improving traffic flow? Because many students were hot on the environment, the ECOS project made classes more exciting. Students also could see that the environment touched everything. Perhaps the best sign that students got that message came when a group of seventh-graders made a presentation about ECOS to the school board. "If you spend so much time on all that," a member of the audience said, "how can you have time for math, English, spelling, and everything else?" "I'm sorry, but you don't understand it at all," one of the seventh-graders answered. "Environmental education is part of the everyday world." By the mid-1970s, schools in many states had adopted the ECOS idea.[64]

The environment also became a focus of extracurricular clubs. A few started before 1970, but Earth Day inspired many more. The story of Protect Your Environment (PYE) illustrates the power of the Earth Day spotlight. The first PYE club formed in spring 1969 after a biology class at a small private school in Connecticut discovered that a nearby marsh had become a dump. The students were appalled that they no longer could use the marsh for field study, and they organized the club to campaign for a law to protect the state's wetlands. The club soon involved most of the school's students. They wrote eight hundred letters to legislators, asked commuters at a local train station to sign petitions on behalf of the bill, and invited officials to tour the site. When the bill passed, their success made local news. *The New York Times* wrote about their campaign in fall 1969. Then a syndicated columnist featured PYE in an Earth Day column, and more national attention followed. By the end of 1970, ninety schools had PYE clubs.[65]

Ecology clubs became even more popular. In the lower grades, the clubs usually focused on awareness. The club at Carthay Center Elementary in Los Angeles formed to put on a play for Earth Day, and then continued to urge students to "Help Our Polluted Earth." The club published *Carthay Ecology News*, a mimeographed magazine with consumer hints, interviews with environmentalists, book reviews, cartoons, songs, poems, and eco-puzzles. The club also organized an environmental art fair. High-school ecology clubs often undertook projects in the community, from pollution surveys to recycling. In Wichita, Kansas, the North High club scouted the city and county for abandoned automobiles, trash heaps in vacant lots, illegal discharge pipes in creeks, backyard incinerators, and more. The club then reported the results to the county health department.[66]

The K–12 initiatives won significant backing from all levels of government. Foundations also supported the cause. The funding meant more opportunities for teachers to get in-service training in environmental education, greater availability of curricular materials, and more publicity for the most successful projects.

The federal Environmental Education Act of 1970 created a grant program that ultimately funded hundreds of projects. When Representative John Brademas and Senator Gaylord Nelson introduced the legislation in late 1969, their staffs saw the bill as worthy but not a top priority. That changed after Earth

Day. The act passed with almost no opposition. Though the Nixon administration initially opposed the measure, the rousing success of Earth Day convinced the president's advisers that environmental education was a cause akin to motherhood. The budget for the first three years was almost $9 million—much less than Brademas and Nelson hoped, but enough to make a difference. In 1971, the new program attracted 2,000 proposals, roughly twice the number officials projected.[67]

The debate over the 1970 act also prompted federal officials to support environmental initiatives with funds from the Elementary and Secondary Education Act of 1965, which included a grant program to encourage curricular innovation. Because the 1965 act was well funded, ESEA grants soon became a major catalyst for environmental-education programs. Beginning in 1974, the government also used ESEA funding to spread the word about the most successful projects. Project ECOS received a grant to run summer workshops for teachers from around the nation.[68]

Several states launched major environmental-education initiatives after Earth Day. Florida made the biggest commitment. A 1970 environmental-education act provided for a state master plan, and a 1973 amendment allowed the department of education to hire six environmental-education specialists. The 1973 act also created a mini-grant program to help school districts and teachers launch projects. The first-year budget was $300,000. By the end of 1975, more than four hundred applicants had received grants.[69]

Though only a few states put a lot of money into environmental education, almost all had a state specialist responsible for helping schools to teach the subject by the end of 1975. In twenty states, that responsibility was assumed by someone already on the state education staff, usually the science specialist. But twenty-two states had a full-time environmental-education position—and six of those states had more than one specialist in the field. Often, the environmental-education specialists oversaw the preparation of state "master plans." The specialists also prepared environmental-education handbooks, conducted workshops for teachers and administrators, and visited schools to help develop programs. In Illinois, the specialist even oversaw the selection of the Environmental Teacher of the Year awards.[70]

At the local level, many school districts sought to ensure that students learned more about the environment. In spring 1970, the Toledo school board hired one of the pioneers in the field, William Stapp of the University of Michigan, to design a K–12 environmental curriculum. Dozens of school districts appointed environmental-education coordinators. Many created facilities for environmental education, from nature centers to eco-labs.[71]

Teachers took the initiative in many districts where the central administration provided no support. They operated on a shoestring. But they knew they were not alone. A national association for environmental educators formed in 1971, and several states soon had similar groups. The National Education Association—the largest teacher's union—began to promote environmental education. In December 1970, the association's journal included a sixteen-page special report on "what schools can do about pollution." The trade publications of the profession also published dozens of stories about innovative environmental-education efforts.[72]

Of course, the most committed environmental educators were not satisfied. As one wrote in 1975, Earth Day was not a second *Sputnik*. The launch of the Soviet satellite in 1957 led to a truly national commitment to improved instruction in math, science, and foreign languages, while the boost to environmental education in the early 1970s was more spotty. But the reforms of the early 1970s were real. The campaign for environmental literacy had begun.[73]

Publishing

In July 1971, a bibliographer at the Library of Congress reported that more books about environmental issues had appeared in the year since the first Earth Day than in all of American history before. He was exaggerating, but he was not alone in marveling at all the new eco-books. By any measure, the rise of what observers began to call "eco-publishing" was breathtaking.[74]

Ballantine alone had twenty-eight eco-titles by mid-1971, with nearly 7 million copies in print. Half of that astounding total came from *The Population Bomb* (two million plus) and *The Environmental Handbook*, an Earth Day tie-in that had sold more than 1.5 million copies. The remaining titles averaged 150,000 copies; that also was amazing. Many of the Ballantine eco-books were published after Earth Day. Several were mass-market editions of older works, including Aldo Leopold's *A Sand County Almanac*. But Ballantine also produced many new books. *The User's Guide to the Protection of the Environment* and *The Voter's Guide to Environmental Politics* both were published in October 1970; *The Nuclear Dilemma* in November 1970; *Teaching for Survival* in January 1971; and *The Environmental Law Handbook* in June 1971. In September 1971, Ballantine also published the first eco-cookbook, Frances Moore Lappé's *Diet for a Small Planet*, which eventually outsold *The Population Bomb* and *The Environmental Handbook* combined.[75]

Though Ballantine unquestionably was the leader in the field, many other publishers had sizable eco-lists. In a survey in August 1971, *Publishers' Weekly* devoted a full page to a publisher-by-publisher summary of the most important offerings. Doubleday was "deeply involved" in the field, and so was Simon & Schuster. Even many of the also-rans had notable titles:

> Dutton has "The Withering Rain," and McKay has "Where Have All the Flowers, Fishes, Birds, Trees, Water and Air Gone?"

Taplinger's "Savage Luxury" and Morrow's "The Crisis of Survival" are often seen on display, along with Nelson's "Brother Earth," Nash's "Ecology Action Guide," Little, Brown's "Terracide," Harper's "The Fitness of Man's Environment," W. W. Norton's "The Breath of Life," Dell's "The Dying Generation" and Macmillan's "Everyman's Guide to Ecological Living."

Like the twenty-eight Ballantine titles, many of the eco-books from other publishers were paperbacks, and many were conceived after Earth Day.[76]

Academic publishers also were pressing to meet the demand. At the 1971 meeting of the American Library Association, the nation's university presses organized a special exhibit with nearly 190 books on ecology and environmental problems. More than thirty publishers were represented. The exhibit manager argued that the display demonstrated that the subject was not a fad: "Enough time has passed so that good, scholarly books are being produced in this field."[77]

Earth Day was critical to the rise of eco-publishing. The millions of Earth Day celebrants convinced publishers that the market would be huge. Earth Day also gave many young people the knowledge and contacts they needed to become authors. But the new enterprise rose on a foundation laid before 1970.

The growth of eco-publishing was tied to a revolution in the role of paperback publishers. Paperback publishers at first were reprinters. They made classic works and recent hardcover bestsellers available to a wider audience. By the 1960s, however, a few paperback houses were publishing "originals," mostly genre fiction. The relative speed of paperback publishing soon encouraged some houses to enter the market for timely nonfiction. By 1970, paperback houses were competing successfully for authors in many fields, including public affairs.[78]

Ian and Betty Ballantine were in the vanguard of the paperback revolution. After a few years running the American branch of Penguin, they started Bantam in 1946 and then Ballantine in 1952. Though Bantam was just a reprinter, Ballantine published mostly originals. Science fiction became the firm's claim to fame, and Ballantine soon had successful lists in mystery, Western, and fantasy. Ballantine also published books about World War II. In 1967, Ian Ballantine began a partnership with David Brower that initially involved only mass-market editions of the Sierra Club's exhibit-format books but quickly led to *The Population Bomb*. By the end of the decade, both Ballantines had concluded that the environment would be one of the great issues of the 1970s.[79]

The Ballantine-Brower relationship grew tighter after Brower established Friends of the Earth. In late 1969 and early 1970, Ballantine brought out five eco-books. Two were reprints, and three were coproductions with Friends of the Earth. Then the adrenaline surge before Earth Day inspired Brower and Ballantine to seek new heights. They announced in March that they intended to produce a "survival series." They brainstormed about what "a survival library" should include, and Brower and his staff set out to recruit authors for the books they envisioned. That was a departure. Though *The Environmental Handbook* was produced from scratch, the other Friends of the Earth books were expanded versions of material already available in a privately produced pamphlet and a *New Yorker* article.[80]

Brower proved to be a tremendous talent scout. He found authors for most of the books he wanted, and their work generally won praise from readers and reviewers. The story of *Teaching for Survival* author Mark Terry illustrates Brower's skill. At a conference in spring 1969, Brower was impressed when Terry challenged the plenary speakers to think more deeply about the nature of environmental education. Though Terry was just a college senior majoring in anthropology, Brower invited him to speak at a high-powered conference that fall at the Aspen Institute. Terry's talk was a hit, and Brower commissioned him to do the Ballantine book, which became a classic.[81]

Garrett De Bell—the editor of *The Environmental Handbook*—was Brower's most important find. Like many of the new eco-authors, De Bell was not an established expert. He had never edited a book, and he had little experience as a writer. He was only twenty-eight. But he was superbly prepared to put together the handbook. As a Stanford undergraduate, he studied with Paul Ehrlich and Donald Kennedy, the future editor of *Science*, and he devoted much of his senior year to independent study of environmental issues. He went to Berkeley to do graduate work in zoology in 1966 but grew disenchanted with the narrowness of academic research, so he began to hang out at the new Berkeley Ecology Center. He also taught a course at the free university on alternatives to environmental disaster—recycling, low-impact transport, energy conservation. Two publishers invited him to submit proposals for a book on the subject, although both rejected his outline. When Brower invited De Bell to edit the handbook after the two met at an environmental conference in November 1969, De Bell was able to produce the manuscript in six weeks. He already had some pieces in mind, he knew what else he wanted to include, he worked with Brower to line up contributors, and he wrote four pieces that he couldn't find anyone to do.[82]

The handbook was a breakthrough. Unlike *Silent Spring* and *The Population Bomb*, De Bell's collection did not focus on one issue. Instead, the handbook addressed three fundamental questions that people had asked again and again at the Berkeley Ecology Center: "What is going wrong? Is there an alternative path? What can I do?" To suggest answers to the first question, De Bell drew mainly from the work of established scholars and scientists. The selections about the path ahead were more eclectic. As De Bell readily acknowledged, "All the answers are not in." The questions were so new, and the necessary changes so wide-ranging, that the handbook could only sketch some possible steps toward "a future that makes ecological sense." Advertising executive Jerry Mander mused on how best to promote a no-growth economy, and *Harper's* columnist John Fischer envisioned a new university dedicated to survival. Poet Gary Snyder outlined how our heads had to change to control population, eliminate pollution, reduce consumption, and reimagine our place in the world. A Berkeley ecologist offered a draft of the sort of legislative agenda an ecological party might propose. In the sections on "Eco-Tactics," De Bell offered manifestos for the League of Conservation Voters and the Ecology Action "Survival Walk." He included descriptions of a soon-to-open "ecology food store" and a new environmental-law organization. A section simply titled "miscellaneous thoughts" offered ideas about what consumers might do to live more lightly on the earth.

Reviewers were divided. To the most matter-of-fact critics, the book exemplified the worst tendencies of the new movement. The editor of *Environment* concluded that the material seemed "randomly collected, conveying little more than a sense of urgency." A science journalist complained about the "hysterical tones," "frequent inaccuracies," and "absurd solutions." But other reviewers lauded the book's overflowing energy. The *New York Times* book critic expected to find the collection as dull as tea on a Sunday afternoon with "a do-gooding maiden aunt," but instead was rapt. "This book is exciting," he concluded, "and it serves its purposes, which are to raise the problems another notch and to introduce the people and organizations that are trying to solve it." Edward Abbey—at the time just a well-regarded novelist and memoirist, not yet the king of the monkey wrenchers—was even more impressed. He argued that the handbook was the best of the new eco-tracts, "a treasury of wit and wisdom, practical and impractical advice, basic ecology and basic philosophy" that posed hard questions with "imagination and spirit."[83]

While the reviews were mixed, the handbook struck many readers as a godsend. High-school and college students discussed it long after Earth Day. So did church groups and garden clubs. People shared it with friends and recommended it to skeptics. A city council member in San Antonio asked his colleagues to read it. In newspaper letters to the editor, people cited the handbook like scripture. "Most of my facts are from 'The Environmental Handbook,'" a Sandusky, Ohio, writer concluded. "I urge you to read it. This problem is real, and can only be solved by people getting together and working together now toward a healthy environment."[84]

For publishers, the success of the handbook suggested the potential of two subgenres. Readers clearly wanted to know more about what they could do to protect the environment. They also seemed eager for more debate about the nature of the environmental crisis. Publishers responded by releasing a bunch of guides to individual action and an even greater number of eco-anthologies. Most were by first-time authors.

The action guides embodied the power of Earth Day to mobilize ordinary people. Many began as locally produced pamphlets. Three members of the Palo Alto chapter of the American Association of University Women created "the little green book": *If You Want to Save the Environment . . . Start at Home*. The first version of *Everyman's Guide to Ecological Living* was twenty photocopied pages prepared by a graduate student and a lab technician at the University of California, Santa Barbara. They began to distribute the pamphlet just before Earth Day, and they soon produced an expanded version with the help of a recent UCSB graduate. After Macmillan agreed to produce a paperback edition, the three authors enlarged the guide again, and the final version was 128 pages. Macmillan printed more than 100,000 copies.[85]

The what-you-can-do-to-save-the-environment books showed how much changed after Earth Day. The conservation movement had never focused on the decisions of consumers. The leader of the Sierra Club in 1970, Michael McCloskey, recalled that he was discomfited by the young activists who suddenly wanted him to avoid paper napkins. Though the counterculture had questioned the costs of affluence, the action guides of the early 1970s were not hippie-dippie. They were written for a mainstream audience, and they sought to make environmentally sensitive lifestyles as wholesome as apple pie. Most were published by well-established presses: Ballantine, Macmillan, Harper & Row, Prentice-Hall, and Little, Brown, among others.[86]

The action guides took several forms. Most assumed that readers already understood the severity of the problem and simply wanted tips about living more lightly on the earth. "This is a manual for those who want to adapt their own lifestyles so as to be less of the environmental deterioration problem and more a part of the solution," *Everyman's Guide to Ecological Living* began. Other guides explained in detail how consumer decisions affected the environment. Paul Swatek's *The User's Guide to the Protection of the Environment* essentially was a primer on the ecology of consumption. In his chapter on energy, for example, he began with a concise tally of the meaning of rising energy use: more oil-rig blowouts like the 1969 Santa Barbara disaster; more spills from oil-tanker accidents; more acid drainage from coal mines; more strip-mined landscapes; "more valleys drowned by hydro-electric dams"; more sulfur dioxide in the air from burning fossil fuels; more radioactive waste; more risk of nuclear-power accidents; more power lines to mar the beauty of the countryside; and more thermal pollution of rivers. A few guides joined practical advice with philosophical argument. Dirck Van Sickle's *The Ecological Citizen* was a plea for a new understanding of community. We needed to "stop being GNP-minded and become planet-minded," he wrote. "GNP rises only from the ashes of the earth's limited life support, including minerals as well as plants and animals, and the supply is much smaller than we think. Furthermore, life support belongs not just to humans or Americans, although in that order we consume by far the greatest share, but to all life on Earth."[87]

Despite the differences, the guides covered a lot of the same ground. They all discussed alternatives to chemical pesticides and detergents. But the similarities went beyond specific suggestions. The guides all pushed readers to ask how much really was enough, although only a few really underscored that point. Almost all of the guides ended with a section on collective action. The authors took for granted that individual decisions—even multiplied a million times—could not end the environmental crisis.

The guides received considerable play in the media. Television talk-show host Steve Allen had one of the authors of *If You Want to Save the Environment . . . Start at Home* as a guest. Barbara Walters interviewed the authors of two other guides on her "Not for Women Only" show. The press coverage was extraordinary: Most newspapers still had a women's section, and editors assumed that the guides would appeal especially to housewives. Almost every how-to-protect-the-planet book was the subject of at least one wire-service story or nationally syndicated column. Local writers summarized the best advice as well. The stories and columns invariably began with a line about the demand after Earth Day for ideas about what individuals could do to make a difference.[88]

The action guides also were cited in newspaper features about local housewives who had gotten the ecology bug. A 1972 story in a Montana newspaper about Mrs. Armand Lohof is a good example. The wife of a high-school teacher and mother of two small children, Mrs. Lohof practiced what she preached in classes at the YWCA on running "an ecologically sound household." To reduce her consumption of gasoline, she biked and took the bus when she could, and she only shopped for groceries once a week. She went to rummage sales to get used clothing, donated newspapers to clubs for recycling, composted kitchen waste, bought oversized quantities of household products to avoid excessive packaging, and made her own no-phosphate laundry soap. She also gave up her dishwasher. "Now my daughter has a chore she needed," she explained, and the family used less electricity, less water, and less damaging dishwashing soap. "We've been brainwashed by the mass media into using all this so-called modern stuff," Mrs. Lohof argued. But people could do a lot to improve the environment "if they just use common sense." She recommended *The User's Guide to the Protection of the Environment*. But she acknowledged that one size didn't fit all. Instead, she concluded, "every homemaker has to make her own decision as to how much she can do."[89]

The eco-anthologies did not get as much media attention as the what-you-can-do-to-save-the-environment books, but the demand was just as great. In the two years after Earth Day, publishers brought out dozens of collections of excerpts from articles, books, pamphlets, and more. Some of the eco-anthologies were mass-market paperbacks; people could buy them in supermarkets and bus stations. Some were reprints of special issues on the environment published by magazines ranging from *Fortune* to *Ramparts*. Most were aimed at students. By one count, seventeen anthologies were available by fall 1972 just "for the ubiquitous new courses in 'Man and His Environment.'" Most of the texts were edited by scientists, but English professors, management experts, and political scientists joined the crowd.[90]

The proliferation of anthologies led to complaints about repetitiveness. "It is nearly to the point where, if you've seen one book of reprinted environmental articles, you've seen them all," one librarian complained. A certain amount of overlap was inevitable. Rachel Carson appeared again and again. Because the new movement had so few superstars, most of the anthologies had something by Paul Ehrlich or Barry Commoner. *The Envi-*

ronmental Handbook canonized one previously neglected essay: Kenneth Boulding's "The Economics of the Coming Spaceship Earth." But the freshness of the subject ensured that the anthologies were not cut like cookies. Editors had no universally accepted template to follow. Instead, they worked more or less simultaneously to figure out what issues to address. They also had a surprising amount of material to consider. Though only a few scholars and journalists had given sustained attention to environmental problems, many had written one or two provocative eco-pieces.[91]

Two mass-market anthologies illustrate the diversity of the genre. *The Arthur Godfrey Environmental Reader* was about consciousness-raising. A radio and television celebrity, Godfrey offered a glimpse of the reading that led him to become a "volunteer for survival." About half of the selections extolled the beauties of nature, and the rest laid out the bad news about the deterioration of the environment. Almost all came from recently published books. Godfrey reprinted an essay he had written for *Esquire* as the introduction, but otherwise let the selections speak for themselves. *The Dying Generations*—edited by science writer Thomas Harney and humanities professor Robert Disch—couldn't have been more different. The editors introduced the collection with a remarkably concise environmental history of the nation. The first section offered different views about how and when humans became estranged from nature, while the second introduced a few prophetic voices from the nineteenth century—a "buried tradition of ecological sanity." The next two sections weighed the unintended costs of our conquest of nature: One focused on the physical challenges to human survival, and the other on the psychological, social, and physiological threats to our quality of life. The fifth section offered a cross spectrum of analyses of "the politics of survival," while the final section offered four utopian visions of a more harmonious world. Though the editors argued that we needed new values and new ways of doing things, they left open for debate exactly what those would be, and how Americans might best get there.[92]

Bookstores were quick to respond to the eco-publishing trend. Many established a new section for "ecology" or "survival" books. The new section often was part of the longstanding "nature" shelf, but sometimes stood alone. Bookstores even used newspaper advertising to promote their environmental sections. "SAVE THE EARTH," a 1971 ad for Kiebel's bookstore in Cedar Rapids, Iowa, proclaimed. "Learn about the many ways you can improve the environment from these and many more books from our ECOLOGY SECTION: Earth Tool Kit, Utopia or Oblivion, Malabar Farm, Ecotactics, Project Survival, The Quiet Crisis, Population Bomb, Roadless Area, No Deposit—No Return." Sales were especially strong at campus stores, but booksellers everywhere reported that books about the environment were popular.[93]

Librarians likewise recognized that people were keen to read about environmental issues. In small cities and towns, librarians touted their acquisition of the latest eco-books in the library columns of local newspapers. "The current talk about pollution and ecology often leaves the man-on-the-street thinking 'Fine, but what can I do about it?'" a 1971 column began. "A new book by Paul Swatek, now available at the Idaho Falls Public Library, attempts to answer that question on a practical, everyday-living level. 'The User's Guide to the Protection of the Environment' gives specific information about . . . gardening, using water, selecting clothing, picking the right brand of detergent, controlling pests safely, and means of transportation, all with an eye to protecting ourselves and the environment around us." Many librarians also set up special displays to showcase their growing eco-collections.[94]

Ecology Centers

Could every day be Earth Day? That seemingly simple question led people in dozens of communities to establish a new kind of environmental organization. The new organizations usually were called "ecology centers," though some had other names. Like Earth Day, they combined education and action.

The ecology center idea predated Earth Day, but not by much. Berkeley pointed the way in 1969. At first, the Berkeley Ecology Center was a more academic version of the city's Ecology Action group, which had formed in 1968 to encourage sustainable living. The Ecology Center served as a kind of coffeehouse, a place where people could rap about the best ways for individuals and communities to meet the challenges of the age. A library and a bookstore sparked conversations, and a speakers' bureau and a publishing operation took the center's ideas into the community.[95]

By Earth Day, activists had launched ecology centers in Little Rock, New Orleans, and Santa Barbara. Then the idea took off. More than twenty centers were open at the end of 1970. A year later, the number was about fifty. Most were in major cities or university towns: Ann Arbor, Austin, Baltimore, Boston, Boulder, Fairbanks, Los Angeles, Madison, Miami, New York, St. Louis, San Diego, and Washington, among others.[96]

The founders mostly were in their twenties. They came of age during a time when many activists were trying to live their ideals, and they wanted to create places that would encourage people to take personal responsibility for solving environmental problems. Several had organized Earth Day events. Though Berkeley inspired some ecology center founders, most did not have a model: They just were looking for a way to nurture local activism.[97]

The ecology centers varied in facilities, hours, and staffing.

Many were storefronts. Some shared space with other nonprofits, and some rented houses as offices. A few were located in university buildings. Some centers were open only on weekends, but most tried to operate full-time. Membership dues, merchandise sales, foundation grants, and special projects provided enough income for some centers to sustain small staffs. Others just had a paid director or relied entirely on volunteers.[98]

The most ambitious ecology centers hoped to be a one-stop resource for anyone eager to know more and do more about environmental problems. They answered telephone questions, maintained libraries, and produced action guides. Some sponsored eco-celebrations or film festivals. Almost all collected recyclables. A few set up model organic gardens or started farmers' markets. Many ecology centers worked with schools to engage young people in the cause. Many also organized community discussions of local environmental issues, and some led campaigns for reform.

Many of the basic ecology center activities might seem humdrum or even obsolete today. But in 1970, those activities were fresh and timely. The libraries are a good example. In the early 1970s, activists could not keep track of the latest eco-developments via the Internet. Instead, much of the most up-to-date and detailed information about environmental activism was available only in newsletters, pamphlets, and magazines that few public libraries had. That material was the raison d'être of the ecology center libraries. Visitors knew that they also would find people with similar interests there.

The recycling operations also had a promise in 1970 that now requires explanation. Before Earth Day, few people had any interest in reducing waste, and recycling was difficult or simply impossible in most places. Local governments did not pick up recyclables. Even if people were willing to haul their cans, bottles, and newspapers to a recycler, many communities did not have anyone willing to accept the goods. But Earth Day created a demand for recycling. Most Americans produced tons of garbage, and recycling was a relatively simple way for individuals to reduce their environmental impact. Thousands of drop-off recycling programs sprang up across the country. Most were run by civic groups, from the Boy Scouts to the League of Women Voters. For some people, taking recyclables to a drop-off site became almost a sacred ritual.[99]

The ecology center operations usually were the most sophisticated and ambitious in their states. Ecology centers were pioneers in curbside recycling. Some took the lead in collecting plastic. Despite wild swings in the market for recyclables in the 1970s, recycling became a major revenue source for many ecology centers. At some centers, the recycling operation trained volunteers to be leaders.

For a time, the number of ecology centers seemed likely to pass one hundred or two hundred or more. In December 1970, representatives of eighteen ecology centers gathered in St. Louis to talk about their common future. That meeting led to the formation of the Ecology Center Communications Council in Washington, D.C. Though always a hand-to-mouth operation, the ECCC helped to publicize the movement. The ecology center idea also got a boost from the environment task force of the White House Conference on Youth. In a 1971 report, the task force argued that the new institutions would help Americans to develop a deeply felt environmental ethic.[100]

Like start-ups of all kinds, however, ecology centers faced many obstacles. Many only lasted a few years. Founders burned out. Because funding was precarious, staff members often received only subsistence wages, and sometimes not even that. As the Earth Day buzz wore off, community interest became harder to sustain.

The most successful ecology centers adapted to changing circumstances in various ways. Some narrowed their focus. In Austin, for example, Ecology Action essentially specialized in recycling. Other ecology centers found new opportunities to make a difference. The stories of New Orleans, Ann Arbor, and Fremont, California, illustrate the different paths taken by centers that survived into the 1980s and beyond.

The Ecology Center of Louisiana was established in 1969 by Winder Monroe Lyons Jr., a Vietnam veteran from a well-connected New Orleans family. During a stay in San Francisco after his military discharge, Lyons was inspired by Ecology Action in Berkeley, and he resolved to create a similar group in his hometown. That took guts: New Orleans was a conservative city, and Louisiana was dominated by the oil and chemical industries.[101]

The Lyons group initially was more a club than a center. The members met at his mother's house. "I just started handing out flyers and sending mailings to my mother's mailing list—she was involved in every social organization in New Orleans," Lyons recalled. "We drew a wonderful mix of folks, from hippies to people who were dropped off by their chauffeurs."

By early 1970, the group had renamed itself, incorporated as a nonprofit, and rented a one-room office at the YMCA. Earth Day helped to solidify the foundation. The center signed up members at a display table at Tulane's Earth Day celebration. Earth Day also helped to make the ecology center seem more mainstream.

At first, the center's focus was consciousness-raising. In March 1970, for example, Lyons led a demonstration against Chevron, the owner of two offshore wells that were spewing oil into the Gulf of Mexico: Lyons publicly cut up a bunch of the company's credit cards. But the center soon evolved into a more policy-oriented organization. The center also ran a recycling program, but that never was a signature project.[102]

Though Lyons founded the organization, the center's dominant force for almost two decades was J. Ross Vincent, a chemical engineer who joined the Lyons group in late 1969. Vincent had done pollution-control research for a chemical and mining company, and that experience politicized him. "I became convinced that the issue wasn't science and technology," he explained. "We had a lot of techniques for solving problems, but we weren't using them. So the real issue had to be elsewhere."[103]

Vincent made the center into Louisiana's foremost environmental organization. He could speak with authority about technical issues, and he was willing to challenge powerful interests. He was a skilled coalition builder: He had as many friends in the Urban League as in the Sierra Club. The center campaigned to protect drinking water from contamination by toxic chemicals, and Vincent advised one of the principal congressional sponsors of the federal Safe Drinking Water Act. The center helped to stop a proposed interstate highway that would have destroyed both wetlands and poor neighborhoods. The center also ensured that environmentalists had a voice in public deliberations on everything from offshore oil leases to industrial waste-discharge permits.[104]

Though widely respected, the center always was close to the edge. The recycling program made very little money. After the center moved its office from the YMCA to an abandoned mansion, several staff members lived there. The staff never was more than five people. "We all did basic clerical work," Vincent recalled. Vincent held everything together. When he left Louisiana in 1988, *The Advocate* in Baton Rouge called him "the rock" of the state's environmental community. The center folded about six months later.[105]

In Ann Arbor, the Ecology Center was established by ENACT, the group that organized the University of Michigan teach-in. The goal was to make the teach-in permanent, with the Berkeley Ecology Center as a model. Because the teach-in ran a $10,000 surplus, ENACT was able to hire a director and rent a two-story office. The spectacular success of the teach-in also ensured that the center would not need to scratch to gain a toehold in the community. In addition to abundant goodwill, the center inherited many passionate and talented volunteers.[106]

That fortunate birth allowed the center to do a lot right away.

The center sponsored a biweekly seminar series, hosted a local radio show, and published a series of guides to eco-action, from "The Consumer and the Environment" to "Bikecology—Wave of the Future." The library was heavily used, and the bookstore was a success. To build esprit de corps, the center organized river and forest cleanups. Volunteers established small parks in deteriorating neighborhoods. The center began a recycling project that now is a multimillion-dollar enterprise. A walkathon raised money—and soon morphed into a popular bikeathon.[107]

The showiest project was a demonstration organic garden. The university lent a seven-acre plot, and the center inaugurated the garden with a community "dig-in." In addition to vegetables, fruits, and herbs, the plantings included hundreds of kinds of flowers. By the end of 1971, about one hundred people visited every day. Schoolchildren took tours. Volunteers came to help and to learn how to sustain a beautiful, productive garden without using chemical pesticides and fertilizers. Many visitors came just to look. In the words of one journalist, the garden's message was "a flower in every pot, a compost pile in every back yard."[108]

From the first, the center drew on the resources of both the university and the community. Almost all of the founders were graduate students or professors, and many volunteers were faculty spouses. But the founders were keen to make the center an Ann Arbor institution. They rented a hundred-year-old commercial building outside the shadow of campus. The center's second director, Mike Schechtman, worked hard to attract board members from the community. After a few years, the center also forged ties to environmental activists around Michigan.[109]

In the 1980s, the center began to work on state environmental policy. In 1985—a year after a leak of toxic chemicals at the Union Carbide plant in Bhopal, India, killed thousands of people—the center pressed for legislation to allow residents to get information about the potential hazards of nearby industrial facilities. The "right-to-know" campaign led to even more ambitious projects. One center campaign now pressures the automobile industry to use greener plastics. Because Michigan is home to Dow Chemical, the center has a "green chemistry" project. The center's environmental-health campaign aims to reduce everyday exposure to environmental hazards, including toys made with toxic materials. In Michigan, the center also is a leading advocate for renewable energy, farmland preservation, and environmental justice.[110]

Though the center's influence now extends far beyond Ann Arbor, the mission has not changed fundamentally. The first projects sought to show how residents could reduce their environmental impact, and many of the center's efforts now are demonstration projects on a larger scale. "Their purpose is to influence individuals and policymakers to integrate green ideas into their lives and institutions," director Mike Garfield explained. "The goal still is to move society toward a greener vision."[111]

The Tri-City Ecology Center in Fremont was the idea of a small group of housewives led by Donna Olsen. Earth Day inspired Olsen to start a local American Association of University Women committee on the environment. The group's fifteen members hoped to make the spirit of Earth Day part of their daily lives. At Christmas, they enclosed eco-tips with their cards. They were keen to recycle their newspapers, glass, and cans. "We wanted to do something hands-on," Olsen recalled. But the women didn't think that they could organize a recycling center by themselves. That would be a ton of work—and more of a mess than they could handle! Olsen met with a doctor who had organized the city's Earth Day lecture series and a biologist who advised the ecology club at the community college. They decided to host a community meeting in January 1971 to gauge interest in the ecology center idea. The meeting drew three hundred people. The two local newspapers gave the organizing effort great play.[112]

By April 1971, the center was a go. The first newsletter appeared. Because the center did not have a headquarters, volunteers established a drop-off recycling site at a Fremont shopping center. The center sponsored an environmental film festival and started a speakers' bureau. With profits from the recycling project, the center helped the public library to create an "Ecology Corner," and the center has donated $1,000 of environmental books to the library every year since 1972. In 1972, the center also produced an environmental info packet for school kids.[113]

The center soon became involved in local environmental politics. In the early 1970s, the center successfully fought for the establishment of a public-transit system in Fremont. At the ribbon-cutting ceremony for the first bus route, Olsen rejoiced that the community had acted to reduce smog. The center helped local officials push for water-conservation measures and sewage-treatment improvements. In 1981, the center hired a land-use attorney to prepare a ballot initiative to limit development in the hills at the edge of the city: Voters approved the measure by a 55–45 margin. The center later was part of a coalition to preserve local wetlands.[114]

The recycling program underwrote everything else for eighteen years, until the city started curbside recycling in 1989. Like all the center's projects, the recycling program was staffed entirely by volunteers. By 1974, roughly eighty people pulled shifts, and another twenty to thirty regularly pitched in as substitutes. In all, the center handled over 13 million pounds of recyclables.[115]

The loss of revenue from recycling might have doomed a different sort of organization. But the center had few overhead expenses—and no paid staff. The volunteer leadership soon found new ways to raise money. In 1994, after twenty-three years without an office, the center put down roots in the Fremont Community Activities Center. The center continues to find new projects. The center even revived Fremont's Earth Day celebration, which had all but died. "Earth Day takes months of planning," Olsen said. "But it's a popular event again. So we've kept the flame alive!"[116]

● Epilogue: The First Green Generation

"Earth Day changed my life."

Though no one can say how many people have thought that, Earth Day inspired a generation of activists. Many high-school and college students changed their career ambitions. Many graduate students changed the focus of their research or abandoned their studies to work full-time on environmental issues. Many adults also decided after Earth Day to devote themselves to the environmental cause. Some eventually turned to other pursuits—but many made a lifelong commitment.

The organizing effort was life-changing for thousands of people. The months of work on Earth Day gave many organizers a new sense of mission. Earth Day also gave many organizers the confidence, skills, and contacts they needed to make a difference. "After we tasted success with this, we were really empowered," high-school organizer Nan Stockholm Walden recalled. "That's a lesson that stayed with many of us throughout our lives, that we didn't just have to throw up our hands in despair, we could do something!"[1]

For some participants, too, Earth Day was transformative. They listened to speeches, they looked at exhibits, they marched or prayed or celebrated—and they resolved to work to protect the environment. Brent Blackwelder is a good example. On Earth

Day, Blackwelder was impressed by the presentations of Friends of the Earth and the League of Conservation Voters, and he decided to serve both groups as a volunteer. That decision proved fateful. Though he had planned to devote his life to teaching college math and philosophy, he soon became a dedicated environmental advocate. He helped to found American Rivers in 1973. In 1994, he became president of Friends of the Earth, and he led the organization for fifteen years.[2]

To make a living as protectors of the environment, the activists of the Earth Day generation often had to chart their own course. Before 1970, natural-resource management and sanitary engineering were the only well-established careers in the field. Earth Day inspired people to create new kinds of jobs and new career paths. Some moved from project to project as freelance environmentalists. Penn State organizer Tim Palmer made a career out of writing and speaking in defense of rivers. Many Earth Day activists formed new organizations—the growth of environmental nonprofits contributed to the stunning expansion of the nonprofit sector of the economy in the 1970s.[3]

Some Earth Day activists found ways to pursue their passion within traditional professions. They became environmental lawyers, green architects, eco-journalists, or environmental-studies professors. Other Earth Day activists joined new government agencies. Philadelphia organizer Ed Furia became the first administrator of one of the U.S. Environmental Protection Agency's ten regions in 1971. New York organizer Pete Grannis abandoned his career as a tax attorney to work for the New York Department of Environmental Conservation. Though he left the DEC to enter politics, he returned as the department's commissioner in 2007 after a thirty-two-year stint in the state legislature. Of course, many Earth Day activists went to work for rapidly growing environmental groups as lobbyists, researchers, media liaisons, and administrators.[4]

The careers of Karim Ahmed, Dorothy Bradley, Nancy Pearlman, and Buck Robinson illustrate the profound influence of Earth Day on many organizers and participants. Ahmed worked as a scientist-advocate for environmental organizations. Bradley championed the environment as a state legislator. Pearlman became a producer of environmental radio and television shows. Robinson started several eco-businesses. Before Earth Day, none planned to follow those paths.

Karim Ahmed

Karim Ahmed came to the University of Minnesota from Pakistan in 1960 with a simple ambition: He would earn a Ph.D. in biochemistry and make great scientific discoveries. "I was apolitical," he recalled. "I never wanted to take time away from my studies, except for cricket." But the preaching of his wife's pastor led him to volunteer at a neighborhood empowerment center run by a black activist couple. He also organized demonstrations against the Vietnam War. When he was arrested after a protest in 1968, he even went on a hunger strike. But his activism did not lead him to think anew about his mission. Even when he led a study of lead poisoning in the black community, he continued to separate his professional work from his social activism. He felt a stir, though, when he heard about Gaylord Nelson's call for a national environmental teach-in. He had read *Silent Spring*, he knew the issues were important, and he began to organize the Minnesota teach-in. The months of intense work on the teach-in were more fulfilling than anything he had done before. The day after Earth Day, he woke up depressed: "There was nothing to do!" That emptiness proved to be the start of a career he had never intended to have.[5]

Ahmed soon found another project. In the fall after Earth Day, he led a campaign to win student support for the establishment of a Public Interest Research Group at the University of

Minnesota. Ralph Nader was promoting PIRGs as a way to bring the energy of young people to bear on environmental, consumer, and social-justice issues. With funding from student fees, a small professional staff would work with students to prepare reports, serve as watchdogs over public agencies, and lobby for policy initiatives. To establish Minnesota PIRG, a majority of students had to approve a $1-per-quarter fee, and Ahmed built on the success of Earth Day by promising that pollution would be a major concern of the new organization. The PIRG organizers secured more than 30,000 signatures on petitions in just two weeks. Minnesota became the second state with a PIRG— Oregon was the first—and Nader used the two states as models in a 1971 guide to student organizing: *Action for a Change*.[6]

MPIRG hired Ahmed as the organization's first research director. That allowed him to get his feet wet as a public scientist. He helped prepare a manual for citizen participation in hearings to set regional air-pollution standards. He pressed the university and the city to halt the use of asbestos in buildings. He weighed in on sewage and public-transit proposals for the metro area.[7]

In 1974, Ahmed joined the staff of the Natural Resources Defense Council. Founded in 1970, NRDC was fast becoming a model of a new kind of expert-driven environmental organization. Though NRDC initially had focused on litigation, the organization soon began to work on legislation and administrative rule making. That required the help of scientists. For Ahmed, the job meant abandoning the dream of doing original research. Instead, he synthesized the discoveries of others in order to shape debate about public policy.[8]

Ahmed immediately helped NRDC launch a campaign to protect the ozone layer in the atmosphere—a critical shield against harmful ultraviolet radiation. In 1974, two scientists reported that chlorofluorocarbons in aerosol sprays destroy atmospheric ozone, and NRDC took the lead in publicizing their research. The organization petitioned the federal Consumer

Product Safety Commission to ban CFC spray cans. Though the agency denied the petition, NRDC's action ensured that the issue continued to receive media attention. NRDC also pressed for legislative bans on CFC aerosols. Ahmed testified before Congress. He urged state legislatures to act. Again and again, he challenged the argument of chemical manufacturers that policymakers should wait for definitive evidence that CFCs did harm. The industry wants to see "a smoking gun," Ahmed told *The New York Times.* "We'll have to wait 25 years for that, and by then the irreparable damage will have been done." As Ahmed predicted, further research strengthened the argument against CFCs. The Environmental Protection Agency banned CFCs in aerosol sprays in 1977. The 1987 Montreal Protocol then began a global phaseout of all CFC use. For the first time, the international community had acknowledged that human activity could cause harm on a planetary scale.[9]

In fourteen years at NRDC, Ahmed worked on everything from air-pollution standards to chemical-plant safety. He drew attention to many neglected issues. In 1982, for example, he coauthored a pioneering expose of the "double standard" in the export of pesticides, pharmaceuticals, and other potentially hazardous materials: American corporations were aggressively seeking markets in developing nations for products banned or severely restricted in the industrialized world.[10]

After leaving NRDC, Ahmed worked for almost a decade as an environmental consultant. He also helped to establish a national organization that lobbies for federal support for environmental research. Recently, he began to teach again. Early in his career, he periodically taught classes on environmental science and policy as an adjunct professor, but now he is enjoying the chance to think more philosophically about our relationship with nature. In 2008, he taught his first class on environmental ethics. "We have to get closer to nature and understand it better," he says, "and that understanding should inform everything we do."[11]

Dorothy Bradley

Dorothy Bradley decided on Earth Day to seek election to the Montana House of Representatives. She was just a year out of college, and she had never imagined running for political office. She hadn't even intended to stay in Montana: She was planning to do graduate work in environmental studies at the University of Wisconsin. But she had begun to build a reputation as an activist. Earlier that year, she helped to found the Bozeman Environmental Task Force. She also helped to organize Bozeman's Earth Day celebration. At a party for Earth Day organizers and speakers, a leader of the state League of Women Voters suggested that Bradley run for a seat in the legislature. A state senator seconded the suggestion. Bradley had three strikes against her, the senator said—she was only twenty-three, she was a woman seeking to enter a man's world, and she was a Democrat in a Republican county—but what did she have to lose?[12]

Like many young Americans in 1970, Bradley was not sure that the system worked. But she saw her campaign as a way to sustain the spirit of Earth Day. She wanted to raise fundamental questions about our relationship to the environment. Her "spiritual platform" was Aldo Leopold's *A Sand County Almanac.* "I don't think people should be allowed to abuse the land any more than they're allowed to abuse their children," she argued. "The morals of a community should extend to the whole land." Bradley also wanted to advance a practical agenda. She was especially keen to promote a statewide zoning law to give public officials more power to control land use.[13]

Bradley's campaign fit her beliefs. She raised money by holding a garage sale. Instead of buying campaign signs and billboard space, she gave away litterbags that people could put in their cars. "DOROTHY IS FOR THE BIRDS," proclaimed one side of the bag, "and the elk, and the bears, and the flowers, and for Montana." The headline invited chuckles. "To keep Montana beautiful," the other side said, "it's up to you." The bag then had a checklist for action: Carpool or bike, wash with low-phosphate detergents, avoid DDT.[14]

From the first, Bradley's candidacy caused a stir. Some observers dismissed her as a "glib hippy kid," and some Democratic Party officials thought her speeches were "too intellectual." But she had strong support in the Montana State University community. She also appealed to hunting and fishing enthusiasts. When she won, she argued that her victory was a sign of the timeliness of her agenda. "I said everything I felt like saying," she said. "The people were ready for a strong environmental pitch."[15]

In her first term, Bradley was the only woman in the 105-member House of Representatives. She also was one of the youngest legislators in Montana history. But she quickly earned the respect of colleagues in both parties. Though she spoke for a cause, she never wasted time on symbolic gestures. She had "ability and courage." Bradley, in turn, came to appreciate that political leadership was not black-and-white. "I've met some fantastic people," she told a reporter at the end of the legislative session. Though legislators had to cater to interest groups, "sometimes they act independently and then try to convince the voters they're right."[16]

Bradley's grit and maturity were even more evident in her second term. A coal boom was beginning to transform Montana, and Bradley feared that the boom would destroy the state's quality of life. In addition to new strip mines, the explosive growth of the coal industry promised to produce perhaps twenty new power plants. As one of Bradley's supporters commented, "the powers-that-be were trying very hard to turn Montana into the boiler room of the nation." Bradley proposed a moratorium on coal development. Before the state made "possibly irreversible decisions," she argued, policymakers needed a chance to study the many issues the boom would bring to the fore. What should the state do to prevent strip-mined wastelands? How should the state determine where power plants and transmission lines could go? What should the state do to control air pollution and protect groundwater? How should the state balance agricultural and industrial interests? The moratorium seemed to have no chance— yet the House approved the measure by one vote, after a passionate debate. The prodevelopment forces counterattacked, and the moratorium was overturned by one vote two days later. But the moratorium was revived as a stick: If legislators did not pass tough laws to protect the environment, the moratorium would get one last vote just before the end of the session. The stick worked. The legislature approved measures to address strip-mine reclamation, power-plant siting, and other critical needs.[17]

Bradley ultimately served eight legislative terms. After four terms, she ran unsuccessfully for Congress, earned a law degree, then won back her seat in the legislature. In her second stint as a representative, she decided that she should broaden her focus. "I took a gulp," she later wrote, "and submerged myself in education, taxation, economic development, welfare, corrections, science and technology, energy, and health care." In 1992, she barely lost a race for governor. If she had won, she would have been the first woman to serve in that office.[18]

Instead, Bradley focused again on environmental work. She directed the Montana Water Center from 1993 to 1999. She still is grateful to have been able to help try to build "an enduring land ethic" in her state. "I always felt lucky," she said in 2008. "My career never would have happened without Earth Day."[19]

Nancy Pearlman

Nancy Pearlman began to develop an environmental consciousness in the late 1960s. She watched as her childhood playgrounds—the orange and walnut groves just beyond her

Southern California suburb—fell to development. She joined Defenders of Wildlife in high school. She read *The Population Bomb* in college. Until Earth Day, however, she was most concerned about the Vietnam War. Even after Earth Day, she was not sure that the environment was her calling. "I tried my hand at feminist work," she recalled. But Pearlman's experience organizing Earth Day at UCLA ultimately became the foundation for a lifelong commitment to the environmental cause.[20]

Earth Day introduced Pearlman to a group of "incredibly important mentors." All were women in their forties, and all were volunteer leaders of local conservation organizations. Margot Feuer had cofounded Stamp Out Smog in 1959. With Jill Swift, she was leading a campaign to preserve the Santa Monica Mountains. Beulah Edmiston was a champion of the tule elk. "I went on hikes with them, I went to meetings in their homes, I went to hearings with them," Pearlman recalled. "That's how I learned about the issues."[21]

Unlike her mentors, though, Pearlman did not want to be a volunteer activist. She hoped to earn her living as an environmentalist. In 1972, a year after graduating from college, she established the Ecology Center of Southern California. Though her mentors all were active in single-issue organizations, Pearlman's model for the center was Earth Day. She envisioned her organization as a source of information, a facilitator of activism, and a place for networking.[22]

As director of the Ecology Center, Pearlman spoke publicly about environmental issues of all kinds. On Earth Day, she had led bicyclists in gas masks on a ride down one of the most famous streets in L.A., and she fought in the early 1970s for the creation of bike lanes. But her forte turned out to be communications, not grassroots activism. She started *Compendium*, a bimonthly calendar of eco-activities in the region. The Ecology Center also published a guide to local recycling centers and a yearly list of environmental organizations in the United States.[23]

Though the center attracted donors and volunteers, Pearlman never was able to secure the kind of major funding needed to sustain a full-time staff. To make ends meet, she worked part-time for the California Coastal Commission, Zero Population Growth, and the League of Conservation Voters. She even coordinated conferences for a surfing group. For a few years in the late 1970s, she taught high school full-time. But she continued to direct the Ecology Center. Her position eventually gave her entrée to the media—and then to local politics.[24]

In 1977, Pearlman launched a weekly environmental program on the number one commercial radio station in L.A. At the time, federal law required radio and television stations to air public affairs programming, and Pearlman often appeared on public affairs broadcasts as the environmental expert from the Ecology Center. She got the radio gig when the station manager asked her to suggest someone to host the program and she suggested herself. Her half-hour interview show—*Environmental Directions*—now is the longest-running eco-program in the country.[25]

Environmental Directions is a continuing teach-in. Pearlman sought from the start to look at our relationship to the environment from as many angles as possible. In her first year, she did programs on music and nature, environmentally sound lifestyles, land-use planning, environmental education, solar energy, corporate responsibility, water supply and demand, poverty and the environment, and much more. When the show was young, many of Pearlman's guests were activists. Now—a sign of the times—most are authors or businesspeople.[26]

Pearlman expanded to cable television in 1984. With a friend from the local PBS station, she worked nights and weekends in a public-access studio to produce *EcoNews*, a half-hour weekly show. At first, *EcoNews* mostly consisted of studio interviews, though the show always included at least one segment from the field. The crew is all volunteer. "The quality isn't what I'd like," Pearlman acknowledged. "But we fill a niche—getting the message out, not trying to do a *National Geographic* wonder every week." The show also enabled Pearlman to secure funding for a few high-quality specials: Her documentary about the Santa Monica Mountains, *Gem in the Heart of the City*, aired on the Discovery Channel and on PBS stations.[27]

Pearlman never gave up the hope of shaping public policy directly. In 1993, she decided to seek a seat on the elected board of trustees of L.A.'s community-college system. She had taught in the district, and she believed fervently that community colleges strengthened democracy. But she ran "to green the system." When she was elected in 2001 after three losing campaigns, she immediately made an impact. The board was about to oversee a $2 billion capital-improvement project, and Pearlman pressed successfully for a requirement that all new buildings meet Leadership in Energy and Environmental Design standards. Because the district is the largest in the country, the LEED decision received national attention. In recent years, the board also has sought to make sustainability a part of the curriculum. The district's nine campuses soon will produce most of their own power, and students will have the opportunity to become experts in renewable energy. Pearlman now chairs the board's infrastructure committee. "I'm constantly pushing to be greener," she said. "I want to create a model."[28]

Buck Robinson

For Buck Robinson, Earth Day came at a time of self-questioning. He was thirty-one, recently divorced, and unfulfilled at work. He had grown up in country-club comfort outside Chicago, and he had started on the road to corporate success by earning a Michigan law degree and a Harvard M.B.A. Then he took a job as assistant dean of business administration at Northeastern University in Boston. That was a rejection of his roots, but not a response to a call. "I was a young man in search of a cause," he recalled. "I was ready for the next step, and, when Earth Day was celebrated in 1970, I knew where to plant my foot. At that point I 'dropped out.' I resigned my university position, sold all my possessions, and honed my life down to a BMW motorcycle and a suitcase." A few months later, he landed in Rockport, Massachusetts, where he established a not-for-profit bookstore to support the environmental cause.[29]

Robinson made the Toad Hall Bookstore into both a community resource and a charitable organization. Incorporated as the Essex County Ecology Center, the store truly became a gathering place for residents and vacationers eager to learn more about the cause. Toad Hall sponsored eco-lectures and films. The local Sierra Club chapter met there. Though the store sold books of all kinds, the ecology section had pride of place, and one of the two window displays always featured environmental books. With the proceeds from the store, the Ecology Center essentially was a small foundation. The center so far has made $150,000 in grants for environmental projects and scholarships for students interested in environmental studies. The beneficiaries include the local recycling group, Kids Against Pollution, and the New England Rivers Center. The center paid student interns to monitor water quality in a nearby river and harbor, sponsored a regional acid-rain conference, and supported the county's greenbelt project. The center also funded the creation of educational materials.[30]

In the late 1970s, Robinson began to focus on the environmental impact of energy. He joined the Clamshell Alliance, a grassroots effort to halt construction of a nuclear power plant in New Hampshire. He worried about proposals to allow oil drilling off the New England coast. But he wanted to do more than protest. In 1978, he and a partner opened an alternative-energy store in a remodeled gas station in Cambridge, Massachusetts. Three years later, Robinson established a wholesale business to supply low-energy equipment to traditional stores. He also produced an award-winning short film about energy that played at many museums, schools, and environmental conferences.[31]

The Cambridge Alternative Power Company attracted a lot of attention. *The New York Times* and *The New Yorker* wrote about the store, which sold furnaces, insulating materials, books, and more. Out-of-towners came—pretending to be customers—to see if they could start similar stores. "The thing we are proudest of is that so much of our store is itself an example of energy conservation," Robinson told *The New Yorker*. "We actually depend for our operation on the equipment we sell." A cast-iron wood-stove provided heat. A forty-three-foot windmill powered the energy-efficient fluorescent lighting. Solar collectors on the roof provided hot water.[32]

The film profiled two alternative-energy pioneers, Amory and Hunter Lovins. Physicist Amory had thrown down a gauntlet in the mid-1970s by arguing that the nation could prosper without building more mega-sized power plants or developing more risky, environmentally destructive energy sources. That was "the hard path." Instead, we needed to focus on efficiency. That meant relying on small-scale technologies to meet many energy needs as well as redesigning our homes and workplaces to use less energy. Lawyer Hunter had worked for the California energy office. Together, they traveled the country pitching "the soft path" to corporate officers, civic groups, and academic audiences. *Lovins on the Soft Path* sought to give voice and image to their transformative agenda. But the thirty-six-minute film also was about demystifying the subject so that ordinary citizens would feel empowered to help build "a sustainable energy future" from the ground up. "People tend to be intimidated by energy, to say that we have to leave this to the experts," Amory says at the start of the film. "It isn't like that at all. The energy problem is the cracks around my window."[33]

Robinson started over again in 1991. He moved to New

Hampshire with his second wife, Caroline, to grow organic berries at the country place where she had grown up. The berry business was not their livelihood, and they moved mainly for family reasons. They wanted a connection to the land. "We came to this work out of a desire to try to live a clean and simple life in a dirty and complex age; to raise our children in wide spaces with plentiful skies; and to eat as many fresh organic berries as we could," Caroline explained. At first, they simply hoped to earn enough to pay the real-estate taxes. But Berry Hill Farm became a showplace.[34]

On the farm, Robinson continued to promote the cause of energy conservation. He was the first hybrid Prius owner in New Hampshire, with the license plate "48+ MPG." Not long before he died in 2003, the family bought a second-generation Prius, with a similarly gleeful tag: "55+ MPG."[35]

● Postscript

I realized early in my work on this book that Earth Day made a green generation, yet I don't think I really understood why until I was nearly done. Now—belatedly—the explanation seems obvious. Earth Day was an educational experience as well as a political demonstration. That rare combination enabled Earth Day to have both a long-term and short-term impact.

The educational experience was most intense for the thousands of Earth Day organizers. They often devoted months to their task, and they had to answer question after question as they worked out what kind of event Earth Day would be. The assignment for the thousands of Earth Day speakers was easier but still challenging. Few could repeat talks they had given before; the rest had to figure out what to say. Earth Day also challenged attendees to decide where they stood on difficult and important issues, and many took that challenge seriously.

Of course, the Earth Day education was informal. No one graded Earth Day organizers or speakers or participants. The educational process was self-motivated and self-directed. As a result, many people learned something about themselves. How much did they care about pollution or population growth? What were they willing to sacrifice to help the environmental cause? And what might they find fulfilling and even exciting

to do? Those questions often proved empowering, even transformative.

None of that was inevitable. Few political demonstrations
are powerful educations. Though a rally or a protest march
might teach participants something about solidarity or en-
trenched power, demonstrations rarely are occasions for debate
or soul-searching. Their goal is not to educate: Most demonstrations aim instead to inspire action, to channel anger, to give hope,
and to express a common will.

Earth Day was different because Gaylord Nelson made two
inspired decisions that allowed the event to be a life-changing
education for many people. Even Nelson's greatest admirers
have not appreciated how inspired those decisions were. Indeed, the most common way of crediting Nelson as the man
behind Earth Day, calling him "Earth Day founder," actually
obscures Nelson's true achievement. "Earth Day" was not Nelson's name for the event, and acknowledging that neglected
fact is critical to appreciating what Nelson did to make Earth
Day so transformative. Nelson envisioned a "nationwide environmental teach-in"—a politically charged educational event—
and the teach-in model allowed Earth Day to be far more
powerful that a traditional political demonstration. Nelson also
decided not to be a micromanager—he did not even object when
the national teach-in staff renamed the event—and Nelson's willingness to let others take ownership of the teach-in made Earth
Day even more powerful.

The teach-in model encouraged an entrepreneurial approach
to problem solving. That might have been a drawback. The open-
ended discussion at most Earth Day events meant that participants did not end up agreeing on a specific agenda. They were
not all ready to lobby for antipollution laws or press corporations
to account for environmental costs or reconsider the nature of
the good life. But the environmental crisis had many causes,
which required many kinds of solutions: No single piece of legis-

lation or change in business practice or new way of thinking could address all the issues of the day. The educational structure of Earth Day allowed participants to decide for themselves how they might make a difference—and then to act, in whatever way they saw fit.

The teach-in model also made Earth Day a youthful event, and again that was a potential weakness that proved to be a source of strength. In 1970, students were not a compelling constituency for most politicians: The voting age still was twenty-one, and student protesters had become a cliché. But young people were ideal participants in a do-it-yourself educational event. They were more likely than their elders to internalize what they learned. They still were forming their values, their priorities, even their sense of themselves. They tended to believe that anything was possible. Because they weren't as constrained by responsibilities, they often could change their plans abruptly without burdening or even disappointing anyone. Earth Day ultimately pointed thousands of young people in new directions.

Nelson might have limited the scope of the Earth Day education, but he chose instead to do the opposite. He let local organizers determine the curriculum. He did not insist that the teach-ins focus on specific issues. Though he was a legislator eager to pass new environmental legislation, he did not insist that the teach-ins promote a specific set of solutions to environmental problems. As a result, Earth Day became a remarkably capacious event, able to attract and inspire a range of people.

Nelson's decision not to micromanage the teach-in also made the local organizing effort more empowering. Because Earth Day events could take any form, the local organizers were more like small-business owners than franchise managers. They did not just implement a business plan devised by higher-ups. They were responsible for everything, and the breadth of their responsibility ensured that they were tested in many ways.

I did not fully appreciate the genius of the first Earth Day until I compared the 1970 event with the twentieth-anniversary celebration in 1990. The 1990 celebration was organized nationally—the only time that has happened since 1970—and the organizers had ambitious goals. They hoped, in the words of lead organizer Denis Hayes, "to galvanize a new outpouring of public support for environmental values and to enlist a new generation of activists in the environmental struggle." The 1990 organizers also sought to make Earth Day a global event, and they managed that brilliantly. In the United States, however, the twentieth anniversary celebration accomplished less than Earth Day 1970, and the reasons why the 1990 effort fell short are instructive.[1]

Hayes proposed a national organizing effort for Earth Day 1990 in a short essay in the Environmental Protection Agency journal in late 1988. At the time, he was a lawyer in California, but he had worked for years on environmental issues, especially energy. His call to arms immediately impressed the leaders of the major national environmental organizations, who offered their support. Hayes then established a not-for-profit organization to promote Earth Day 1990. He took a leave of absence from his law firm to serve as the organization's CEO, and he hired a thirty-five-year-old lawyer and political strategist, Christina Desser, as executive director. A $3 million budget allowed Desser to run a remarkably professional operation. In addition to a sizable staff, Desser had the help of a talented group of consultants—and most donated their time or worked at reduced rates. The coordinator of television, print, and radio advertising had created the "Everything you always wanted in a beer. And less" campaign for Miller Lite. Other consultants brought expertise in direct-mail fund-raising, polling, publicity, lobbying, event planning, and merchandising.[2]

Desser envisioned the organizational effort as "a national political campaign without the politicians." The staff used focus groups and test mailings to hone the Earth Day 1990 message.

The event had a logo and slogan: "Who says you can't change the world?" The promotional campaign aimed to match Hollywood's prerelease hype for blockbusters. "I want Earth Day to be as well known on April 22 as 'Batman' was the day it opened," consultant Josh Baran said. To counter the stereotype that environmentalism only appealed to the privileged, the organizing effort included outreach to labor unions and social-justice groups. Field operatives worked with grassroots groups to produce local events that served the national mission. Though the organizers encouraged students to celebrate Earth Day, they put much more effort into off-campus events: Big turnouts at attention-getting celebrations in community venues would demonstrate the breadth of support for the environmental cause.[3]

The organizers stressed the need for direct action. A test of the direct-mail operation, for example, asked a million people to take the Earth Day Green Pledge. Would they promise to recycle, conserve energy, buy products with smaller environmental impacts, and vote for pro-environment candidates? Of course the mailing also asked recipients to support the Earth Day 1990 campaign with a contribution. Though the pledge did not become a major part of the organizing effort, the basic message of the national campaign did not change. "We are trying to generate as much interest as we can for people to start doing things immediately—at home, at work and at school," communications director Diana Aldridge said.[4]

The Earth Day 1990 organizers accomplished all of their immediate goals. The turnout at Earth Day events in many major cities was far greater than in 1970. More than a million people attended the celebration in Central Park in New York City, and a rally and concert on the steps of the Capitol in Washington, D.C., drew 200,000. The media gave "saturation coverage" to the environment in the run-up to Earth Day, and the subject continued to receive unprecedented media attention for the next two years. Membership in many national environmental organizations reached all-time highs in the early 1990s. Earth Day 1990 also encouraged millions of people to think about how they could reduce their environmental footprint. The most conspicuous example of the heightened interest in individual eco-action was the astonishing success of *50 Simple Things You Can Do to Save the Earth*, a privately published pamphlet that came out just before Earth Day 1990 and soon sold more than 5 million copies.[5]

But Earth Day 1990 did not match the long-term impact of the 1970 event. Even Denis Hayes acknowledges that. Though circumstances seemed to be favorable for national legislation to address climate change, biodiversity, and other pressing issues, Earth Day 1990 did not lead to a second "environmental decade." I am less sure about the institutional and individual legacies, but Earth Day 1990 evidently did not engender the same kind of entrepreneurial activism as the 1970 event. The young people inspired by Earth Day 1990 mostly joined established environmental organizations, agencies, and professions.[6]

Why was Earth Day 1990 less successful than the 1970 event, despite a much bigger and more professional organizing effort?

Perhaps the limited long-term impact of Earth Day 1990 was inevitable. Because the idea was not new, the organizing effort largely lacked the freshness of discovery. Some of the national organizers were veterans of Earth Day 1970, and all already had a sense of what an Earth Day event should be. The local organizing effort relied on established organizations, not ad-hoc groups formed to plan Earth Day events.

But the problem went beyond the difficulty of making a sequel more compelling than the original. The organizational effort in 1990 was more top-down and more directive than in 1970. The models were political and marketing campaigns, which fail if they prompt lots of questions. In politics and marketing, the goal is yes or no—a vote for or against a candidate or a decision to buy one product rather than another. Though the Earth

Day 1990 organizers did not promote a specific policy agenda, they framed the event in ways that pushed people to make simple, immediate, and conspicuous demonstrations of commitment to the environmental cause. They sought to "enlist" people in a well-defined movement, not to empower them to work out their own vision of how they might make a difference. No one called the discussions at Earth Day 1990 events "soul-searching."

That was not an accident. Desser argued that Earth Day 1990 needed to be about action, not education. "The challenge in 1970 was educating people that the environment was an issue," she explained. "The challenge now is: What are we going to do about it? How can I change my behavior? How can I get corporations, the government, to change their behavior?"[7]

Of course, that contrast derived from a serious misreading of what the first Earth Day accomplished. The first Earth Day was about action as well as awareness, and the two were related in ways that the 1990 organizers failed to appreciate. People only change because they have learned something important—and hard-won lessons are the most transformative.

Desser's suggestion that the time for education had passed also speaks to a more profound misunderstanding. For the 1990 organizers, the only important question was whether people had the will to "change the world." Yet a willingness to act only is meaningful if people have a clear goal, and the goal of eco-action never is a given. Though human existence ultimately depends on the health of natural systems, humans can survive and even thrive in many kinds of environments, so the kind of environment people prefer always will be a complicated question of individual values, social circumstances, and cultural traditions. Whose preferences count the most also is a critical question. The simple exhortation to save the planet avoids the hard questions that are the foundation of true commitment.

I take no pleasure in criticizing the 1990 organizers. Hayes and Desser have continued to work on environmental issues, and I appreciate their dedication. But understanding the short-comings of the twentieth-anniversary celebration is not just useful in appreciating the genius of Earth Day 1970. The differences in the two great Earth Day celebrations offer insight into the predicaments of the contemporary environmental movement.

Like the Earth Day 1990 organizers, the professionals on the staffs of the major environmental organizations today are much better at leading campaigns than asking questions. They are adept at marshaling scientific evidence, making legal arguments, framing messages, and assessing environmental costs. They also know how to raise money—the sine qua non of not-for-profit advocacy. But they seldom inspire the deep reflection that might make the environmental movement dramatically bigger and stronger.

That sort of reflection begins with questions. What are the most important reasons why we have environmental problems? What environments do we value most? Who should decide how best to use the resources of the earth? What are the most effective ways to build a more sustainable future? As Earth Day 1970 demonstrated, those questions really can change the world. We need to ask them more often.

● Note on Sources

The Gaylord Nelson Papers at the Wisconsin Historical Society were indispensable. Because the Earth Day files were being processed when I visited the society in 2007, I cannot provide box and folder information for material I found there: I simply indicate that the material came from the Gaylord Nelson Papers. Now many of the documents I used are available online via a website I helped to create: http://nelsonearthday.net/. The website is a joint project of the Nelson Institute for Environmental Studies at the University of Wisconsin and the Wisconsin Historical Society, and I encourage every reader to explore it!

The private collection of Steve Cotton also was indispensable. Cotton was the press coordinator for the national teach-in office, and he saved press releases, speeches, meeting minutes, memos, correspondence, field notes, newspaper and magazine articles, and much more. Cotton used that material in 1970 to write a never-published history of Earth Day, and the collection includes draft fragments from that manuscript. The collection also includes multiple versions of a case study of the Earth Day organizing effort that Cotton cowrote for the Kennedy School of Government. Cotton lent me the collection for one frenzied weekend—and I could copy anything I wanted. The collection is not organized, so I sometimes can provide only a generic description of the material I used. That is especially true for the material Cotton wrote himself. In every case, however, I cite the source as the Steve Cotton collection.

I relied heavily on newspaper articles, which I found in different ways. Material from *The New York Times* came from the ProQuest Historical Newspapers database. So did some of the material I cite from the *Chicago Tribune*. The page numbers in that database occasionally take a different form than in the original newspapers. Though I used microfilm to look at Earth Day coverage in thirty-three metropolitan newspapers, most of my newspaper material came from the NewspaperArchive.com database. In both cases, I was able to see the articles in full-page form. For material since the late 1980s, I relied on the NewsBank and LexisNexis Academic databases, which often do not include page numbers. For those articles, I indicate in my notes that I viewed the material online.

I interviewed more than 120 people, and I had three rules of thumb about whether to use the recollections of my interviewees. I often was able to find corroborating material on the Web or in print. I also used information if more than one interviewee had the same recollection. In a few cases, I used interview material that I could not corroborate, but I did that only when I was able to verify similar recollections from that interview and when I was using the material essentially to give texture to my story rather than to support an argument.

● Notes

Prologue: "Give Earth a Chance"

1. *The Michigan Daily* and *The Ann Arbor News* had dozens of stories about the teach-in. The Douglas D. Crary Papers in the University of Michigan's Bentley Library include a huge clipping file: See Box 18, Enact Teach-In folder. The crowd estimate was from a *News* story on March 12, 1970.
2. *Time* 95 (February 2, 1970).
3. Barry Commoner Keynote Address, March 11, 1970, in the collection of the University of Michigan's Bentley Library, Ecology Center of Ann Arbor Box 5, Teach-In on the Environment 1970–72 folder.
4. The reporter for the student-run *Michigan Daily* kept extensive files about the planning of the teach-in, and those files are in the university's Bentley Library: David Chudwin Papers Box 1, ENACT Environmental Teach-In folder. I draw here on the first ENACT newsletter, a handout about the organizing effort, the minutes of the February 16, 1970, steering committee meeting, a February 19, 1970, letter to the *Daily* by co-chair Doug Scott about the conflict with the black-power group, and the RE-ENACT pamphlet produced by SDS. The records of university administrators in the Bentley Library also have important material on the teach-in. The budget figure is from a December 22, 1969, letter to the university's vice president for research, A. G. Norman, in Vice-President for Research Box 5, ENACT folder. The official teach-in program is in Assistant to the President (U of M) Box 39, ENACT Program folder. I also am drawing here on interviews with ENACT organizers Doug Scott (August 28, 2007), David Allan (August 20, 2007), Arthur Hanson (August 29, 2007), and John Turner (August 30, 2007).

5. I am drawing on the clippings, planning documents, and program in the Crary Papers Box 18, Enact Teach-In folder; Chudwin Papers Box 1, EN-ACT Environmental Teach-In folder; Assistant to the President (U of M) Box 39, ENACT Program folder.

6. *New York Times* (March 16, 1970): 31; Luther J. Carter, "Environmental Teach-In: University of Michigan Meeting Links Concerns About Pollution and 'Upside-Down Society,'" *Science* 167 (March 20, 1970): 1594–95; Raymond R. Coffey, "Teach-In on the Environment: Prelude to 'Earth Day,'" *Nation* 210 (April 6, 1970): 390–92; "Students Call It Dirty Business," *Business Week* (March 21, 1970): 29–30; Barry Commoner, "Beyond the Teach-In," *Saturday Review* 53 (April 4, 1970): 50–52, 62–64; *Washington Post* (March 12, 1970): A19; *San Francisco Chronicle* (March 22, 1970): 25A; *Chicago Tribune* (March 22, 1970) (online); *ABC Evening News* (March 11, 1970); *CBS Evening News* (March 12, 1970); *San Francisco Chronicle* (April 22, 1970): 44; *Christian Science Monitor* (April 22, 1970): 6; Group W "Give Earth a Chance" Press Kit, Gaylord Nelson Papers. The ABC and CBS reports are summarized in the Vanderbilt Television News Archive.

7. George Coling interview (December 5, 2008); John Russell interview (May 18, 2010); Mike Schechtman interview (August 20, 2010); Doug Fulton, "'What Can I Do?' Rings Loud and Clear," *Ann Arbor News* (March 22, 1970), in the Crary Papers Box 18, Enact Teach-In folder; J. David Allan and Arthur J. Hanson, eds., *Recycle This Book! Ecology, Society, and Man* (Belmont, CA: Wadsworth, 1972).

8. John Turner interview.

9. Interviews with Doug Scott, David Allan, and Arthur Hanson.

1. The Prehistory of Earth Day

1. I checked several databases for the phrase "the environmental movement," and the first two uses I found were in stories about preparations for Earth Day: "Ecology on the Campus," *Science News* 96 (December 20, 1969): 576; *New York Times* (February 23, 1970): 25. The historical literature on the environmental movement is vast. For an overview, see Thomas R. Wellock, *Preserving the Nation: The Conservation and Environmental Movements, 1870–2000* (Wheeling, IL: Harlan Davidson, 2007).

2. I first wrote about the activism of liberals, middle-class women, and young critics of American institutions in "'Give Earth a Chance': The Environmental Movement and the Sixties," *Journal of American History* 90 (September 2003): 525–54.

3. Arthur M. Schlesinger Jr. made the case for a new liberalism most notably in three essays: "The Future of Liberalism: The Challenge of Abundance," *Reporter* 14 (May 3, 1956): 8–11; "Where Does the Liberal Go From Here?" *New York Times Magazine* (August 4, 1957): 7, 36, 38; and "The New Mood in Politics," *Esquire* 53 (January 1960): 58–60. John Kenneth Galbraith's key work was *The Affluent Society* (Boston: Houghton Mifflin, 1958). For the political involvement of the two men, see John Kenneth Galbraith, *A Life in Our Times: Memoirs* (Boston: Houghton Mifflin, 1981), 289, 340, 357–59; Steven M. Gillon, *Politics and Vision: The ADA and American Liberalism, 1947–1985* (New York: Oxford University Press, 1987), 124–27.

4. Schlesinger, "Future of Liberalism," 9; Galbraith, *Affluent Society*, 255.

5. Schlesinger, "Future of Liberalism," 10.

6. Galbraith, *Affluent Society*, 253.

7. Allan M. Winkler, *Life Under a Cloud: American Anxiety about the Atom* (New York: Oxford University Press, 1993), 84–108; Adam Rome, *The Bulldozer in the Countryside: Suburban Sprawl and the Rise of American Environmentalism* (New York: Cambridge University Press, 2001), 119–52; Scott Hamilton Dewey, *Don't Breathe the Air: Air Pollution and U.S. Environmental Politics, 1945–1970* (College Station: Texas A&M University Press, 2000), 37–110; Richard H. K. Vietor, *Environmental Politics and the Coal Coalition* (College Station: Texas A&M University Press, 1980), 131–32; Donald E. Carr, *Death of the Sweet Waters* (New York: W. W. Norton, 1966), 157–80.

8. In the second edition of *The Affluent Society*, Galbraith noted that the uproar over *Sputnik* had helped sales of the book. For the response to Galbraith's work, see Charles H. Hession, *John Kenneth Galbraith and His Critics* (New York: New American Library, 1972), 66–68, 110–13. The *Life* and *New York Times* essays were reprinted in John K. Jessup et al., *The National Purpose* (New York: Holt, Rinehart and Winston, 1960). The other core texts from the great debate are President's Commission on National Goals, *Goals for Americans: Programs for Action in the Sixties* (Englewood Cliffs, NJ: Prentice-Hall, 1960); and Rockefeller Brothers Fund, *Prospect for America: The Rockefeller Panel Reports* (Garden City, NY: Doubleday, 1961). In addition, see John W. Jeffries, "The 'Quest for National Purpose' of 1960," *American Quarterly* 30 (1978): 451–70.

9. *New York Times* (March 13, 1960): Section 4, 5; *New York Times* (February 7, 1960): 1, 42. Both stories were cited by other participants in the debate. See Eric Larrabee, *The Self-Conscious Society* (New York:

Doubleday, 1960), 157; Vance Packard, *The Waste Makers* (New York: David McKay, 1960), 296.

10. Jessup, *National Purpose*, 27, 88.

11. President's Commission on National Goals, *Goals for Americans*, 239–41. The quotation is on page 228.

12. Packard, *The Waste Makers*, 294–98, 299–300, 307, 313. For the response to Packard's trilogy, see Daniel Horowitz, *Vance Packard and American Social Criticism* (Chapel Hill: University of North Carolina Press, 1994), 132–222.

13. John F. Kennedy, "We Must Climb to the Hilltop," *Life* 49 (August 22, 1960): 70B–77. The quotation is on page 75. In addition, see Richard M. Nixon, "Our Resolve Is Running Strong," *Life* 49 (August 29, 1960): 87–94. The Kennedy and Nixon articles were reprinted in Oscar Handlin, ed., *American Principles and Issues: The National Purpose* (New York: Holt, Rinehart and Winston, 1961), 3–17. For Walter Lippmann's views, see Jessup, *National Purpose*, 132–33; *New York Times* (March 13, 1960): Section 4, 5; *New York Times* (February 7, 1960): 1.

14. Thomas G. Smith, "John Kennedy, Stewart Udall, and New Frontier Conservation," *Pacific Historical Review* 64 (1995): 329–62.

15. Stewart L. Udall, *The Quiet Crisis* (New York: Holt, Rinehart and Winston, 1963), viii, 189; Martin V. Melosi, "Lyndon Johnson and Environmental Policy," in *The Johnson Years: Vietnam, the Environment, and Science*, edited by Robert A. Divine (Lawrence: University Press of Kansas, 1987), 117; James MacGregor Burns, ed., *To Heal and to Build: The Programs of President Lyndon B. Johnson* (New York: McGraw-Hill, 1968), 290.

16. Gillon, *Politics and Vision*, 152; David Vogel, *Fluctuating Fortunes: The Political Power of Business in America* (New York: Basic Books, 1989), 32, 39.

17. The best discussion of Johnson's interest in the environment is Melosi, "Lyndon Johnson and Environmental Policy," 119–23.

18. Robert Dallek, *Flawed Giant: Lyndon Johnson and His Times, 1961–1973* (New York: Oxford University Press, 1998), 80–84.

19. Eric F. Goldman, *The Tragedy of Lyndon Johnson* (New York: Alfred A. Knopf, 1969), 164. In addition, see Eric F. Goldman, *The Crucial Decade—and After: America, 1945–1960* (New York: Vintage, 1960), 345.

20. Richard N. Goodwin, *Remembering America: A Voice from the Sixties* (Boston: Little, Brown, 1988), 273. In addition, see *New York Times* (July 25, 1965): 51.

21. Lyndon B. Johnson, "Remarks at the University of Michigan, May 22, 1964," *Public Papers of the Presidents of the United States: Lyndon B.*

Johnson, 1963–1964 (2 volumes) (Washington, DC: U.S. Government Printing Office, 1965), I, 704–5.

22. Dallek, *Flawed Giant*, 229. For assessments of the Johnson initiatives, see Melosi, "Lyndon Johnson and Environmental Policy," 113–49; Irving Bernstein, *Guns or Butter: The Presidency of Lyndon Johnson* (New York: Oxford University Press, 1996), 261–306; G. Calvin Mackenzie and Robert Weisbrot, *The Liberal Hour: Washington and the Politics of Change in the 1960s* (New York: Penguin, 2008), 184–227.

23. James L. Sundquist, *Politics and Policy: The Eisenhower, Kennedy, and Johnson Years* (Washington, DC: Brookings Institution, 1968), 323. For the agenda-setting role of the new pollution agencies, see J. Clarence Davies III, *The Politics of Pollution* (New York: Pegasus, 1970), 23.

24. *Time* 95 (February 2, 1970).

25. Ehrlich appeared on *The Tonight Show* more than twenty times. See Tom Turner, "The Vindication of a Public Scholar: Forty Years After *The Population Bomb* Ignited Controversy, Paul Ehrlich Continues to Stir Debate," *Earth Island Journal* (Summer 2009) (online).

26. *New York Times* (August 10, 1969): 53.

27. Barry Commoner, *Science and Survival* (New York: Ballantine, 1970), 151.

28. Michael Egan, *Barry Commoner and the Science of Survival: The Remaking of American Environmentalism* (Cambridge, MA: MIT Press, 2007), 20, 26, 35–43.

29. "Social Aspects of Science: Preliminary Report of AAAS Interim Committee," *Science* 125 (January 25, 1957): 145; "Science and Human Welfare," *Science* 132 (July 8, 1960): 68–73.

30. Egan, *Barry Commoner*, 43, 60, 66–72, 97.

31. Ibid., 76.

32. Glenn Paulson interview (June 25, 2009); *New York Times* (January 9, 1969): 95; *Bridgeport* (CT) *Telegram* (September 14, 1968): 4; Les Leopold, *The Man Who Hated Work and Loved Labor: The Life and Times of Tony Mazzocchi* (White River Junction, VT: Chelsea Green, 2007), 240–42, 245–52.

33. Rachel Carson, *Silent Spring* (Boston: Houghton Mifflin, 1962), 5–6.

34. Richard S. Miller, "Summary Report of the Ecology Study Committee with Recommendations for the Future of Ecology and the Ecological Society of America," *Bulletin of the Ecological Society of America* 46 (June 1965): 71–73.

35. Ibid., 71.

36. Ibid., 72–73.

37. *BioScience* 14 (July 1964): 9, 10, 12, 13, 16.

38. Thomas B. Robertson, "The Population Bomb: Population Growth, Globalization, and American Environmentalism" (Ph.D. dissertation, University of Wisconsin, 2005), 147–49.

39. Paul R. Ehrlich, "The Biological Revolution," *Stanford Review* (September–October 1965): 47.

40. For the origins of *The Population Bomb*, see Turner, "The Vindication of a Public Scholar." The sales figure is from "Ecology's Angry Lobbyist," *Look* 34 (April 21, 1970): 42. In addition, see Alan Caruba, "Ecology Books: A Doomsday Bibliography," *Publishers' Weekly* 200 (August 16, 1971): 29.

41. Paul Ehrlich, *The Population Bomb* (New York: Ballantine, 1968), 11, 169–70.

42. Editors of *Playboy*, *Project Survival* (Chicago: Playboy Press, 1971), 77; "Ecology: The New Jeremiahs," *Time* 94 (August 15, 1969): 38–40.

43. *Science* 152 (May 20, 1966): 1117–8; *Science* 155 (January 20, 1967): 271.

44. Wes Jackson, *Man and the Environment* (Dubuque, IA: Wm. C. Brown, 1971), xvii. I also am drawing here on interviews with Jackson in 1988 and 1989, when I was a journalist in Kansas.

45. The historical literature on the activism of women in the Progressive Era now is sizable. For pioneering analyses, see Suellen M. Hoy, "'Municipal Housekeeping': The Role of Women in Improving Urban Sanitation Practices, 1880–1917," in *Pollution and Reform in American Cities, 1870–1930*, edited by Martin V. Melosi (Austin: University of Texas Press, 1980), 173–98; Carolyn Merchant, *Earthcare: Women and the Environment* (New York: Routledge, 1995), 109–36.

46. Carr, *Death of the Sweet Waters*, 12; Louise M. Young, *In the Public Interest: The League of Women Voters, 1920–1970* (Westport, CT: Greenwood Press, 1989), 174–77; League of Women Voters Education Fund, *The Big Water Fight: Trials and Triumphs in Citizen Action on Problems of Supply, Pollution, Floods, and Planning Across the U.S.A.* (Brattleboro, VT: Stephen Greene, 1966), 5–8, 34–77; Alvin B. Toffler, "Danger in Your Drinking Water," *Good Housekeeping* 150 (January 1960): 130; Polly Welts Kaufman, *National Parks and the Woman's Voice: A History* (Albuquerque: University of New Mexico Press, 1996), 199–200; Davies, *Politics of Pollution*, 87; Samuel P. Hays, *Beauty, Health, and Permanence: Environmental Politics in the United States, 1955–1985* (New York: Cambridge University Press, 1987), 460; Terrianne K. Schulte, "Grassroots at the Water's Edge: The League of Women Voters and the Struggle to Save Lake Erie, 1956–1970" (Ph.D. dissertation, State University of New York–Buffalo, 2006).

47. John J. Berger, *Restoring the Earth: How Americans Are Working to Renew Our Damaged Environment* (New York: Anchor Press/Doubleday, 1979), 9–25; Odom Fanning, *Man and His Environment: Citizen Action* (New York: Harper & Row, 1975), 1–24.

48. Mrs. Carter F. Henderson, "What You Can Do to Combat Air Pollution," *Parents' Magazine and Better Homemaking* 41 (October 1966): 76–77, 96–98; Mary Joy Breton, *Women Pioneers for the Environment* (Boston: Northeastern University Press, 1998), 193. In addition, see Charles O. Jones, *Clean Air: The Policies and Politics of Pollution Control* (Pittsburgh: University of Pittsburgh Press, 1975), 149–51; Dewey, *Don't Breathe the Air*, 97–98, 191–92, 201–2, 234.

49. Amy Swerdlow, *Women Strike for Peace: Traditional Motherhood and Radical Politics in the 1960s* (Chicago: University of Chicago Press, 1993), 83, 111.

50. Vera Norwood, *Made From This Earth: American Women and Nature* (Chapel Hill: University of North Carolina Press, 1993), 147–48, 153–57, 162–64, 167–68. The quotation is on page 153.

51. Andrew Hurley, *Environmental Inequalities: Class, Race, and Industrial Pollution in Gary, Indiana, 1945–1980* (Chapel Hill: University of North Carolina Press, 1995), 46–76; Ann Vileisis, *Discovering the Unknown Landscape: A History of America's Wetlands* (Washington, DC: Island Press, 1997), 212–15; Cam Cavanaugh, *Saving the Great Swamp: The People, the Powerbrokers, and an Urban Wilderness* (Frenchtown, NJ: Columbia Publishing Company, 1978), 97–110; Kaufman, *National Parks and the Woman's Voice*, 187–93, 197–206; Fanning, *Man and His Environment*, 193–98. The quotation is from James Nathan Miller, "To Save the Landscape," *National Civic Review* 53 (July 1964): 355.

52. Lewis L. Gould, *Lady Bird Johnson and the Environment* (Lawrence: University Press of Kansas, 1988); Robert Easton, *Black Tide: The Santa Barbara Oil Spill and Its Consequences* (New York: Delacorte 1972), 46, 222; Mel Horwitch, *Clipped Wings: The American SST Conflict* (Cambridge, MA: MIT Press, 1982), 284; "Women of the Month: Environmental Life Preservers," *Ladies' Home Journal* 93 (April 1976): 59; Thomas Raymond Wellock, *Critical Masses: Opposition to Nuclear Power in California, 1958–1978* (Madison: University of Wisconsin Press, 1998), 49–51; Hurley, *Environmental Inequalities*, 46–76.

53. I am summarizing the argument of chapters 3 and 4 of my first book, *The Bulldozer in the Countryside*, 87–152. For the statistics, see page 8.

54. For the role of gender expectations in shaping the activism of women

environmentalists after World War II, see Hurley, *Environmental Inequalities*, 56–57. I also am drawing on the sizable historical literature on maternalist politics.

55. Ruth Carson, "How Safe Is Your Drinking Water?" *Redbook* 117 (August 1961): 47–48, 86; Milton J. E. Senn with Evan McLeod Wylie, "We Must Stop Contaminating Our Water," *American Home* 66 (Winter 1963): 45–46, 72–74; Alvin B. Toffler, "Danger in Your Drinking Water," *Good Housekeeping* 150 (January 1960): 42–43, 128–30. The quotation is from Toffler, 130.

56. Betty Ann Ottinger, *What Every Woman Should Know—and Do—About Pollution: A Guide to Good Global Housekeeping* (New York: EP Press, 1970), 11–12. In addition, see Terence Kehoe, *Cleaning Up the Great Lakes: From Cooperation to Confrontation* (DeKalb: Northern Illinois University Press, 1997), 110, 144. *The Feminine Mystique* was published in 1963.

57. Kay Franklin and Norma Schaeffer, *Duel for the Dunes: Land Use Conflict on the Shores of Lake Michigan* (Urbana: University of Illinois Press, 1983), 214–15.

58. Swerdlow, *Women Strike for Peace*, 4, 9.

59. Stephen Fox, *The American Conservation Movement: John Muir and His Legacy* (Madison: University of Wisconsin Press, 1985), 344; Jones, *Clean Air*, 151. In addition, see William O. Douglas, *The Three Hundred Year War: A Chronicle of Ecological Disaster* (New York: Random House, 1972), 193–94; Breton, *Women Pioneers for the Environment*, 89–92. Rachel Carson also faced gender-based charges of hysterical exaggeration. See Michael B. Smith, "'Silence, Miss Carson!': Science, Gender, and the Reception of *Silent Spring*," *Feminist Studies* 27 (2001): 733–52.

60. Patrick Kiger, "The Perennial Campaigner: Stepping Out with Michelle Madoff," *Pittsburgh Magazine* 11 (July 1980): 20, 23; Dana Jackson, "Women for the Earth," *Land Report* (Fall 1979): 17; Fox, *American Conservation Movement*, 344; Hazel Henderson, *Creating Alternative Futures: The End of Economics* (New York: Perigree, 1980), 1–8. I also am drawing on biographical material I gathered—mostly online—about women who won the American Motors Conservation Award from 1960 to 1970.

61. *Lawton* (OK) *Constitution* (November 27, 1969): 2D; *New York Times* (November 30, 1969): 1, 57; "New Bag on Campus," *Newsweek* 74 (December 22, 1969): 72.

62. Though many members of the 1960s generation ultimately rebelled against the suburbs and the universities, that rebellion often intensified their commitment to the ideal of harmony with nature. I discuss the impor-

tance of forests and fields as suburban playgrounds in *The Bulldozer in the Countryside*, 127–28, 149–50. The 1967 film *The Graduate* first prompted me to think about the significance of the college landscape: When Dustin Hoffman goes to find his true love at the University of California, the cinematography emphasizes the pastoral harmony of the campus.

63. Joyce Maynard, *Looking Back: A Chronicle of Growing Up Old in the Sixties* (Garden City, NY: Doubleday, 1973), 122; Margaret Mead, *Culture and Commitment: A Study of the Generation Gap* (Garden City, NY: Natural History Press/Doubleday, 1970), 58–59. For the nuclear nightmares of the sixties generation, see Landon Y. Jones, *Great Expectations: America and the Baby Boom Generation* (New York: Coward, McCann & Geoghegan, 1980), 52–53; Todd Gitlin, *The Sixties: Years of Hope, Days of Rage* (New York: Bantam, 1987), 22–24; Lawrence Wright, *In the New World: Growing Up with America from the Sixties to the Eighties* (New York: Vintage, 1989), 53–54. The rhetoric of "survival" was everywhere. People taught courses in survival studies, demonstrated in survival marches, and offered survival agendas. The word also appeared often in the titles of eco-readers. See Editors of *The Progressive*, *The Crisis of Survival* (Glenview, IL: Scott, Foresman, 1970); Glen A. Love and Rhoda M. Love, eds., *Ecological Crisis: Readings for Survival* (New York: Harcourt Brace Jovanovich, 1970); Robert Disch, ed., *The Ecological Conscience: Values for Survival* (Englewood Cliffs, NJ: Prentice-Hall, 1970); Clifton Fadiman and Jean White, eds., *Ecocide—and Thoughts Toward Survival* (Santa Barbara: Center for the Study of Democratic Institutions, 1971).

64. For the differences in environmental attitudes among the young, see Daniel Yankelovich, Inc., *The Changing Values on Campus: Political and Personal Attitudes of Today's College Students* (New York: Washington Square Press, 1972), 73–74.

65. Jack Kerouac, *The Dharma Bums* (New York: Penguin, 1976), 97–98. According to Allen Ginsberg, the intellectual core of the Beat movement was "the return to nature and the revolt against the machine." See Bruce Cook, *The Beat Generation* (New York: Charles Scribner's Sons, 1971), 104. For Gary Snyder's importance to young environmentalists in the 1960s, see John G. Mitchell and Constance L. Stallings, eds., *Ecotactics: The Sierra Club Handbook for Environment Activists* (New York: Pocket Books, 1970), 84-87.

66. The quotation is from Keith Melville, *Communes in the Counter Culture: Origins, Theories, Styles of Life* (New York: William Morrow, 1972), 134–35. For the urban scene, see Helen Swick Perry, *The Human Be-In* (New

York: Basic Books, 1970); Don McNeill, *Moving Through Here* (New York: Alfred A. Knopf, 1970); Charles Perry, *The Haight-Ashbury: A History* (New York: Rolling Stone Press, 1984). For the rural movement, I drew on Timothy Miller, *The 60s Communes: Hippies and Beyond* (Syracuse, NY: Syracuse University Press, 1999).

67. Maurice Isserman and Michael Kazin, *America Divided: The Civil War of the 1960s* (New York: Oxford University Press, 2000), 158; Geoffrey O'Brien, *Dream Time: Chapters from the Sixties* (New York: Penguin, 1989), 74–76. For similar accounts, see Leonard Wolf, *Voices from the Love Generation* (Boston: Little, Brown, 1968), 151–52; Stephen Diamond, *What the Trees Said: Life on a New Age Farm* (New York: Dell, 1971), 75–89; Nick Bromell, *Tomorrow Never Knows: Rock and Psychedelics in the 1960s* (Chicago: University of Chicago Press, 2000), 69–71.

68. Raymond Mungo, *Famous Long Ago: My Life and Hard Times with Liberation News Service* (Boston: Beacon Press, 1970), 108. Mungo did not provide a source for the warning not to drink the water or breathe the air, but the phrase almost certainly came from Tom Lehrer's 1965 song "Pollution." For the text, see Jim Morse and Nancy Mathews, eds., *The Sierra Club Survival Songbook* (San Francisco: Sierra Club Books, 1971), 18–21. Paul Goodman captured the apocalyptic vision of many commune members in a short science-fiction piece, "Rural Life: 1984." See Paul Goodman, *"People or Personnel: Decentralizing and the Mixed Systems" and "Like a Conquered Province: The Moral Ambiguity of America"* (New York: Vintage Books, 1968), 412–22.

69. For the estimate of commune participants, see Hugh Gardner, *The Children of Prosperity: Thirteen Modern American Communes* (New York: St. Martin's, 1978), v. The examples of hippie activism are from William Hedgepeth and Dennis Stock, *The Alternative: Communal Life in New America* (New York: Collier Books, 1970), 117; McNeill, *Moving Through Here*, 118–20, 123–27; Terry H. Anderson, *The Movement and the Sixties* (New York: Oxford University Press, 1995), 266; Timothy Miller, *The Hippies and American Values* (Knoxville: University of Tennessee Press, 1991), 109. For a succinct discussion of the dissemination of hippie values, see Miller, *60s Communes*, 15–16.

70. For *The Port Huron Statement*, see James Miller, *"Democracy Is in the Streets": From Port Huron to the Siege of Chicago* (New York: Simon and Schuster, 1987), 329–74. The quotation is on page 330. The New Left critique of Earth Day is exemplified by James Ridgeway, *The Politics of Ecology* (New York: E. P. Dutton, 1970), 204; Mitchell Goodman, ed., *The*

Movement Toward a New America (New York and Philadelphia: Alfred A. Knopf/Pilgrim Press, 1970), 519; Editors of *Ramparts, Eco-Catastrophe* (New York: Harper & Row, 1970), vii.

71. The quotations are from Ralph Nader, *Unsafe at Any Speed: The Designed-In Dangers of the American Automobile* (New York, 1965), 147–69; Massimo Teodori, ed., *The New Left: A Documentary History* (Indianapolis: Bobbs-Merrill, 1969), 194; Garrett De Bell, ed., *The Environmental Handbook* (New York: Ballantine, 1970), 5–7; Editors of *Ramparts, Eco-Catastrophe,* v. In addition, see Goodman, *The Movement Toward a New America,* 519; Ridgeway, *The Politics of Ecology,* 208; Disch, *The Ecological Conscience,* 154–60, 167; Barry Weisberg, *Beyond Repair: The Ecology of Capitalism* (Boston: Beacon Press, 1971); Theodore Roszak, ed., *Sources: An Anthology of Contemporary Materials Useful for Preserving Personal Sanity While Braving the Great Technological Wilderness* (New York: Harper Colophon, 1972), 388.

72. Goodman, *The Movement Toward a New America,* 518, 529; Editors of *Ramparts, Eco-Catastrophe,* 84–105. The quotation is from page 84 in the *Ramparts* collection.

73. Goodman, *The Movement Toward a New America,* 509. In addition, see Weisberg, *Beyond Repair,* 166; Roszak, *Sources,* 393. Michael Rossman's 1969 poem about People's Park also illustrates the conjunction of radical politics and reverence for nature. See Michael Rossman, *The Wedding Within the War* (Garden City, NY: Doubleday, 1971), 349–69. For a photographic record of the struggle, see Alan Copeland, ed., *People's Park* (New York: Ballantine, 1969). In 1969, activists at the University of Texas waged a similar struggle over the fate of a campus creek, but the battle in Austin did not receive national attention. See Doug Rossinow, *The Politics of Authenticity: Liberalism, Christianity, and the New Left in America* (New York: Columbia University Press, 1998), 274–76.

74. Barry Weisberg, ed., *Ecocide in Indochina: The Ecology of War* (San Francisco: Canfield, 1970); John Lewallen, *Ecology of Devastation: Indochina* (Baltimore: Penguin, 1971). In addition, see Susan R. Schrepfer, *The Fight to Save the Redwoods: A History of Environmental Reform, 1917–1978* (Madison: University of Wisconsin Press, 1983), 165–66; Robert Gottlieb, *Forcing the Spring: The Transformation of the American Environmental Movement* (Washington, DC: Island Press, 1993), 96.

75. Weisberg, *Ecocide in Indochina,* vi–vii; Environmental Action, *Earth Day—The Beginning* (New York: Arno Press, 1970), 86; Susan Sontag, *Styles of Radical Will* (New York: Farrar, Straus and Giroux, 1987), 203. In

addition, see Edward P. Morgan, *The 60s Experience: Hard Lessons About Modern America* (Philadelphia: Temple University Press, 1991), 131–32.

76. Mitchell and Stallings, *Ecotactics*, 54, 57, 59, 161–68; Kenneth R. Bowling, "The New Conservationist," *Journal of Environmental Education* 1 (Spring 1970): 79.

77. Judy Clavir and John Spitzer, eds., *The Conspiracy Trial* (Indianapolis: Bobbs-Merrill, 1970), 296; Judith Clavir Albert and Stewart Edward Albert, eds., *The Sixties Papers: Documents of a Rebellious Decade* (New York: Praeger, 1984), 429; Abbie Hoffman, *Revolution for the Hell of It* (New York: Dial, 1968), 168.

78. For examples of Life-versus-Death rhetoric, see Editors of *The Progressive*, *The Crisis of Survival*, 211; Mitchell and Stallings, *Ecotactics*, 45–46; Thomas R. Harney and Robert Disch, eds., *The Dying Generations: Perspectives on the Environmental Crisis* (New York: Dell, 1971), 354; Tom Hayden, *Trial* (New York: Holt, Rinehart and Winston, 1970), 37; Clavir and Spitzer, *Conspiracy Trial*, 349; Environmental Action, *Earth Day—The Beginning*, 165; Jerry Hopkins, ed., *The Hippie Papers: Notes from the Underground Press* (New York: Signet, 1968), 105. The most vivid example, however, is the 1971 movie *Harold and Maude*.

79. Diane di Prima, *Revolutionary Letters Etc* (San Francisco: City Lights Books, 1971), 17, 46; James Simon Kunen, *The Strawberry Statement: Notes of a College Revolutionary* (New York: Random House, 1969), 4; Paul Potter, *A Name for Ourselves* (Boston: Little, Brown, 1971), 116–17, 205. Potter moved to the country in the late 1960s to be closer to nature. He was not unique. See Diamond, *What the Trees Said*; Raymond Mungo, *Total Loss Farm: A Year in the Life* (New York: E. P. Dutton, 1970).

80. Yankelovich, *Changing Values on Campus*, 167–85.

81. Grant McConnell, "The Conservation Movement—Past and Present," *Western Political Quarterly* 7 (September 1954): 475; Christopher J. Bosso, *Environment, Inc.: From Grassroots to Beltway* (Lawrence: University Press of Kansas, 2005), 35.

82. Bosso, *Environment, Inc.*, 35.

83. Thomas B. Allen, *Guardian of the Wild: The Story of the National Wildlife Federation, 1936–1986* (Bloomington: University of Indiana Press, 1987).

84. Ibid., 69.

85. Ibid., 84.

86. Bosso, *Environment, Inc.*, 35.

87. *National Wildlife* 1 (October–November 1963): 8–11. In addition, see

National Wildlife 2 (October–November 1964): 38–43; *National Wildlife* 4 (April–May 1966): 12–15.

88. *National Wildlife* 2 (February–March 1964): 14–15; *National Wildlife* 2 (October–November 1964): 43.

89. *National Wildlife* 2 (December–January 1964): 8–9; *National Wildlife* 3 (December–January 1965): 3; *National Wildlife* 4 (December–January 1966): 3–10.

90. *National Wildlife* 2 (August–September 1965): 2–9; *National Wildlife* 4 (June–July 1966): 4–9.

91. *National Wildlife* 7 (August–September 1969): 2–13; *National Wildlife* 8 (February–March 1970): 13; *National Wildlife* 8 (June–July 1970): 30; Allen, *Guardian*, 79.

92. "From Birdwatching to the Total Environment," *Audubon* 71 (May 1969): 4.

93. Thomas R. Dunlap, *DDT: Scientists, Citizens, and Public Policy* (Princeton: Princeton University Press, 1981), 78, 91, 140–41; Frank Graham Jr. with Carl W. Buchheister, *The Audubon Ark: A History of the National Audubon Society* (New York: Alfred A. Knopf, 1990), 187, 224–27, 231–32.

94. "The Great Swamp and the 'Good Life,'" *Audubon* 63 (March–April 1967): 5; "The Everglades Are Jeopardized Again," *Audubon* 71 (May 1969): 89. In addition, see Gene Marine, *America the Raped* (New York: Avon, 1970), 183–203.

95. "The Great Swamp and the 'Good Life,'" 5.

96. Paul Brooks, "Superjetport or Everglades," *Audubon* 71 (July 1969): 4–11 (quotation on 11); Editors of *Fortune*, *The Environment: A National Mission for the Seventies* (New York: Harper & Row, 1970), 169.

97. Michael P. Cohen, *The History of the Sierra Club, 1892–1970* (San Francisco: Sierra Club Books, 1988), 439–40. For the club's evolving position on nuclear power, see Wellock, *Critical Masses*.

98. Cohen, *Sierra Club*, 355–65, 413; "Fighting Sierrans," *Newsweek* 70 (December 25, 1967): 51; "Call of the Wild," *Time* 83 (March 24, 1964): 54; Scott Thurber, "Conservation Comes of Age," *Nation* 204 (February 27, 1967): 273–74; Robert A. Jones, "Fratricide in the Sierra Club," *Nation* 208 (May 5, 1969): 568.

99. Schrepfer, *The Fight to Save the Redwoods*, 133; Finis Dunaway, *Natural Visions: The Power of Images in American Environmental Reform* (Chicago: University of Chicago Press, 2005), 117–93.

100. The quotation is from Terry and Renny Russell, *On the Loose* (Layton, UT: Gibbs-Smith, 2001), 99. In addition, see Dunaway, *Natural Visions*, 185–89. For the campus outreach, see "An Orgy of Interest," *Sierra Club Bulletin* 55

(February 1970): 2; Connie Flateboe, "Environmental Teach-In," *Sierra Club Bulletin* 55 (March 1970): 14–15.

101. Jones, "Fratricide in the Sierra Club," 568. For Brower's appeal to the counterculture, see also Dunaway, *Natural Visions*, 172, 185–89.
102. Bowling, "The New Conservationist," 79.
103. For the making of *Ecotactics*, see Cohen, *Sierra Club*, 442. I discuss *The Environmental Handbook* in chapter 5. For the sales figures, see Caruba, "Ecology Books," 28; *Sierra Club Bulletin* 55 (April 1970): 22.

2. Organizers

1. Bill Christofferson, *The Man from Clear Lake: Earth Day Founder Senator Gaylord Nelson* (Madison: University of Wisconsin Press, 2004), 303; *Tri-City* (WA) *Herald* (September 21, 1969): 2; *Delta* (MS) *Democrat-Times* (October 9, 1969): 13.
2. Christofferson, *The Man from Clear Lake*, 305.
3. Lucy G. Barber, *Marching on Washington: The Forging of an American Political Tradition* (Berkeley: University of California Press, 2002), 141–78; Melvin Small, *Antiwarriors: The Vietnam War and the Battle for America's Hearts and Minds* (Wilmington, DE: Scholarly Resources, 2002), 106–7, 110–11.
4. Christofferson, *The Man from Clear Lake*, 30. I am indebted to Christofferson's fine biography, which provided most of the material for my account of Nelson's childhood and early career.
5. Ibid., 20, 31, 33, 36, 38. The quotation is from Nelson's obituary in the *Milwaukee Journal Sentinel* (July 4, 2005) (online).
6. Christofferson, *The Man from Clear Lake*, 41, 52, 57.
7. Ibid., 100.
8. Ibid., 13, 24–26.
9. Thomas R. Huffman, *Protectors of the Land and Water: Environmentalism in Wisconsin, 1961–1968* (Chapel Hill: University of North Carolina Press, 1994), 18–20; Christofferson, *The Man from Clear Lake*, 25–26.
10. Huffman, *Protectors of the Land and Water*, 35.
11. Huffman, *Protectors of the Land and Water*, 35–41; Christofferson, *The Man from Clear Lake*, 138–47.
12. Huffman, *Protectors of the Land and Water*, 39, 42, 45. For the concern about the loss of open space, see Adam Rome, *The Bulldozer in the Countryside: Suburban Sprawl and the Rise of American Environmentalism* (New York: Cambridge University Press, 2001), 119–52.

13. Christofferson, *The Man from Clear Lake*, 168–69.

14. The letter is reproduced in Gaylord Nelson, with Susan Campbell and Paul Wozniak, *Beyond Earth Day: Fulfilling the Promise* (Madison: University of Wisconsin Press, 2002), 163–68.

15. Christofferson, *The Man from Clear Lake*, 180–86.

16. Christofferson, *The Man from Clear Lake*, 266; Huffman, *Protectors of the Land and Water*, 56.

17. *New York Times* (July 4, 2005): B6; Christofferson, *The Man from Clear Lake*, 172–73.

18. Christofferson, *The Man from Clear Lake*, 265–69.

19. Ibid., 276–77.

20. Ibid., 302. For Nelson's views on Vietnam, see 282–301.

21. For the teach-ins, see Louis Menashe and Ronald Radosh, eds., *Teach-Ins: U.S.A.* (New York: Praeger, 1967).

22. I relied for Dutton's career on a memorial website: http://freddutton.com /history/bio/Fred_Dutton_Bio.htm.

23. Fred Dutton, "Prospectus for a National Teach In on Our Worsening Environment," Gaylord Nelson Papers.

24. John Heritage interview (August 3, 2007).

25. John Heritage interview (August 3, 2007); John Heritage interview (August 4, 2007).

26. The Gaylord Nelson Papers include files for speaking engagements. The AFL-CIO talk was September 26, 1969. The symposium for young professionals was October 24. The engineering conference talk was part of a Wisconsin tour in mid-October, according to a press release in the Nelson papers. A news clip in the Nelson papers described the congressional conference in early November. Nelson also touted the teach-in in print. See, for example, Gaylord A. Nelson, "Our Polluted Planet," *Progressive* 33 (November 1969): 17. Nelson cited the meeting with network executives in an April 7, 1971, letter to CBS president Frank Stanton in the Nelson papers. Though the Nelson papers include teach-in financial statements, the handiest source for the donations is Christofferson, *The Man from Clear Lake*, 303.

27. Christofferson, *The Man from Clear Lake*, 310.

28. *San Mateo (CA) Times* (April 27, 1970): 17; *San Mateo Times* (June 26, 1963): 6; *San Mateo Times* (October 28, 1965): 29; *San Mateo Times* (December 9, 1966): 33; *San Mateo Times* (November 30, 1967): 33.

29. John Heritage interview (August 3, 2007); *New York Times* (October 20, 1984): 7; *New York Times* (April 14, 1996): 39; *Los Angeles Times* (May 10,

1996) (online). For the Conservation Foundation, see Robert Gottlieb, *Forcing the Spring: The Transformation of the American Environmental Movement* (Washington, DC: Island Press, 1993), 38–39; Rome, *Bulldozer in the Countryside*, 185.

30. The Gaylord Nelson Papers include press releases about the steering committee as well as Scott's memo. In addition, I drew a few details from interviews with Harold Jordahl (December 8, 2008), Doug Scott (August 28, 2007), Glenn Paulson (June 25, 2009), and Daniel Lufkin (January 25, 2010).

31. The minutes of steering committee meetings are part of the private Earth Day collection of Steve Cotton. I did not see them in the Gaylord Nelson Papers, but they may be there too. I also interviewed Linda Billings (January 18, 2010).

32. The Gaylord Nelson Papers include letters inquiring about the teach-in.

33. The Gaylord Nelson Papers include the November 25 letter from Steve Schmiuki of Waukesha, WI, and the memos of Rozanne Weissman. I also interviewed Weissman (March 10, 2008).

34. "America the Befouled," *Time* 94 (October 10, 1969) (online); *New York Times* (November 30, 1969): 1, 57; *New York Times* (December 7, 1969): E10; "New Bag on Campus," *Newsweek* 74 (December 22, 1969): 72. The quotation is from my August 3, 2007, interview with John Heritage.

35. *Congressional Record*, 91st Congress, Second Session, January 19, 1970; Gaylord Nelson, *America's Last Chance* (Waukesha, WI: Country Beautiful, 1970); "'Teach-In' to Save the Earth," *Reader's Digest* 96 (April 1970): 110–12; Manitowoc (WI) *Herald-Times* (April 21, 1970): T7; Christofferson, *The Man from Clear Lake*, 307–9. The quotation is from an April 3, 1970 press release about the speaking tour in the Gaylord Nelson Papers.

36. Denis Hayes interview (April 18, 2008); *New York Times* (April 23, 1970): 30; *Long Beach* (CA) *Independent* (March 29, 1970): A18. Hayes has told the story of his travels often. See, for example, *Seattle Times* (April 21, 2002) (online) and *Puget Sound Business Journal* (April 22, 2007) (online). For Hayes at Stanford, see *New York Times* (September 1, 1968): E9; *Palo Alto Weekly* (April 13, 1994) (online).

37. Denis Hayes described the Harvard program to me in an e-mail sent April 21, 2008. I also am drawing on my interviews with Andrew Garling (August 23, 2007) and Steve Cotton (August 16, 2007). For Taubman, see *New York Times* (March 2, 1970): 18.

38. Andrew Garling interview.

39. Steve Cotton interview; *New York Times* (February 26, 1969): 49. For the history of the *Southern Courier*, see http://southerncourier.org.

40. Steve Cotton interview; Bryce Hamilton interview (August 5, 2007); Barbara Reid Alexander interview (July 27, 2007); Arturo Sandoval interview (August 2, 2007).

41. Bryce Hamilton interview; *New York Times* (March 2, 1970): 18; *Des Moines Register* (February 15, 1970): 1, 5.

42. Barbara Reid Alexander interview; Madison *Capital Times* (April 28, 1970): 2.

43. Sam Love interview (July 18, 2007); *Delta Democrat-Times* (August 28, 1968): 4; *Delta Democrat-Times* (October 20, 1968): 7; *Delta Democrat-Times* (September 12, 1969): 1; *Delta Democrat-Times* (October 13, 1969): 1; *Delta Democrat-Times* (November 9, 1969): 5A; *Delta Democrat-Times* (November 14, 1969): 3; *Delta Democrat-Times* (December 23, 1969): 4.

44. Arturo Sandoval interview; Arturo Sandoval, "Tierra Sagrada," *Wilderness Magazine* (2004) (online). I also used material from a 2006 University of New Mexico press release about the founding of the Chicano studies program; the release was online but no longer is available.

45. For Conrad, see *Minneapolis Tribune* (January 11, 1970): 14B. I also am relying on lists of staff members in the Steve Cotton collection.

46. *New York Times* (January 18, 1970): 163. Nelson's biographer only notes that the ad was prepared "by a top New York advertising agency," which provided several possibilities. See Christofferson, *The Man from Clear Lake*, 307. Denis Hayes told me that Koenig was the advertising guru who suggested "Earth Day" in a September 4, 2006, e-mail, in response to an e-mail I sent to say that I might write a book about Earth Day. He repeated that in my 2008 interview with him. But Steve Cotton could not recall the name of the advertising agency when I interviewed him in 2007. I finally decided to accept the attribution when Koenig's daughter Sarah Koenig did a piece on the public radio show *This American Life* about her father's role in renaming the environmental teach-in "Earth Day." The show aired on June 19, 2009, and the transcript is online: http://www.thisamericanlife.org/radio-archives/episode/383/transcript. That show inspired Hayes to e-mail Sarah Koenig on August 8, 2010, with a lengthy recollection. I had talked earlier with Koenig about her father, and she forwarded the Hayes e-mail to me.

47. *New York Times* (April 23, 1970): 30; "A Day Devoted to a Better Earth," *Life* 68 (April 24, 1970): 41. The Cotton quote is from a draft of Cotton's unpublished Earth Day history in the Steve Cotton collection.

48. The Steve Cotton collection includes the remarks Hayes made at the news conference on January 20, 1970.

49. The staff debated the name change for seventeen days, according to a draft of Steve Cotton's never-published history of Earth Day in the Cotton collection. "Nightly staff meetings, mostly devoted to the name," Cotton wrote. "Will the Senator get upset if we change the name? What difference does it make?" The staff also talked to the media about their frustration with the "teach-in" label. See James R. Wagner, "Environmental Teach-In," *National Journal* 2 (February 21, 1970): 410.

50. *Greeley* (CO) *Tribune* (April 17, 1970): 2; *New York Times* (February 23, 1970): 25; *Long Beach* (CA) *Independent* (March 29, 1970): A18. The Steve Cotton collection also has material about the efforts of the staff to be rid of "the Nelson albatross"—the idea that they were "Senator Nelson's kids."

51. The quotation is from the first Environmental Teach-In, Inc., Fact Sheet. The undated fact sheet is in the Gaylord Nelson Papers.

52. I thank Bryce Hamilton for sending me a copy of the letter from fifth-grader Jerry Murphy. He quoted the letter often, and so did the media. See, for example, *Des Moines Register* (February 15, 1970): 5; *Greeley* (CO) *Tribune* (April 17, 1970): 4. Hamilton's information letter is in the Gaylord Nelson Papers. For a short version, see "Happy Earth Day to You," *Senior Scholastic* 96 (April 6, 1970): 14. Kids also wrote to Gaylord Nelson. See Gaylord Nelson, ed., *What Are Me and You Gonna Do? Childrens's Letters to Senator Gaylord Nelson About the Environment* (New York: Ballantine, 1971).

53. Barbara Reid Alexander interview. The Steve Cotton collection includes field notes and correspondence of the regional coordinators for the Midwest (Barbara Reid) and Northeast (Andrew Garling). I also am drawing on my interviews with Garling, Sam Love, and Arturo Sandoval.

54. Steve Cotton and Andrew Garling discussed the decision to put more effort into events in big cities in a case study of Earth Day they wrote for the Kennedy School of Government at Harvard University. The Cotton collection includes multiple versions of the case study.

55. The Steve Cotton collection includes Reid's invitation to the March meeting, which she attended. The Cotton collection also includes memos of her telephone conversations with Karaganis and a report to the staff on the coalition-building meeting. For the Earth Week Committee, see *Chicago Tribune* (April 22, 1970): 1. The crowd estimates in news reports varied. See *Chicago Tribune* (April 23, 1970): 1; *Christian Science Monitor*

(April 24, 1970): 3. Andrew Garling tried to spark big events in several New England cities, but his efforts were not successful. The Cotton collection includes a summary of his disappointments.

56. The Steve Cotton collection has notes about the origins of the newsletter. The notes also give the size of the mailing list. The staff touted the UAW contribution to the media: See, for example, *New York Times* (March 2, 1970): 18. I also am drawing here on my interviews with Sam Love and Denis Hayes. The reports on the Northwestern and Michigan teach-ins were in the January 31 and March 26 newsletter issues. The first eco-film list was in the February 18 issue—and the April 2 issue reported that most films were no longer available for late April. The February 18 issue also was the first to list pending environmental legislation.

57. I reviewed the complete run of the newletter: January 31, February 18, March 3, March 12, March 19, March 26, April 2, April 9, and April 16.

58. Oxnard (CA) *Press-Courier* (February 9, 1970): 4; Elyria (OH) *Chronicle-Telegram* (February 22, 1970): C12; *Florence* (SC) *Morning News* (February 21, 1970): TV News 1; *New York Times* (March 2, 1970): 18; *Washington Post* (March 15, 1970): A1, A4; *Idaho State Journal* (March 11, 1970): A4. All of these pieces ran in many newspapers.

59. Steve Cotton writes about the decision to steer the media to off-campus activities in a draft of his never-published history of Earth Day. I also am drawing on my interview with Cotton. For the response to Ehrlich in Minnesota, see *Minneapolis Tribune* (April 24, 1970): 22.

60. *Albuquerque Journal* (April 19, 1979): D1; transcript of CBS News Special, "Earth Day: A Question of Survival," April 22, 1970, Gaylord Nelson Papers.

61. *Albuquerque Journal* (April 23, 1970): A1-2; CBS News Special transcript.

62. Environmental Action, *Earth Day—The Beginning* (New York: Arno Press, 1970), 246–47.

63. *Minnesota Daily* (April 23, 1970): 10, 12; Barbara Reid Alexander interview.

64. Environmental Action, *Earth Day—The Beginning*, 165–66; Madison *Capital Times* (April 28, 1970): 2.

65. The Steve Cotton collection has memos and notes about the staff debates about what to do in Washington. I also am drawing here on my interviews with Andrew Garling, Sam Love, and Steve Cotton.

66. *New York Times* (April 23, 1970): 1, 30; *Washington Post* (April 23, 1970): A20.

67. Environmental Action, *Earth Day—The Beginning*, 73, 87–88, 239; *Washington Post* (April 23, 1970): A20.

68. Hayes spoke in Santa Barbara on January 28 and at the National Wildlife Federation meeting on March 21. The texts are in the Steve Cotton collection. The Earth Day speech appeared in Environmental Action, *Earth Day—The Beginning*, xv–xvii.

69. Environmental Action, *Earth Day—The Beginning*, xv–xvii.

70. I devoted more effort to researching this section than any other part of the book. To identify Earth Day organizers, I searched the year 1970 in NewspaperArchive.com for "Earth Day organizer," "Earth Day coordinator," "teach-in organizer," and "teach-in coordinator," and that search produced more than a hundred stories. Some simply identified or quoted the organizers. But dozens of stories described how the organizers became involved and how they planned events. I made a similar Google search of the Web. I also found many stories about organizers when I reviewed Earth Day coverage in thirty-five metropolitan newspapers. I then located and interviewed fifty-five organizers.

71. The account of SECS mostly comes from my interview with Herman Sievering (June 12, 2009). In addition to published accounts of teach-in organizers, I base my generalizations on interviews with Karim Ahmed (March 28, 2008), Ross McCluney (October 30, 2007), Dennis Sustare (July 30, 2009), Jerry Yudelson (June 15, 2009), and Richard Mural (July 20, 2011).

72. The Iowa State organizing effort was the subject of a feature in the *Ames Daily Tribune* (July 30, 1970): 12. In addition to published accounts of teach-in organizers, I base my generalizations on interviews with Tim Palmer (August 2, 2007), Ed Beckwith (August 6, 2007), David Boeri (February 17, 2008), Robert Yaro (February 19, 2008), Nancy Pearlman (May 3, 2008), Tee Guidotti (May 9, 2008), Dick Roop (May 29, 2008), Curt Freese (June 17, 2009), Eric Jones (November 19, 2009), Sunni Eckhardt (February 1, 2010), Tom Hudspeth (June 30, 2011), and Walt Pomeroy (July 11, 2011).

73. Alan Strahler interview (April 8, 2008); Morgantown *Dominion-Post* (March 1, 1970): 1B; Ed Beckwith interview. The quote is from *The Montana Standard* (April 20, 1970): 12.

74. *Commerce* (TX) *Journal* (March 19, 1970): 9. In addition to published accounts of teach-in organizers, I base my generalizations on interviews with Alan Strahler, David Trauger (June 8, 2009), Edward Clebsch (January 29, 2010), and David Yetman (January 22, 2010).

75. As I explain in the first note to this section, my analysis of the organizing

effort is based on many newspaper and Web accounts. For examples of news stories about college and university organizers, see *New York Times* (February 23, 1970): 1, 25; *Tucson Daily Citizen* (April 17, 1970): 29; *Bennington* (VT) *Banner* (January 15, 1970): 7. I also interviewed thirty-two organizers of college and university events.

76. *Ames Daily Tribune* (January 30, 1970): 16; Pennsylvania State University *Daily Collegian* (January 13, 1970): 5.

77. Tom Smith interview (June 2, 2010); Lifestyle on Trial program in the Gaylord Nelson Papers.

78. *Atlanta Constitution* (April 23, 1970): 4A, 19A; *Brownsville* (TX) *Herald* (April 19, 1970): 16A; Richard Mural interview; Jim Harb interview (January 11, 2010); Edward Clebsch interview.

79. *Montana Standard* (April 20, 1970): 12; *Montana Standard* (April 24, 1970): 18.

80. Paul Wegener, "Caltech's EcoWeek," *Engineering and Science* 33 (May 1970): 20–21.

81. CBS News Special transcript; *Albuquerque Journal* (April 16, 1970): 20; Cleveland *Plain Dealer* (April 25, 1970): 13A; *Billings Gazette* (April 21, 1970): 17; *Ruston* (LA) *Daily Leader* (April 23, 1970): 15; *Minnesota Daily* (April 23, 1970): 2.

82. *Industry Week* 166 (April 13, 1970): 13; *Business Week* (April 25, 1970): 30.

83. Alan Strahler interview. For organizers eager to avoid partisanship, see *Brownsville* (TX) *Herald* (April 19, 1970): 16A.

84. Karim Ahmed interview; *Minnesota Daily* (April 23, 1970): 9; *Minnesota Daily* (April 27, 1970): 1.

85. Soon after Earth Day, Environmental Action surveyed roughly five hundred organizers about their budgets, fund-raising, promotional efforts, and much more. A draft summary of the survey results is in the Steve Cotton collection. The summary did not record how many organizers responded to the survey, though the return rate was termed "rather good." I also draw here on my interviews with organizers.

86. Jim Harb interview; David Trauger interview.

87. *Ames Daily Tribune* (April 21, 1970): 4; *Montana Standard* (April 20, 1970): 12; Herman Sievering interview; David Trauger interview; Karim Ahmed interview; Tom Smith interview; Doug Scott interview (August 21, 2007). The Environmental Action survey of Earth Day organizers in the Steve Cotton collection also provides information about administrative support, including provision of office space.

88. As I explain in the first note to this section, my analysis of the organizing

effort is based on many newspaper and Web accounts. For examples of news stories about high-school organizers, see *Chicago Tribune* (April 19, 1970): 1A; *Frederick* (MD) *Post* (April 20, 1970): 1, A5; *Denton* (TX) *Record-Chronicle* (April 21, 1970): 1–2. I also drew on interviews with twelve high-school organizers; four were planners of the San Mateo event, which I discuss below. The quotation is from my interview with Pan Conrad (January 11, 2008).

89. Ed Radatz interview (May 30, 2008); Steve Landfried interview (July 8, 2009). For the national renown of the Pollution Control Center, see *Chicago Tribune* (April 20, 1972): 8; "A Pollution Control Center Raising Environmental Consciousness," *Environmentalist* 2 (1982): 259–261.

90. *Washington Post* (March 15, 1970): A4; *Centre* (PA) *Daily Times* (April 21, 1970): Section 2, 11; *Danville* (VA) *Register* (April 19, 1970): 7D.

91. Raymond Bruzan, "Conservation Education in an Illinois High School," *American Biology Teacher* 33 (September 1971): 339–41.

92. The quotation is from my interview with Chris Bowman (May 4, 2008). I also interviewed three other organizers: Gary Wakai (January 15, 2010), Susan Obata (July 23, 2011), and Ed Holm (June 6, 2008). In addition, see *San Mateo* (CA) *Times* (April 18, 1970): 2A, 4A. Bowman gave me copies of roughly seventy-five documents about the teach-in, including the program, stories from the school newspaper, and memos about ecology club activities. His collection was invaluable.

93. Susan Obata interview.

94. For the quotation, see *San Mateo* (CA) *Times* (April 18, 1970): 4A.

95. The comment about the New York organizers is from my interview with Fred Kent (December 10, 2007). I also interviewed organizers of community events in Philadelphia, Cleveland, St. Louis, Birmingham, and Houston.

96. Joan Morrison and Robert K. Morrison, *From Camelot to Kent State: The Sixties Experience in the Words of Those Who Lived It* (New York: Times Books, 1987), 191; *Charleston* (WV) *Daily Mail* (June 10, 1971), 21; Dorothy Slusser interview (April 9, 2008).

97. *Charleston* (WV) *Gazette* (February 3, 1970): 16; *Charleston Gazette* (February 18, 1970): 5; *Charleston Gazette* (April 15, 1970): 9; *Charleston Gazette* (April 16, 1970): 22.

98. CBS did a fifteen-minute feature on the Philadelphia event. The quotation is from the CBS News Special transcript in the Gaylord Nelson Papers. The official program was fifty glossy pages: John Zeh, ed., *Earth Week '70* (Philadelphia: Philadelphia Earth Week Committee, 1970). The

1970 documentary *Circuit Earth*—available from Bullfrog Films—has footage of Earth Week events.

99. Austan Librach interview (April 29, 2008); Ed Furia interview (May 2, 2008); Zeh, *Earth Week '70*, 34.

100. *Philadelphia Inquirer* (March 17, 1970): 10; Zeh, *Earth Week '70*, 42; Ed Furia interview; Austan Librach interview.

101. Ed Furia interview; Austan Librach interview; Frank Herbert, ed., *New World or No World* (New York: Ace Books, 1970), 146–147; CBS News Special transcript; *Philadelphia Inquirer* (April 12, 1970): Section 2, 12; Zeh, *Earth Week '70*, 34, 49.

102. Zeh, *Earth Week '70*, 13, 32–33; CBS News Special transcript; Ed Furia interview; Austan Librach interview. For a different account of Einhorn's role, see Steven Levy, *The Unicorn's Secret: Murder in the Age of Aquarius* (New York: Prentice Hall, 1988), 114–120. Einhorn later was convicted of murdering his girlfriend, and critics of Earth Day have claimed that he organized Earth Week in Philadelphia to tarnish the event. As I make clear in the text, that claim is false.

103. Philadelphia Earth Week Committee, *The Delaware Valley Environment: Status and Prospects* (Philadelphia: Earth Week Committee, 1970), Section 1: 3.

104. Ed Furia interview; Austan Librach interview. The unscenic tour was especially notable. See *Philadelphia Inquirer* (April 19, 1970): Section 2, 9; CBS News Special transcript.

105. Dorothy Slusser interview; Curt Freese interview.

3. Events

1. "A Memento Mori to the Earth," *Time* 95 (May 4, 1970): 16–18. *Long Beach (CA) Independent* (April 23, 1970): 1, 8; *Oshkosh Daily Northwestern* (April 23, 1970): 8.

2. *New York Times* (March 19, 1970): 1, 95; Fred Kent interview (December 10, 2007).

3. Garrett De Bell, ed., *The Environmental Handbook* (New York: Ballantine Books, 1970), 197–213; *Albuquerque Journal* (April 16, 1970): B6.

4. *New York Times* (April 23, 1970): 30.

5. Vincent J. Cannato, *The Ungovernable City: John Lindsay and His Struggle to Save New York* (New York: Basic Books, 2001), 44; *Washington Post* (April 23, 1970): A21; New York *Daily News* (April 23, 1970): 3, 4.

6. New York *Daily News* (April 23, 1970): 3.

7. New York *Daily News* (April 23, 1970): 1; *New York Times* (April 23, 1970): 1; *Washington Post* (April 23, 1970): A21; *San Francisco Chronicle* (April 23, 1970): 1; Vanderbilt Television News Archive abstracts for the ABC, CBS, and NBC nightly news broadcasts on April 22, 1970.

8. New York *Daily News* (April 23, 1970): 5; Samuel G. Freedman, *The Inheritance: How Three Families and the American Political Majority Moved from Left to Right* (New York: Touchstone, 1998), 249–50.

9. New York *Daily News* (April 23, 1970): 4, 5; *Washington Post* (April 23, 1970): A21.

10. New York *Daily News* (April 23, 1970): 5.

11. *New York Times* (April 23, 1970): 30, 32; Freedman, *The Inheritance*, 249; Environmental Action, *Earth Day—The Beginning* (New York: Arno Press, 1970), 244–45.

12. *New York Times* (April 23, 1970): 30; *Washington Post* (April 23, 1970): A21; New York *Daily News* (April 23, 1970): 5.

13. Joan Morrison and Robert K. Morrison, *From Camelot to Kent State: The Sixties Experience in the Words of Those Who Lived It* (New York: Times Books, 1987), 193, 191; Bridget O'Brian, "The Birth of Earth Day," Columbia University *Record* 32 (April 16, 2007): 1, 8.

14. *Newsday* (April 23, 1970): 2, 12.

15. Barbara M. Kelly, *Expanding the American Dream: Building and Rebuilding Levittown* (Albany: State University of New York Press, 1993), 112–13. I also am drawing on interviews with two Levittown teachers, Ron Zoia (January 16, 2008) and Regina LaMarca (January 16, 2008).

16. Milly Dawson interview (January 22, 2008); *Newsday* (April 23, 1970): 2; Holly Berger interview (April 29, 2008).

17. *Salina* (KS) *Journal* (September 5, 1969): T5; *New Castle* (PA) *News* (September 12, 1969): 19; *Las Cruces* (NM) *Sun-News* (October 2, 1969): 9; *Ogden* (UT) *Standard-Examiner* (November 29, 1969): 4TV; *Portsmouth* (NH) *Herald* (September 27, 1969): 4; *Muscatine* (IA) *Journal* (October 4, 1969): 4.

18. *Newsday* (April 23, 1970): 2.

19. *Newsday* (April 23, 1970): 12.

20. Ibid.

21. Ron Zoia interview; *Newsday* (April 23, 1970): 12.

22. The *Newsday* story does not describe the film, so my description comes from my own viewing of it. The film is in the media collection of Pennsylvania State University.

23. *Newsday* (April 23, 1970): 12.

24. Ibid.

25. *Miami Herald* (April 22, 1970): 6A; *Miami Herald* (April 20, 1970): 28C; *Fort Pierce* (FL) *News Tribune* (April 13, 1970): 8; Luther P. Gerlach and Virginia H. Hine, *Lifeway Leap: The Dynamics of Change in America* (Minneapolis: University of Minnesota Press, 1973), 191–218. I thank Jack Davis for suggesting that I look at the Gerlach and Hine book, which was a superb guide to Miami's environmental politics in the Earth Day period.

26. *Miami Herald* (April 23, 1970): 30A; *Miami News* (April 22, 1970): 12A; *Albuquerque Journal* (December 10, 1970): B7.

27. Sam Love and David Obst, eds., *Ecotage!* (New York: Pocket Books, 1972), 164–68.

28. *Miami Herald* (April 23, 1970): 30A; *Miami News* (April 23, 1970): 3D; *Tucson Daily Citizen* (April 23, 1970): 36. CBS and NET (the predecessor of PBS) featured the parade in Earth Day broadcasts. See Vanderbilt Television News Archive; *New York Times* (April 22, 1970): 72. For the New Party, see *Panama City* (FL) *News-Herald* (May 18, 1970): 1B.

29. *Miami News* (April 22, 1970): 12A; *Miami Herald* (April 23, 1970): 30A.

30. *Miami News* (April 28, 1970): 6A; *Miami News* (April 21, 1970): 5A.

31. Joyce Tarnow interview (October 31, 2007); Ross McCluney interview (October 30, 2007); William Ross McCluney, ed., *The Environmental Destruction of South Florida* (Coral Gables: University of Miami Press, 1971); Gerlach and Hine, *Lifeway Leap*, 216. For the Eco Commandos, see *Albuquerque News* (December 10, 1970), B7; "Cheerful Sabotage," *Time* 99 (January 31, 1972); and Love and Obst, *Ecotage!*, 160–70.

32. Gerlach and Hine, *Lifeway Leap*, 210. The Miami newspapers also illustrate the fears among some older supporters of the environmental cause about the style of the new activists. The *News* and the *Herald* campaigned against pollution, yet both warned after Earth Day that activists should not go too far. See *Miami News* (April 22, 1970): 22A; *Miami Herald* (April 25, 1970): 6A.

33. Gerlach and Hine, *Lifeway Leap*, 191–218.

34. Sam Love interview (July 18, 2007).

35. *Birmingham News* (April 19, 1970): 4; *Birmingham News* (April 22, 1970): 67; Cameron McDonald Vowell interview (July 31, 2007); Patrick J. Sloyan, "The Day They Shut Down Birmingham," *Washington Monthly* 3 (May 1972): 44–45.

36. Cameron McDonald Vowell interview; Clara Ruth Hayman, *Protecting Alabama: A History of the Alabama Environmental Council* (Birmingham: Alabama Environmental Council, 1997), 1–11; Ben Branscomb interview (October 16, 2007); *Birmingham News* (March 3, 1970): 1, 4.

37. *Birmingham News* (April 16, 1970): 17; Cameron McDonald Vowell interview; Marshall Brewer interview (August 2, 2011); Sam Love interview.

38. *Birmingham News* (April 16, 1970): 4B, 17, 20; *Birmingham News* (April 18, 1970): 3; *Birmingham News* (April 22, 1970): 30, 53.

39. *Birmingham News* (April 23, 1970): 8. In March, Russakoff had been removed from his position as head of the county medical society's air-pollution committee, and his dismissal was a front-page news story. See *Birmingham News* (March 3, 1970): 1, 4; *Birmingham News* (March 8, 1970): 1, 3.

40. *Birmingham News* (April 22, 1970): 1, 4; *Birmingham News* (April 16, 1970): 17.

41. *Birmingham News* (April 16, 1970): 8; *Birmingham News* (April 20, 1970): 10; *Birmingham News* (April 21, 1970): 12; *Birmingham News* (April 22, 1970): 10; *Birmingham News* (April 27, 1970): 10. The city's second newspaper took a similar stand: See *Birmingham Post-Herald* (April 15, 1970): 12.

42. Cameron McDonald Vowell interview; *Birmingham News* (April 23, 1970): 39.

43. The Penn State student newspaper is *The Daily Collegian*, and I will refer to it solely by that name in this section. For the Penn State protests, see *Daily Collegian* (April 17, 1970): 1, 3; *Daily Collegian* (April 21, 1970): 1; *Daily Collegian* (April 22, 1970): 1; *Daily Collegian* (April 24, 1970): 1. For a wire-service report on campus unrest across the country, see *Wisconsin State Journal* (April 25, 1970): 1–2.

44. Thomas G. Smith, *Green Republican: John Saylor and the Preservation of America's Wilderness* (Pittsburgh: University of Pittsburgh Press, 2006).

45. Saylor's speech was published in full in the *Barnesboro Star* in May 1970. I thank Saylor biographer Tom Smith for providing me a copy of the article.

46. Michael Bezilla, *Penn State: An Illustrated History* (University Park: Pennsylvania State University Press, 1985), 309–10. The Penn State chapter of Young Americans for Freedom was the biggest in the nation in the late 1960s. See Rebecca E. Klatch, *A Generation Divided: The New Left, the New Right, and the 1960s* (Berkeley: University of California Press, 1999), 123.

47. Ed Beckwith interview (August 6, 2007); *Daily Collegian* (November 12, 1969): 3; *Daily Collegian* (May 30, 1968): 6; *Daily Collegian* (May 27, 1969): 3; *Daily Collegian* (November 11, 1969): 5.

48. Tim Palmer interview (August 2, 2007); *Daily Collegian* (January 7, 1970): 1; *Daily Collegian* (January 13, 1970): 5.

49. *Daily Collegian* (April 3, 1970): 1; *Daily Collegian* (April 21, 1970): 3–4; Ed Beckwith interview; Tim Palmer interview.

50. *Daily Collegian* (April 9, 1970): 1.

51. Ed Beckwith interview; *Centre Daily Times* (February 25, 1970): 12; *Daily Collegian* (April 3, 1970): 1.

52. *Daily Collegian* (April 24, 1970): 2; *Daily Collegian* (April 21, 1970): 1. The local newspaper noted that Kunstler drew students away from Earth Week activities, but the newspaper still devoted a tremendous amount of space to Earth Week coverage. See *Centre Daily Times* (April 20, 1970): Second Section, 13.

53. The *Cleveland Press* put the flower logo on every story about Crisis in the Environment Week. The paper's editorial cartoonist also depicted the flower growing tall again in a cartoon entitled "Flower Power." See *Cleveland Press* (April 21, 1970): A8.

54. Both the Cleveland *Plain Dealer* and the *Cleveland Press* reported at length on all of these events. For a summary, see *Cleveland Press* (April 21, 1970): A8.

55. Laurence Aurbach interview (July 24, 2007). Aurbach provided me a copy of the minutes of the first steering committee meeting, January 31, 1970. In addition, see the profile of Aurbach in the *Cleveland Press* (April 16, 1970): B7.

56. Betty Klaric interview (October 19, 2007); Cleveland *Plain Dealer* (April 19, 1970): 4A; David Beach, "Environmentalism," *The Encyclopedia of Cleveland History* (online); Jonathan H. Adler, "Fables of the Cuyahoga: Reconstructing a History of Environmental Protection," *Fordham Environmental Law Journal* 14 (2002): 107–8; Terrianne K. Schulte, "Grassroots at the Water's Edge: The League of Women Voters and the Struggle to Save Lake Erie, 1956–1970" (Ph.D. dissertation, State University of New York–Buffalo, 2006), 68–72; *Cleveland Press* (April 21, 1970): A8.

57. Laurence Aurbach interview; Betty Klaric interview; *Cleveland Press* (April 21, 1970): A4; Schulte, "Grassroots at the Water's Edge," 61.

58. Laurence Aurbach interview.

59. Cleveland *Plain Dealer* (April 16, 1970): 7A; *Cleveland Press* (April 15, 1970): G10; Laurence Aurbach interview.

60. *Cleveland Press* (April 15, 1970): G10; Adler, "Fables of the Cuyahoga," 108. For Richard Hatcher, see Andrew Hurley, *Environmental Inequalities: Class, Race, and Industrial Pollution in Gary, Indiana, 1945–1980*

(Chapel Hill: University of North Carolina Press, 1995), 111–12, 129–35, 140.

61. Cleveland *Plain Dealer* (April 21, 1970): 6A; *Plain Dealer* (April 23, 1970): 1, 6.

62. Cleveland *Plain Dealer* (April 23, 1970): 6A; *Plain Dealer* (April 20, 1970): B1; *Cleveland Press* (April 18, 1970): A7; *Plain Dealer* (April 19, 1970): 4A; *Cleveland Press* (April 20, 1970): 1. The complete calendar of events is in the Gaylord Nelson Papers.

63. *Cleveland Press* (April 21, 1970): B1; *Cleveland Press* (April 22, 1970): A1; *Cleveland Press* (April 13, 1970): D1; *Environmental Action* 1 (January 31, 1970): 3; Environmental Crisis Week Calendar of Events, Gaylord Nelson Papers.

64. *Salina Journal* (April 22, 1970): 1–2; *Salina Journal* (April 19, 1970): 35. In 1988 and 1989, when I was a journalist in Kansas, I interviewed four members of the group—Dana Jackson, Penny Geis, Terry Evans, and Ivy Marsh—and my characterization of the membership derives from those interviews.

65. *Salina Journal* (April 22, 1970): 1–2.

66. Environmental Action, *Earth Day—The Beginning*, 71; *Great Bend* (KS) *Daily Tribune* (April 23, 1970): 1.

67. *Salina Journal* (April 23, 1970): 8; *Salina Journal* (April 17, 1970): 17.

68. *Salina Journal* (April 23, 1970): 2. I also am drawing here on interviews in 1988 and 1989 with Jackson and several of his colleagues at Kansas Wesleyan.

69. *Salina Journal* (April 23, 1970): 1, 2.

70. *Salina Journal* (May 1, 1970): 1; *Salina Journal* (May 5, 1970): 6; *Salina Journal* (June 16, 1970): 8; *Salina Journal* (September 6, 1970): 8.

71. *Salina Journal* (September 9, 1970): 10; *Salina Journal* (October 29, 1970): 8; *Salina Journal* (September 6, 1970): 8; *Salina Journal* (April 21, 1971): 12.

72. *Salina Journal* (July 25, 1971): 8.

73. Steven V. Roberts, "The Better Earth," *New York Times Magazine* (March 29, 1970): 8, 53–55; Larry Borowsky, "The Consummate Recycler," in *Learning to Listen to the Land*, edited by Bill Willers (Washington, DC: Island Press, 1991), 248–54. The most prominent reading of Humphrey's Declaration of Interdependence was the kickoff of Earth Week in Philadelphia. See John Zeh, ed., *Earth Week '70* (Philadelphia: Philadelphia Earth Week Committee, 1970), 29. *Mother Earth News* published the Declaration in the March–April 1970 issue (online).

74. *Washington Post* (March 15, 1970): A5. Humphrey's "manifesto" for the walk was included in De Bell, *The Environmental Handbook*, 307–9.

75. *Los Angeles Times* (April 22, 1970): Section 2, 1; *Long Beach* (CA) *Independent* (May 1, 1970): A16; Tom Clingman interview (December 12, 2007).

76. *San Francisco Chronicle* (March 14, 1970): 7; *Long Beach* (CA) *Independent* (May 1, 1970): A16; *Fresno Bee* (March 25, 1970): 1.

77. *Washington Post* (April 23, 1970): A20.

78. Ibid.

79. *Modesto Bee* (March 22, 1970): 1; *Fresno Bee* (March 30, 1970): 1.

80. *Oakland Tribune* (April 1, 1970): 2F; *Fresno Bee* (March 30, 1970): 1; *Fresno Bee* (April 1, 1970): 1D, 9D; *Long Beach* (CA) *Independent* (May 1, 1970): A16; Tom Clingman interview.

81. *Modesto Bee* (May 3, 1970): C4; *Los Angeles Times* (April 22, 1970): Section 2, 1; *San Francisco Chronicle* (March 14, 1970): 7.

82. *Modesto Bee* (July 31, 1970): B1; *Modesto Bee* (July 22, 1970): D1.

83. Ibid.

84. Margaret M. McGlynn, "The Town's Hooked on Garbage Power!" *Look* 35 (May 1971): 26–30.

85. John McPhee, *Coming into the Country* (New York: Farrar, Straus and Giroux, 1977), 105; Peter A. Coates, *The Trans-Alaska Pipeline Controversy: Technology, Conservation, and the Frontier* (Bethlehem, PA: Lehigh University Press, 1991), 189–90; *Fairbanks Daily News-Miner* (April 25, 1970): 1.

86. Terrence Cole, *The Cornerstone on College Hill: An Illustrated History of the University of Alaska Fairbanks* (Fairbanks: University of Alaska Press, 1994), 238–41. In addition, see Coates, *The Trans-Alaska Pipeline Controversy*, 122, 203, 265. I thank Ross Coen for sending me the material from the Cole history. Coen also sent material from the student newspaper and yearbook.

87. University of Alaska *Polar Star* (April 16, 1970): 6; *Fairbanks Daily News-Miner* (April 21, 1970): 3; *Fairbanks Daily News-Miner* (April 28, 1970): A1–A2.

88. *Fairbanks Daily News-Miner* (April 18, 1970): 4. Vogler also took out display ads with a similar argument. See *Fairbanks Daily News-Miner* (April 21, 1970): 4; *Fairbanks Daily News-Miner* (April 22, 1970): 11.

89. *Fairbanks Daily News-Miner* (April 22, 1970): 13; *Fairbanks Daily News-Miner* (April 21, 1970): 4.

90. Frank Keim interview (November 28, 2007).

91. University of Alaska *Polar Star* (April 24, 1970): 5.

92. *Fairbanks Daily News-Miner* (April 23, 1970): 3; University of Alaska *Polar Star* (April 24, 1970): 4.

93. U.S. Department of the Interior News Release, April 22, 1970. I thank Walter Hickel's Anchorage office for providing me a copy of the release.

94. Pat Ryan, "The Earth as Seen from Alaska," *Sports Illustrated* 32 (May 4, 1970): 26–31; *Florence* (SC) *Morning News* (April 24, 1970): 12A; *New York Times* (April 25, 1970): 27; *Fairbanks Daily News-Miner* (April 24, 1970): 4.

95. *Fairbanks Daily News-Miner* (April 30, 1970): 4; *Fairbanks Daily News-Miner* (April 28, 1970): 4; *Fairbanks Daily News-Miner* (April 25, 1970): 4.

96. Coates, *The Trans-Alaska Pipeline Controversy*, 203.

97. *New York Times* (April 22, 1970): 72.

98. *Wall Street Journal* (April 23, 1970): 1; *New York Times* (April 22, 1970): 73. The transcripts of several of the environmental special reports and talk shows are in the Gaylord Nelson Papers.

99. Frank Herbert, ed., *New World or No World* (New York: Ace Books, 1970). NBC actively promoted the broadcasts. See, for example, *Kittanning* (PA) *Leader-Times* (April 9, 1970): 17.

100. Herbert, *New World or No World*, 19–20.

101. Ibid., 33, 63.

102. *Long Beach* (CA) *Independent* (April 22, 1970): C16.

103. Herbert, *New World or No World*, 39–42.

104. Ibid., 71–75.

105. Ibid., 160–62.

106. Ibid., 238–39.

107. Ibid., 253.

4. Speakers

1. I estimate that at least 15,000 people spoke at colleges and universities and 20,000 people at K–12 events. The college and university figure assumes an average of ten speakers at 1,500 events. Many events had dozens of speakers, so I have no doubt that my college and university estimate is conservative. The K–12 estimate assumes an average of two speakers for 10,000 events. Though some school events had no speakers, some schools had extensive programs. I did not estimate the number of speakers at community events; that decision also ensures that my overall estimate is conservative.

2. The generalizations in this paragraph—and the rest of the introduction

to this chapter—come from a survey of the Earth Day programs of dozens of colleges and universities. Many newspapers printed the complete programs of local events. The Gaylord Nelson Papers also include many Earth Day programs.

3. The La Crosse program is in the Gaylord Nelson Papers. For the Grambling program, see *Ruston* (LA) *Daily Leader* (April 21, 1970): 6.

4. For the number of Interior speakers, see *Birmingham News* (April 22, 1970): 53; Walter J. Hickel, *Who Owns America?* (Englewood Cliffs, NJ: Prentice-Hall, 1971), 240.

5. *New York Times* (April 23, 1970): 30; *Atlanta Constitution* (April 23, 1970): 1, 19A.

6. Furman College *Paladin* (May 1, 1970): 4; UCLA teach-in program in the Gaylord Nelson Papers; *Pittsburgh Post-Gazette* (April 21, 1970): Section 2, 1; *Anderson* (IN) *Daily Herald* (April 20, 1970): 8; *Los Angeles Times* (April 21, 1970): Supplement 5, 1; Environmental Action, *Earth Day—The Beginning* (New York: Arno Press, 1970), 77–78.

7. *Washington Post* (April 23, 1970): 20; "A Giant Step—Or a Springtime Skip?" *Newsweek* 75 (May 4, 1970): 27.

8. Barry Commoner wrote about the conflicting arguments people made on Earth Day about the root causes of environmental problems: See *The Closing Circle: Nature, Man and Technology* (New York: Bantam, 1972), 1–7.

9. Cole was included in a list of "eco-celebrities from academe" just before Earth Day. See Luther J. Carter, "Environmental Teach-In: University of Michigan Meeting Links Concerns about Pollution and 'Upside-Down Society,'" *Science* 167 (March 20, 1970): 1594. In early 1970, Cole spoke at major teach-ins at Northwestern and the University of Michigan, and both of those speeches were published: See Robert C. Gesteland and John B. Putnam, eds., *Project Survival* (Evanston, IL: Project Survival Press, 1970), 3–8; J. David Allan and Arthur J. Hanson, eds., *Recycle This Book! Ecology, Society, and Man* (Belmont, CA: Wadsworth, 1972), 19–23.

10. Editors of *Playboy, Project Survival* (Chicago: Playboy Press, 1971), 15.

11. I did not find a short biography of Cole. My summary of his credentials derives from a variety of materials. Many of the basic facts are in his obituary in the *Syracuse Post-Standard* (June 6, 1978): 18C.

12. LaMont C. Cole, "The Ecosphere," *Scientific American* 198 (April 1958): 92; LaMont C. Cole, "The Impending Emergence of Ecological Thought," *BioScience* 14 (July 1964): 32.

13. LaMont C. Cole, "Protect the Friendly Microbes," *Saturday Review* 49 (May 7, 1966): 47.

14. LaMont C. Cole, "Can the World Be Saved?" *BioScience* 18 (July 1968): 679–84.

15. Ibid.

16. LaMont C. Cole, "Can the World Be Saved?" *New York Times Magazine* (March 31, 1968): 34–35, 95–96, 100, 106–8; "Oxygen Crisis," *Newsweek* 71 (January 8, 1968): 45; *Cedar Rapids* (IA) *Gazette* (March 2, 1969): 7A; "Fighting to Save the Earth from Man," *Time* 95 (February 2, 1970): 62; *Delaware County* (PA) *Daily Times* (February 17, 1970): 6; *Nashua* (NH) *Telegraph* (March 2, 1970): 13.

17. LaMont Cole, "In Unison," in *Earth Day—The Beginning*, 26–38.

18. "Fighting to Save the Earth from Man," 61; *Delaware County* (PA) *Daily Times* (February 17, 1970): 6.

19. The text of Claypool's sermon is printed in Henlee H. Barnette, *The Church and the Ecological Crisis* (Grand Rapids, MI: William B. Eerdmans, 1972), 98–107.

20. Lynn White Jr., "The Historical Roots of Our Ecological Crisis," *Science* 155 (March 10, 1967): 1203–1207. The 1970 works include Frederick Elder, *Crisis in Eden: A Religious Study of Man and the Environment* (Nashville: Abingdon Press, 1970); H. Paul Santmire, *Brother Earth: Nature, God and Ecology in Time of Crisis* (New York: Thomas Nelson, 1970). Roderick Frazier Nash discusses the debate over White's work in *The Rights of Nature: A History of Environmental Ethics* (Madison: University of Wisconsin Press, 1989), 87–120. For examples of religious leaders inspired by White, see Michael Hamilton, ed., *This Little Planet* (New York: Charles Scribner's Sons, 1970), vii–viii; *Billings Gazette* (April 18, 1970): 18.

21. Leigh Eric Schmidt, "From Arbor Day to the Environmental Sabbath: Nature, Liturgy, and American Protestantism," *Harvard Theological Review* 84 (July 1991): 317–18; H. Paul Santmire, "The Struggle for an Ecological Theology," *Christian Century* 87 (March 4, 1970): 275–77; *New York Times* (January 4, 1970): 145; *Port Arthur* (TX) *News* (April 18, 1970): 2; *Ontario-Upland* (CA) *Daily Report* (May 23, 1970): A6.

22. John T. Claypool, *Opening Blind Eyes* (Nashville: Abingdon Press, 1983), 36, 37, 39, 41; Reggie R. Ogea, "The Crescent Hill Years: The Impact of Historical Context on the Preaching of John Rowan Claypool, 1960–1971" (Doctor of Theology dissertation, New Orleans Baptist Theological Seminary, 1984), 89, 97–99, 113–14, 125–27.

23. Ogea, "The Crescent Hill Years," 19.

24. Leonard Silk, *The Economists* (New York: Basic Books, 1976), 191–239.

25. Kenneth E. Boulding, *The Meaning of the Twentieth Century: The Great Transition* (New York: Harper Colophon, 1965).

26. Kenneth E. Boulding, "The Economics of the Coming Spaceship Earth," in *Environmental Quality in a Growing Economy: Essays from the Sixth RFF Forum*, edited by Henry Jarrett (Baltimore, MD: Johns Hopkins University Press, 1966), 3–4.

27. Ibid., 4, 9.

28. Ibid., 11.

29. Ibid.

30. Ibid., 12–13.

31. In the late 1960s, Boulding developed his ideas in two short works: Kenneth E. Boulding, "The Prospects of Economic Abundance," in *The Control of the Environment*, edited by John D. Roslansky (Amsterdam: North-Holland Publishing Company, 1967), 40–57; Kenneth E. Boulding, "Is Scarcity Dead?" *The Public Interest* 5 (Fall 1966): 36–44. The reprint was Garrett De Bell, ed., *The Environmental Handbook* (New York: Ballantine Books, 1970), 96–101. For reports on Boulding's talks in early 1970, see *Holland* (MI) *Evening Sentinel* (February 13, 1970): 8; *Wisconsin State Journal* (February 5, 1970): 50; *Centralia* (WA) *Daily Chronicle* (April 13, 1970): 3. My list of Boulding's teach-in speeches comes from Earth Day programs.

32. The Environmental Action collection of Earth Day speeches includes a snippet from Boulding, "What Is the GNP Worth?" See *Earth Day—The Beginning*, 163–64. My analysis here draws mainly on another version of his GNP talk: Kenneth E. Boulding, "Fun and Games with the Gross National Product—The Role of Misleading Indicators in Social Policy," in *The Environmental Crisis: Man's Struggle to Live with Himself*, edited by Harold W. Helfrich Jr. (New Haven: Yale University Press, 1970), 157–70. The quotation is on page 157.

33. Boulding, *The Meaning of the Twentieth Century*, 13.

34. Boulding, "Fun and Games with the Gross National Product," 160.

35. Ibid., 163.

36. Ibid., 166.

37. Ibid., 169.

38. Environmental Action, *Earth Day—The Beginning*, 164.

39. Stephanie Mills, *Whatever Happened to Ecology?* (San Francisco: Sierra Club Books, 1989), 19–20, 35–36.

40. Ibid., 51.

41. Paul C. Light, *Baby Boomers* (New York: W. W. Norton, 1988), 131. The

Population Bomb was a bestseller on college campuses. See Alan Caruba, "Ecology Books: A Doomsday Bibliography," *Publishers' Weekly* 200 (August 16, 1971): 29.

42. *Oakland Tribune* (June 5, 1969): 17; Stephanie Mills, "Ecology: A Commitment," in *No Deposit—No Return: Man and His Environment: A View Toward Survival*, edited by Huey D. Johnson (Reading, MA: Addison-Wesley, 1970), 292.

43. Stephanie Mills, "Mills College Valedictory Address," in *American Earth: Environmental Writing Since Thoreau*, edited by Bill McKibben (New York: Library of America, 2008), 469–71.

44. *New York Times* (June 15, 1969): 54; *San Antonio Express/News* (June 8, 1969): 10E; *Oakland Tribune* (June 5, 1969): 11F.

45. Mills, *Whatever Happened to Ecology?* 52, 60–61; *Oakland Tribune* (June 12, 1969): 14; *Oakland Tribune* (June 5, 1969): 11F; Rasa Gustaitis, *Wholly Round* (New York: Holt, Rinehart and Winston, 1973), 33.

46. Mills, *Whatever Happened to Ecology?* 56, 59–60, 63; *Charleston* (WV) *Gazette* (April 25, 1970): 14; *Oxnard* (CA) *Press-Courier* (November 24, 1969): 3; *Washington Post* (April 29, 1970), B1, B4; "Miss Stephanie Mills vs. Motherhood," *Look* 34 (April 21, 1970): 58–59; *Morgantown* (WV) *Dominion-Post* (April 19, 1970): 3A; transcript of CBS News Special *Earth Day: A Question of Survival*, April 22, 1970, Gaylord Nelson Papers; transcript of ABC News Special *Mission Possible*, March 20, 1970, Gaylord Nelson Papers. "Four Changes" is in De Bell, *The Environmental Handbook*, 323–33.

47. Mills, *Whatever Happened to Ecology?* 58.

48. Stephanie Mills, ". . . O and all the little babies in the Alameda gardens Yes . . . ," in *Ecotactics: The Sierra Club Handbook for Environmental Activists*, edited by John G. Mitchell with Constance L. Stallings (New York: Pocket Books, 1970), 79–80; Stephanie Mills, "Action Imperatives for Population Control: A Woman's View," in *Agenda for Survival: The Environmental Crisis—2*, edited by Harold W. Helfrich Jr. (New Haven: Yale University Press, 1971), 120–21.

49. Mills, "Action Imperatives for Population Control," 124–25.

50. Ibid., 123, 127.

51. Ibid., 128–29.

52. *Stanford Daily* (April 23, 1970): 1; *Morgantown* (WV) *Dominion-Post* (April 19, 1970): 3A.

53. *Stanford Daily* (April 23, 1970): 1; Mills, "O and all the little babies," 83; *Earth Times* 1 (April 1970): 3; *Earth Times* 1 (May 1970): 4.

54. Richard J. Lazarus, *The Making of Environmental Law* (Chicago: University of Chicago Press, 2004), 47–49; *New York Times* (December 20, 1969): 33; *New York Times* (March 23, 1970): 41; *Ann Arbor News* (March 11, 1970), in the collection of the University of Michigan's Bentley Library, Douglas D. Crary Papers Box 18, Enact Teach-In folder; *Syracuse* (NY) *Post-Standard* (April 18, 1970): 8.

55. Gilbert Rogin, "All He Wants to Save Is the World," *Sports Illustrated* 30 (February 3, 1969), 26; Editors of *Playboy*, *Project Survival*, 21; Robert C. Gesteland and John B. Putnam, eds., *Project Survival* (Evanston, IL: Project Survival Press, 1970), 54; Harmon Henkin, Martin Merta, and James Staples, *The Environment, the Establishment, and the Law* (Boston: Houghton Mifflin, 1971): 15–16.

56. *New York Times* (September 14, 1969): 78; Norman J. Landau and Paul D. Rheingold, *The Environmental Law Handbook* (New York: Friends of the Earth/Ballantine Books, 1971), 8.

57. Thomas R. Dunlap, *DDT: Scientists, Citizens, and Public Policy* (Princeton: Princeton University Press, 1981), 144–54; *Tucson Daily Citizen* (October 15, 1969): 27.

58. Rogin, "All He Wants to Save Is the World," 29.

59. The literature on the Scenic Hudson case is considerable. For a good overview, see Allan R. Talbot, *Power Along the Hudson: The Storm King Case and the Birth of Environmentalism* (New York: E. P. Dutton, 1972).

60. Marion Lane Rogers, *Acorn Days: The Environmental Defense Fund and How It Grew* (New York: Environmental Defense Fund, 1990), 36.

61. Luther J. Carter, "Environmental Pollution: Scientists Go to Court," *Science* 158 (December 22, 1967): 1556; Malcolm F. Baldwin and James K. Page Jr., eds., *Law and the Environment* (New York: Walker, 1970), 94–95, 262–63; "Environmental Defense Fund: Yannacone Out as Ringmaster," *Science* 166 (December 26, 1969): 1603.

62. Rogin, "All He Wants to Save Is the World," 24–29; "Vic Yannacone: Natural Man," *Playboy* 16 (November 1969): 205; Creighton Peet, "The Effluent of the Affluent," *American Forests* 75 (May 1969): 16–19, 37–38; Editors of *Playboy*, *Project Survival*, 20–21; *Bennington* (VT) *Banner* (October 17, 1969): 1, 12.

63. Yannacone's speech, "Sue the Bastards!" is in Environmental Action, *Earth Day—The Beginning*, 199–215.

64. Samuel G. Freedman, *The Inheritance: How Three Families and the American Political Majority Moved from Left to Right* (New York: Touchstone,

1998), 40–55, 69–84, 119–41. Garrett is a major protagonist in Freedman's wonderful book, and I could not have written this section without his excellent reporting.

65. Ibid., 233, 237.

66. Ibid., 231–33.

67. Ibid., 231–32, 235–36. For Boyle's view of the association, see Robert H. Boyle, *The Hudson River: A Natural and Unnatural History* (New York: W. W. Norton, 1969), 278–81.

68. Freedman, *The Inheritance*, 243–51; Boyle, *The Hudson River*, 99–103, 170, 177–81.

69. The quotations from Garrett's speech all come from Freedman, *The Inheritance*, 250–51. I asked Freedman if he could provide me a copy of the speech, and he generously offered to dig it out from storage, but I decided not to trouble him and to rely on his published account instead.

70. Freedman, *The Inheritance*, 234, 243–44; Boyle, *The Hudson River*, 101–3.

71. Freedman, *The Inheritance*, 243–47. The expressway battle received considerable attention. See Talbot, *Power Along the Hudson*, 162–82; Joseph L. Sax, *Defending the Environment: A Strategy for Citizen Action* (New York: Alfred A. Knopf, 1971), 64–82.

72. *New York Times* (October 17, 1968): 64; Talbot, *Power Along the Hudson*, 150.

73. Neal R. Peirce, *The Mountain States of America: People, Politics, and Power in the Eight Rocky Mountain States* (New York: W. W. Norton, 1972), 116–17; *Billings Gazette* (January 8, 1969): 12.

74. *Billings Gazette* (January 8, 1969): 12; *Billings Gazette* (December 18, 1969): 15; Helena *Independent Record* (March 4, 1970): 4.

75. Peirce, *The Mountain States of America*, 105–7; Helena *Independent Record* (April 24, 1970): 4.

76. The full text of the speech was published in the *Billings Gazette* (April 23, 1970): 5.

77. Gaylord Nelson made a similar argument in one of his Earth Day speeches. See Bill Christofferson, *The Man from Clear Lake: Earth Day Founder Senator Gaylord Nelson* (Madison: University of Wisconsin Press, 2004), 311. For other examples of liberal Democrat rhetoric about the inseparability of environmental and social problems, see Environmental Action, *Earth Day—The Beginning*, 43, 90–92, 232, 241.

78. *Montana Standard* (April 29, 1970), 4; *Billings Gazette* (April 23, 1970): 4; Helena *Independent Record* (April 24, 1970): 4; *Missoulian* (April 24, 1970): 6.

79. *Billings Gazette* (January 5, 1971), 3; K. Ross Toole, *The Rape of the Great Plains: Northwest America, Cattle and Coal* (Boston: Little, Brown, 1976), 2–3, 214–26.

5. The New Eco-Infrastructure

1. *New York Times* (April 23, 1970): 30.
2. Council on Environmental Quality, *Environmental Quality: The Fourth Annual Report of the Council on Environmental Quality* (Washington, DC: U.S. Government Printing Office, 1973), 396–97.
3. *Greeley* (CO) *Tribune* (April 30, 1970): 29; *Fairbanks* (AK) *Daily News-Miner* (February 17, 1971): 8; Walt Pomeroy interview (July 11, 2011); Environmental Action, *Earth Day—The Beginning* (New York: Arno Press, 1970); Environmental Action, *Earth Tool Kit: A Field Guide for Environmental Action* (New York: Pocket Books, 1971); *Scottsbluff* (NE) *Star Herald* (July 29, 2001): 55.
4. Frank Graham Jr. with Carl W. Buchheister, *The Audubon Ark: A History of the National Audubon Society* (New York: Alfred A. Knopf, 1990), 232, 240–42; Thomas B. Allen, *Guardian of the Wild: The Story of the National Wildlife Federation, 1936–1986* (Bloomington: University of Indiana Press, 1987), 147–49; Mark Harvey, *Wilderness Forever: Howard Zahniser and the Path to the Wilderness Act* (Seattle: University of Washington Press, 2005), 208.
5. *New York Times* (September 17, 1969): 21.
6. The major national newspapers and the wire services reported the decision of the teach-in staff to stay in business. See, for example, *New York Times* (April 22, 1970): 35; *Greeley* (CO) *Tribune* (August 25, 1970): 4; *Centralia* (WA) *Daily Chronicle* (April 27, 1970): 12.
7. *New York Times* (August 16, 1970): 49; *New York Times* (September 26, 1970): 75; *Chicago Tribune* (December 13, 1970): N3.
8. Garrett De Bell, ed., *The Voter's Guide to Environmental Politics: Before, During, and After the Election* (New York: Ballantine, 1970), 6, 211–32.
9. *Bridgeport* (CT) *Telegram* (September 3, 1970): 11.
10. "E.A. Joins Campaign Effort," *Environmental Action* 2 (June 11, 1970): 5; "The Dirty Dozen," *Environmental Action* 2 (September 19, 1970): 11–13; Frank Wallick, "Elections Decimate EA's 'Dirty Dozen,'" *Environmental Action* 2 (November 14, 1970): 5.
11. Daniel Nelson, *A Passion for the Land: John F. Seiberling and the*

Environmental Movement (Kent, OH: Kent State University Press, 2009), 43–68; *New York Times* (August 22, 1970): 10.

12. *New York Times* (September 26, 1970): 1, 75.

13. *New York Times* (November 6, 1970): 34; *New York Times* (November 5, 1970): 37.

14. "How the Ecologists Defeated Aspinall," *Business Week* (September 23, 1972): 27; *New York Times* (September 16, 1972): 12; *New York Times* (October 1, 1972): 46; *New York Times* (November 12, 1972): 41; *New York Times* (May 16, 1974): 44; *New York Times* (October 28, 1974): 27; *New York Times* (November 7, 1974): 31.

15. Mark Dowie, *Losing Ground: American Environmentalism at the Close of the Twentieth Century* (Cambridge, MA: MIT Press, 1996), 59; De Bell, *Voter's Guide*, 283–84; Jamie Heard, "Friends of the Earth Give Environmental Interests an Active Voice," *National Journal* 2 (August 8, 1970): 1718; James R. Wagner, "Environment Groups Shift Tactics from Demonstrations to Politics, Local Action," *National Journal* 3 (July 24, 1971): 1557–64.

16. *New York Times* (September 3, 1971): 33; Wagner, "Environment Groups," 1560; Richard Corrigan, "Muskie Plays Dominant Role in Writing Tough New Air Pollution Law," *National Journal* 3 (January 2, 1971): 30.

17. Harry Lenhart Jr., "SST Foes Confident of Votes to Clip Program's Wings Again Before Spring," *National Journal* 3 (January 9, 1971): 43–58; Mel Horwitch, *Clipped Wings: The American SST Conflict* (Cambridge, MA: MIT Press, 1982), 275–327.

18. Lenhart Jr., "SST Foes Confident," 43–48; Heard, "Friends of the Earth," 1712–14; Horwitch, *Clipped Wings*, 275–327.

19. The boomdoggle charge is from William A. Shurcliff, *The S/S/T and Sonic Boom Handbook* (New York: Ballantine, 1970), 104.

20. *New York Times* (August 16, 1970): 49; Horwitch, *Clipped Wings*, 295–97.

21. *New York Times* (September 3, 1971): 33; Horwitch, *Clipped Wings*, 346; Marc Mowrey and Tim Redmond, *Not in Our Backyard: The People and Events that Shaped America's Modern Environmental Movement* (New York: William Morrow, 1993), 60–69.

22. *Annapolis* (MD) *Evening Capital* (November 25, 1970): 4. The Environmental Action plan for clean air is in the Gaylord Nelson Papers, along with many other documents from the Clean Air Act lobbying effort. For an overview of the campaign, see Environmental Action, *Earth Tool Kit*, 309–24.

23. *Arizona Republic* (June 28, 1970): B9.

24. *Delaware County* (PA) *Daily Times* (August 29, 1970): 2; *Southern Illinoisan* (August 30, 1970): 6. In addition, see Charles O. Jones, *Clean Air: The Policies and Politics of Pollution Control* (Pittsburgh: University of Pittsburgh Press, 1975), 196, 207.

25. Marchant Wentworth interview (May 8, 2008); Clean Air Coalition files in the Gaylord Nelson Papers; Environmental Action, *Earth Tool Kit*, 309–24.

26. Paul Charles Milazzo, *Unlikely Environmentalists: Congress and Clean Water, 1945–1972* (Lawrence: University Press of Kansas, 2006), 148–49, 202–5; Jeffrey M. Berry, *Lobbying for the People: The Political Behavior of Public Interest Groups* (Princeton: Princeton University Press, 1977), 257; Wagner, "Environment Groups," 1563.

27. "Eco-Journalism," *Newsweek* 77 (February 1, 1971): 43–44; *Rocky Mountain News* (October 28, 1997) (online).

28. David M. Rubin and David P. Sachs, *Mass Media and the Environment: Water Resources, Land Use and Atomic Energy in California* (New York: Praeger, 1973), 54–55; A. Clay Schoenfeld, "The Press and NEPA: The Case of the Missing Agenda," *Journalism Quarterly* 56 (Autumn 1979): 577–85.

29. G. Ray Funkhouser, "The Issues of the Sixties: An Exploratory Study of the Dynamics of Public Opinion," *Public Opinion Quarterly* 37 (Spring 1973): 68; A. Clay Schoenfeld, Robert F. Meier, and Robert J. Griffin, "Constructing a Social Problem: The Press and the Environment," *Social Problems* 27 (October 1979): 45, 46, 48; Rubin and Sachs, *Mass Media and the Environment*, 59–60.

30. William Witt, "The Environmental Reporter on U.S. Daily Newspapers," *Journalism Quarterly* 51 (Winter 1974): 697–704; John De Mott and Emmanuel Tom, "The Press Corps of Spaceship Earth: A Trend Analysis, 1968–1988," *Newspaper Research Journal* 11 (Fall 1990): 15.

31. "Environmental Writers," *Editor & Publisher* 103 (August 8, 1970): 45. The circulation figures are from *Editor & Publisher, The 1971 Editor & Publisher International Year Book* (New York: Editor & Publisher, 1971).

32. *Chicago Sun-Times* (April 19, 1970): 8; *Chicago Tribune* (April 22, 1970): C24.

33. *Long Beach* (CA) *Independent* (March 9, 1970): B2; *Long Beach Independent* (May 29, 1970): C7; *Long Beach Independent* (July 17, 1970): C7.

34. Larry Pryor, "The Ecology Thicket," *Journal of Environmental Education* 4 (Winter 1972): 55; *Editor & Publisher, The 1973 Editor & Publisher International Year Book* (New York: Editor & Publisher, 1973).

35. The *Editor & Publisher International Year Book* lists beat reporters at

every newspaper, and I reviewed the volumes from 1969 through 1975. I found very few papers with a race-relations or civil-rights writer. Though many newspapers had women's pages, few if any had writers who wrote regularly about gender roles. The first major stories about the women's liberation movement appeared in late 1969 and early 1970. See Susan J. Douglas, *Where the Girls Are: Growing Up Female with the Mass Media* (New York: Times Books, 1995), 163–91.

36. John C. Maloney and Lynn Slovonsky, "The Pollution Issue: A Survey of Editorial Judgments," in *The Politics of Ecosuicide*, edited by Leslie L. Roos Jr. (New York: Holt, Rinehart and Winston, 1971), 69–70.

37. Mary Kiss interview (March 11, 2011). For examples of Kiss's front-page stories, see *Kingsport* (TN) *Times* (April 13, 1971) and *Kingsport* (TN) *Times-News* (May 2, 1971).

38. Witt, "The Environmental Reporter," 698. I also base my generalizations on interviews with Jo-Ann Albers (March 11, 2011), Peg Breen (March 25, 2011), Cornelia Carrier (January 14, 2011), Paul Hayes (March 18, 2001), Mary Kiss (March 11, 2011), Richard Krantz (March 22, 2011), Larry Pryor (June 27, 2011), Ben Rubendall (March 11, 2011), Doug Turner (March 17, 2011), and Mary Walton (January 13, 2011). In addition, I found lengthy obituaries for Bruce Ingersoll, Bob Rothe, Harold Scarlett, and Fred Thomas. Many newspapers described the credentials of their new environmental beat reporters.

39. *Albuquerque Journal* (August 16, 1970): 1; *Cincinnati Enquirer* (December 12, 1971): 31; *Kingsport* (TN) *Times-News* (May 2, 1971): 1. For environmental special projects before 1970, see Mark Neuzil, *The Environment and the Press: From Adventure Writing to Advocacy* (Evanston, IL: Northwestern University Press, 2008), 185.

40. Richard Krantz interview; Robert Frederiksen, *Our Dirty Water* (Providence, RI: Providence Journal Company, 1971). The Meeman awards for environmental reporting give a good sense of the kinds of projects the new beat reporters did. See *Albuquerque Tribune* (March 10, 1972): A7; *El Paso Herald-Post* (March 16, 1973): B11.

41. The columns I mention were written by Susan Conte, Morgantown (WV) *Dominion News*; Florence Schaffhausen, *Doylestown* (PA) *Daily Intelligencer*; John Read, *Eureka* (CA) *Times Standard*; Fritz Thompson, *Albuquerque Journal*; Peg Breen, *Albany Knickerbocker News*; Peggy Frizzell, *Northwest Arkansas Times*; Casey Bukro, *Chicago Tribune*; Fred Thomas, *Omaha World-Herald*; and Gil Bailey, *Long Beach* (CA) *Independent* and *Long Beach Press-Telegram*.

42. *Charleston* (WV) *Gazette* (August 17, 1970): 13; *Charleston Gazette* (November 2, 1970): 15.

43. *Charleston* (WV) *Gazette* (October 14, 1971): 6; Mary Walton interview.

44. Peg Breen interview; Witt, "The Environmental Reporter," 700.

45. For reports by *Wisconsin State Journal* environmental reporter Dennis Madigan in other Wisconsin papers, see *Sheboygan Press* (August 28, 1970): 21; *Fond du Lac Commonwealth Reporter* (June 27, 1970): 8.

46. *Terre Haute* (IN) *Tribune* (October 29, 1970): 31; *Lowell* (MA) *Sun* (November 17, 1970): 20; *Arizona Republic* (December 28, 1971): 34; *Tucson Daily Citizen* (September 5, 1972): 29.

47. Edward Flattau, *Evolution of a Columnist: The 40-Year Intellectual Journey of America's Senior Nationally Syndicated Environmental Commentator* (Xlibris, 2003), 126–27; *San Antonio Sunday Light* (February 7, 1971): 1.

48. Morgantown (WV) *Dominion-News* (January 16, 1970): 8A; *Cumberland* (MD) *Evening Times* (September 16, 1970): 1; *Charleston* (WV) *Gazette* (September 28, 1970): 13; *Cedar Rapids* (IA) *Gazette* (December 13, 1970): 8A.

49. *New York Times* (December 30, 1979): DX10.

50. Council on Environmental Quality, *Environmental Quality: The First Annual Report of the Council on Environmental Quality* (Washington, DC: U.S. Government Printing Office, 1970), vii.

51. Malcolm G. Scully, "Environmental Problems Will Be the Central Concern of New University of Wisconsin at Green Bay," *Chronicle of Higher Education* (November 24, 1969): 1, 8; Samuel A. Eliot, "Maine's College of Human Ecology," *Journal of Environmental Education* 4 (Spring 1973): 16; Clay Schoenfeld and John Disinger, eds., *Environmental Education in Action—II: Case Studies of Environmental Studies Programs in Colleges and Universities Today* (Columbus, OH: Educational Resources Information Center/Science, Mathematics and Environmental Education Analysis Center, 1978), 391; *New York Times* (November 30, 1969): 1, 57; *Lawton* (OK) *Constitution* (November 27, 1969): 2D; "Big Class" Press Release, January 9, 1970, University of Oregon Libraries Digital Collections (online).

52. A. Clay Schoenfeld, "The University-Environmental Movement Marriage," *Journal of Higher Education* 50 (May–June 1979): 302. For an overview of the new programs, see Schoenfeld and Disinger, *Environmental Education in Action—II*.

53. *Albuquerque Journal* (February 17, 1972): B4; Arden L. Pratt, *Environmental Education in the Community College* (Washington, DC: American Association of Junior Colleges, 1971), 34.

54. Pratt, *Environmental Education in the Community College*, 27–33; Robert H. McCabe and R. F. Mines, eds., *Man and Environment* (two volumes) (Englewood Cliffs, NJ: Prentice-Hall, 1972 and 1974).

55. *Harrison* (AR) *Daily Times* (August 22, 1972): 10; *Bennington* (VT) *Banner* (September 14, 1973): 14; *Bucks County* (PA) *Courier Times* (February 5, 1973): 16; Dee Brock and Linda Resnik, "Courseware," *Alternative Higher Education* 2 (1978): 245–46.

56. Arden L. Pratt, ed., *Selected Environmental Education Programs in North American Higher Education* (Miami, FL: National Association for Environmental Education, 1974), 79–80; Lynton K. Caldwell, "The Human Environment: A Growing Challenge to Higher Education," *Journal of Higher Education* 37 (1966): 149–55; Lynton Keith Caldwell, *Environment: A Challenge to Modern Society* (Garden City, NY: Natural History Press, 1970).

57. Noel McInnis and Don Albrecht, eds., *What Makes Education Environmental?* (Louisville, KY: Data Courier and Environmental Educators, 1975), 111–12; Carl Reidel interview (June 13, 2011); *Salina Journal* (July 25, 1971): 8. I also am drawing on interviews with Wes Jackson from the late 1980s, when I was a journalist in Kansas.

58. Herman Sievering interview (June 12, 2009). In addition, see *Edwardsville* (IL) *Intelligencer* (July 7, 1971): 73.

59. Schoenfeld and Disinger, *Environmental Education in Action—II*, 291, 464; interviews with Wes Jackson.

60. Schoenfeld and Disinger, *Environmental Education in Action—II*, 134; Pratt, *Selected Environmental Education Programs*, 21.

61. Eliot, "Maine's College of Human Ecology," 16–19. The College of the Atlantic was featured in news stories as well. See, for example, *Tucson Daily Citizen* (July 6, 1972): 59. For the programs at Evergreen College and the Huxley College of Environmental Studies at Western Washington State University, see Schoenfeld and Disinger, *Environmental Education in Action—II*, 320–30, 391–404. I discuss the University of Wisconsin–Green Bay in the next paragraph.

62. Scully, "Environmental Problems Will Be the Central Concern of New University of Wisconsin at Green Bay," 8; John Fischer, "Survival U Is Alive and Burgeoning in Green Bay, Wisconsin," *Harper's* 242 (February 1971): 20–27; "Ecology U," *Newsweek* 77 (June 14, 1971): 77; *New York*

Times (December 9, 1970): 41; "'Eco-Freaks,'" *Inside UW–Green Bay* 33 (May 2007): 2–9. The quotation is on page 8 of the *Inside UW* story.

63. Clay Schoenfeld and John Disinger, eds., *Environmental Education in Action—I: Case Studies of Selected Public School and Public Action Programs* (Columbus, OH: ERIC Information Analysis Center for Science, Mathematics, and Environmental Education, 1977), 105–42; Michael L. Blim, "KARE For the Environment," *American Education* 12 (January–February 1976): 23–28.

64. Leslie Rich, "The Rudiments of Good Nestkeeping," *American Education* 14 (April 1978): 16–20.

65. *New York Times* (October 5, 1969): 69; *Charleston* (WV) *Daily Mail* (April 14, 1970): 4; *Tucson Daily Citizen* (January 4, 1971): 24; "What Schools Can Do About Pollution," *Today's Education* 59 (December 1970), 24.

66. Cornelius J. Troost and Harold Altman, eds., *Environmental Education: A Sourcebook* (New York: John Wiley & Sons, 1972), 286–305; George Potts interview (January 31, 2008). Potts also provided me with clippings about club activities from the *Wichita Beacon*.

67. Dennis W. Brezina and Allen Overmyer, *Congress in Action: The Environmental Education Act* (New York: Free Press, 1974), 34–35, 56, 99, 125, 127, 129, 168–69.

68. John F. Disinger and Mary Lynne Brown, eds., *Environmental Education 1975: A State-by-State Report* (Columbus, OH: ERIC Center for Science, Mathematics, and Environmental Education, 1975) provides information about the source of funding for school programs in every state. In addition, see Wilhelmina Hill, "Model Environmental Education Programs," *Journal of Environmental Education* 3 (Spring 1972): 28–31; Council on Environmental Quality, *Environmental Quality: The Third Annual Report of the Council on Environmental Quality* (Washington, DC: U.S. Government Printing Office, 1972), 145. Newspapers often reported when teachers received grants to attend ECOS workshops. See, for example, *Florence* (SC) *Morning News* (May 23, 1975): 2A.

69. John E. Stefany, "Environmental Education in Florida's Schools," *AIA (American Institute of Architects) Journal* 64 (September 1975): 40–42. California, Indiana, Minnesota, and Montana also had well-funded programs. See Disinger and Brown, *Environmental Education 1975*.

70. I base this analysis on a review of the state reports in Disinger and Brown, *Environmental Education 1975*.

71. James A. Swan and William B. Stapp, eds., *Environmental Education: Strategies Toward a More Livable Future* (New York: John Wiley & Sons,

1974), 83–87. The state-by-state reports in Disinger and Brown, *Environmental Education 1975*, provide information about some local initiatives, including the construction of facilities.

72. Disinger and Brown, *Environmental Education 1975*, cite state associations for environmental educators in Michigan and New Jersey, among others. The NEA special report is "What Schools Can Do About Pollution," 15–29. For an example of the articles on environmental-education initiatives in professional journals, see Haven Kolb, "The Role of Secondary Education in Solving Environmental Problems," *American Biology Teacher* 33 (April 1971): 214–19.

73. McInnis and Albrecht, *What Makes Education Environmental?* 34–35.

74. George Siehl, "Literature Subsequent to the Ecology Nova," *Library Journal* 96 (July 1971): 2266. In addition, see *New York Times* (March 29, 1970), 233; Sheldon Novick, "Ecopublishing," *Environment* 12 (May 1970): 28–30.

75. Alan Caruba, "Ecology Books: A Doomsday Bibliography," *Publishers' Weekly* 200 (August 16, 1971): 28. For the Ballantine originals I cite, see Paul Swatek, *The User's Guide to the Protection of the Environment* (1970); Garrett De Bell, *The Voter's Guide to Environmental Politics* (1970); Gene Bryerton, *The Nuclear Dilemma* (1970); Mark Terry, *Teaching for Survival* (1971); Norman J. Landau and Paul D. Rheingold, *The Environmental Law Handbook* (1971). Frances Moore Lappé discusses the origins of *Diet for a Small Planet* in the introductory chapter of the twentieth-anniversary edition, published in 1991.

76. Caruba, "Ecology Books," 30.

77. Ibid.

78. *New York Times Book Review* (February 15, 1970): 1, 26.

79. Ian Ballantine and Betty Ballantine, "From the Two-Bit Beginning," *New York Times Book Review* (April 30, 1989): 25, 46; *New York Times* (March 10, 1995): B7.

80. Ballantine and Brower describe the survival library in an appendix to De Bell, *The Voter's Guide*, 279–80. The 1960s reprints were Wesley Marx, *The Frail Ocean* (October 1969) and Robert and Leona Train Rienow, *Moment in the Sun* (October 1969). William A. Shurcliff, *The S/S/T and Sonic Boom Handbook* (February 1970) originally was a pamphlet; Thomas Whiteside, *Defoliation* (March 1970) had appeared in *The New Yorker*.

81. *New York Times Book Review* (February 21, 1971): 3; Caruba, "Ecology Books," 28. For the origins of Terry's book, see his profile on the website

of the Northwest School in Seattle, which he cofounded: http://www
.northwestschool.org/faculty/profiles/mark.shtml.

82. Garrett De Bell interview (July 8, 2010).

83. Novick, "Ecopublishing," 29; *Chicago Tribune* (August 16, 1970): U4; Edward Abbey, "How to Live on This Planet Called Earth," *New York Times Book Review* (April 19, 1970), 318; *New York Times* (April 22, 1970): 43.

84. *Sandusky Register* (May 22, 1970): 4.

85. Greg Cailliet interview (July 19, 2010); Paulette Setzer interview (July 8, 2010); Milton Love interview (May 16, 2010); Carroll Harrington interview (July 20, 2010). In addition, see Carroll Harrington, Marie Niemeyer, Joyce Leonard, and Linda Fischman, *If You Want to Save Your Environment . . . Start at Home!* (New York: Hawthorn Books, 1970); Greg Cailliet, Paulette Setzer, and Milton Love, *Everyman's Guide to Ecological Living* (New York: Macmillan, 1971).

86. I discuss three guides in the next paragraph. In addition, see "Ecology Action Guides—Manuals for Participation," *American Libraries* 4 (July–August 1973): 427–30. That story misses one of the most often-discussed guides: Julia Percivall and Pixie Burger, *Household Ecology* (Englewood Cliffs, NJ: Prentice-Hall, 1971). For the McCloskey quote, see Philip Shabecoff, *A Fierce Green Fire: The American Environmental Movement* (New York: Hill and Wang, 1994), 119.

87. Cailliet, Setzer, and Love, *Everyman's Guide to Ecological Living*, 1; Paul Swatek, *The User's Guide to the Protection of the Environment* (New York: Ballantine, 1970), 83–84; Dirck Van Sickle, *The Ecological Citizen* (New York: Perennial, 1971), xviii–xix.

88. Carroll Harrington interview; Paul Swatek interview (July 7, 2010). For examples of the dozens of stories about the how-to guides, see *Charleston* (WV) *Gazette* (December 8, 1970): 13; *Berkshire* (MA) *Eagle* (March 5, 1971): 12; *Ames* (IA) *Daily Tribune* (July 8, 1971): 6; *Long Beach* (CA) *Independent* (July 18, 1971), B6; *Montana Standard* (September 5, 1971): 13; *Panama City* (FL) *News-Herald* (September 22, 1971): 4A; *Lubbock* (TX) *Avalanche-Journal* (March 15, 1973): 6B.

89. *Billings Gazette* (October 16, 1972): 9.

90. Clay Schoenfeld, "Irruption in Environmental Communications," *American Forests* 78 (October 1972): 53.

91. Siehl, "Literature Subsequent to the Environmental Nova," 2270. I looked at roughly twenty anthologies.

92. Arthur Godfrey, ed., *The Arthur Godfrey Environmental Reader* (New York: Ballantine, 1970); Thomas R. Harney and Robert Disch, eds., *The*

Dying Generations: Perspectives on the Environmental Crisis (New York: Dell, 1971).

93. *Cedar Rapids* (IA) *Gazette* (August 29, 1971): 13B; Caruba, "Ecology Books," 30.

94. *Idaho Falls Post-Register* (May 13, 1971): A7.

95. *Fresno Bee* (March 1, 1970): 5C.

96. White House Conference on Youth, *Recommendations and Resolutions: 1971 White House Conference on Youth* (Washington, DC: U.S. Government Printing Office, 1971), 155; Ecology Center Communications Center files (given to the author by George Coling).

97. I found newspaper articles and Web accounts about the founding of roughly twenty ecology centers. I also drew on an unpublished 1973 study of ecology centers given to me by George Coling.

98. Again, I base my generalizations on newspaper and Web accounts of roughly twenty ecology centers. I also drew on an unpublished 1973 study provided by George Coling and a brief description of ecology center activities in White House Conference on Youth, *Recommendations and Resolutions*, 155.

99. Neil Seldman, *The United States Recycling Movement, 1968 to 1986: A Review* (Washington, DC: Institute for Local Self-Reliance, 1986), 6; Susan Strasser, *Waste and Want: A Social History of Trash* (New York: Metropolitan Books, 1999), 283–84.

100. George Coling interview (December 5, 2008); White House Conference on Youth, *Recommendations and Resolutions*, 154–57. The task force report and the ECCC were the subjects of newspaper stories. See, for example, *Charleston* (WV) *Gazette* (December 25, 1971): 12A.

101. Winder Lyons interview (July 26, 2009).

102. *Big Springs* (TX) *Daily Herald* (March 24, 1970): B1.

103. Ross Vincent interview (July 14, 2009).

104. *Baton Rouge Advocate* (January 4, 1988) (online); *Port Arthur* (TX) *News* (July 16, 1970): 18; *Del Rio* (TX) *News-Herald* (June 7, 1974): 6A; George Coling interview; Ross Vincent interview.

105. *Baton Rouge Advocate* (January 4, 1988) (online).

106. Arthur Hanson interview (August 29, 2007); Bill Kopper interview (August 18, 2010).

107. ENACT Ecology Center 1970 Annual Report, in the collection of the University of Michigan's Bentley Library, Assistant to the President (U of M) Box 39, ENACT Program folder. In addition, see *Charleston* (WV) *Gazette* (May 13, 1972): 10A.

108. Judith Serrin, "'Earth Day' Year Around." *American Education* 8 (January 1972): 26–30.

109. Bill Kopper interview; Mike Schechtman interview (August 20, 2010). The *Ann Arbor Observer* "Then and Now" website has a story about the Ecology Center building: http://aaobserver.aadl.org/aaobserver/17442.

110. Mike Garfield interview (September 9, 2010). The Ecology Center website has information on current projects: http://www.ecocenter.org/.

111. Mike Garfield interview.

112. *Hayward* (CA) *Daily Review* (January 16, 1971): 3; *Hayward Daily Review* (January 28, 1971): 18; Fremont-Newark (CA) *Argus* (February 4, 1971): 8; Donna Olsen interview (December 10, 2008).

113. *Hayward* (CA) *Daily Review* (September 1, 1971): 8; *Hayward Daily Review* (September 14, 1971): 12; Fremont-Newark (CA) *Argus* (March 22, 1972): 4; *Hayward Daily Review* (April 19, 1972): 10; *Hayward Daily Review* (November 13, 1973): 11; Donna Olsen interview.

114. *Hayward* (CA) *Daily Review* (November 13, 1974): 1; *Tri-City Voice* (March 14, 2006) [http://www.tricityvoice.com/articledisplay.php?a=4856]; Donna Olsen interview.

115. Fremont-Newark (CA) *Argus* (April 12, 1974): 1.

116. Donna Olsen interview.

Epilogue: The First Green Generation

1. Nan Stockholm Walden interview (May 27, 2008).

2. Brent Blackwelder interview with *Grist*, 2004, http://www.grist.org/article/blackwelder.

3. For Tim Palmer's career, see http://www.timpalmer.org/about_tim. The growth of nonprofits in the 1970s is detailed in Michael O'Neill, *The Third America: The Emergence of the Nonprofit Sector in the United States* (San Francisco: Jossey-Bass, 1989).

4. Ed Furia interview (May 2, 2008); Pete Grannis, "Earth Day," *New York State Conservationist* 64 (April 2010): 32.

5. Karim Ahmed interview (March 28, 2008).

6. Kelley Griffin, *Ralph Nader Presents More Action for a Change* (New York: Dembner Books, 1987), 171–75; Ralph Nader and Donald Ross, *Action for a Change: A Student's Manual for Public Interest Organizing* (New York: Grossman, 1971); *Winona* (MN) *Daily News* (November 12, 1970): 1b.

7. Karim Ahmed interview (December 29, 2008); Griffin, *Ralph Nader*

Presents More Action for a Change, 13, 171–75. Ralph Nader and Donald Ross, *Action for a Change: A Student's Manual for Public Interest Organizing* (revised edition) (New York: Grossman, 1972), 65.

8. For the Natural Resources Defense Council, see Christopher J. Bosso, *Environment, Inc.: From Grassroots to Beltway* (Lawrence: University Press of Kansas, 2005), 43–44.

9. Karim Ahmed interview (December 29, 2008); *New York Times* (November 21, 1974): 29; *New York Times* (June 22, 1975): 149; David Doniger and Michelle Quibell, *Back from the Brink: How NRDC Helped Save the Ozone Layer* (New York: Natural Resources Defense Council, 2007).

10. Ruth Norris, ed., *Pills, Pesticides & Profits: The International Trade in Toxic Substances* (Croton-on-Hudson, NY: North River Press, 1982); Frederica P. Perera and A. Karim Ahmed, *Respirable Particles: Impact of Airborne Fine Particulates on Health and the Environment* (Cambridge, MA: Ballinger, 1979); *New York Times* (August 18, 1985): E1; *New York Times* (October 13, 1985): C11.

11. Karim Ahmed interview (December 29, 2008).

12. Dorothy Bradley letter to Gaylord Nelson, December 23, 1970, Gaylord Nelson Papers; *Billings Gazette* (May 29, 1970): 11; *Billings Gazette* (November 26, 1970): 57; Dorothy Bradley interview (December 4, 2008); Harry Mitchell interview (December 20, 2008).

13. Dorothy Bradley, "Stegner and Contemporary Western Politics of the Land," in *Wallace Stegner and the Continental Vision: Essays on Literature, History, and Landscape*, edited by Curt Meine (Washington, DC: Island Press, 1997), 201; *Billings Gazette* (November 8, 1970): 28.

14. *Billings Gazette* (November 8, 1970): 28; *Billings Gazette* (November 26, 1970): 57.

15. *Billings Gazette* (May 29, 1970): 11; *Billings Gazette* (November 26, 1970): 57; *Montana Standard* (February 21, 1971): 21; Dorothy Bradley interview.

16. *Montana Standard* (February 21, 1971): 21.

17. *Billings Gazette* (March 10, 1973): 10; *Helena Independent Record* (January 4, 1973): 6; *Billings Gazette* (February 20, 1973): 11; Bradley, "Stegner," 202–205; Gordon Whirry interview (December 20, 2008).

18. The quotation is from a profile of Bradley on the website of the Burton Wheeler Center for the Exploration of Montana Issues when she served on the board. The website no longer is active.

19. Bradley, "Stegner," 201.

20. Nancy Pearlman interviews (May 3, 2008; December 21, 2008).

21. Ibid. For a brief account of the careers of Feuer and Swift, see Polly Welts Kaufman, *National Parks and the Woman's Voice: A History* (Albuquerque: University of New Mexico Press, 1996), 204–206. For an example of Edmiston's activism, see *Long Beach* (CA) *Independent* (March 19, 1970): A22.

22. Nancy Pearlman interview (May 3, 2008).

23. *Orange County* (CA) *Register* (April 15, 1990) (online); *Anderson* (CA) *Daily Bulletin* (August 20, 1971): 7; Nancy Pearlman interviews (May 3, 2008; December 21, 2008).

24. Nancy Pearlman interview (December 21, 2008).

25. Ibid.

26. The complete list of Environmental Directions programs is on Nancy Pearlman's website: http://www.ecoprojects.org/envdir.htm.

27. Nancy Pearlman interview (December 21, 2008). The complete list of EcoNews programs is on Pearlman's website: http://www.ecoprojects.org/econews.htm. I found TV listings for the "Gem in the Heart of the City" program in several newspapers in 1988 and 1989.

28. Nancy Pearlman interview (December 21, 2008); *Los Angeles Times* (June 7, 2001): B4; Leslie Berliant, "LA Community College System Heads for Energy Independence," Solve Climate blog post, June 17, 2009. The site is no longer active.

29. David Wheeler interview (December 9, 2008); *Lowell Sun* (January 25, 1974): 30. The quotation is from the Founder's Message on the Toad Hall Bookstore website, http://toadhallbooks.org/about-toadhall/founders-message/.

30. *Boston Globe* (March 6, 1994) (online); Toad Hall Bookstore 25th Anniversary Flyer (given to the author by Caroline Robinson).

31. Caroline Robinson interview (December 9, 2008); Al Kraft interview (December 10, 2008); David Wheeler interview; Laurie Hawkins interview (December 18, 2008); *Portsmouth Herald* (December 18, 2003) (online).

32. *New York Times* (July 26, 1979): C6; E. J. Kahn, "Alternatives," *New Yorker* (January 14, 1980): 24–25.

33. "Lovins on the Soft Path: An Energy Future with a Future," Bullfrog Films, 1982.

34. *New Hampshire Union Leader* (July 23, 2001) (online); transcript of the memorial service for Buck Robinson, December 21, 2003 (given to the author by Caroline Robinson).

35. *Portsmouth Herald* (December 18, 2003) (online).

Postscript

1. Robert Cahn and Patricia Cahn, "Did Earth Day Change the World?" *Environment* 32 (September 1990): 19.

2. Cahn and Cahn, "Did Earth Day Change the World?" 19–20, 36; *New York Times* (November 12, 1989): F4; *Los Angeles Times* (October 26, 1989) (online).

3. Cahn and Cahn, "Did Earth Day Change the World?" 20, 36; *New York Times* (November 12, 1989): F4.

4. Cahn and Cahn, "Did Earth Day Change the World?" 20; *Los Angeles Times* (October 26, 1989) (online).

5. Cahn and Cahn, "Did Earth Day Change the World?" 37; Ronald G. Shaiko, *Voices and Echoes for the Environment: Public Interest Representation in the 1990s and Beyond* (New York: Columbia University Press, 1999), 36, 42; Joel Makower, "The Death and Rebirth of '50 Simple Things You Can Do to Save the Earth,'" http://makower.typepad.com /joel_makower/2008/03/the-death-and-r.html.

6. For a critical view of Earth Day 1990's accomplishments, see Robert Gottlieb, *Forcing the Spring: The Transformation of the American Environmental Movement* (Washington, DC: Island Press, 1993), 201–4. Cahn and Cahn offer a more positive spin in "Did Earth Day Change the World?" 39–40. In an April 25, 2012, comment on a Web blog, Denis Hayes wrote: "In 1990, Earth Day was larger domestically than in 1970—though its impact was not as great." See http://alltagsgeschichte .wordpress.com/2012/04/23/who-actually-founded-earth-day/.

7. *Los Angeles Times* (October 26, 1989) (online).

● Acknowledgments

The deepest roots of this book go back to the mid-1980s, when I worked at the *Wichita* (KS) *Eagle-Beacon*. I became fascinated by a mom-and-pop environmental center in Salina, the Land Institute, that grew out of the activism of the Earth Day era, and I decided to write a book about the institute's founders, Wes and Dana Jackson. Though I never finished that book, I continued to think about the Jacksons as a graduate student and then a young professor, and my reflections eventually led to a September 2003 article in the *Journal of American History*, " 'Give Earth a Chance': The Environmental Movement and the Sixties," that provided roughly three-fifths of the material for chapter 1 of this book. I also drew on my research on the Jacksons in chapters 3 and 5. I am grateful to Wes and Dana for their willingness to share their stories so many years ago.

I also am indebted to the Jacksons for introducing me to my mentor, Donald Worster. When I met Don in 1989, I already had read his revelatory history of the Dust Bowl, so I knew he was a brilliant scholar. Thanks to the Jacksons, I was able to see that Don was a wonderful person. When I decided to go back to school to study environmental history, I was sure that I would love working with him, and I did. Don continues to be a sage adviser and a great friend. I am thrilled to be able to dedicate this book to him.

Soon after I began to plan this book, Mark Harvey introduced me to Doug Scott, one of the organizers of the ENACT teach-in at the University of Michigan, and I can't thank Mark enough for that introduction. Doug's recollections of the ENACT organizing effort helped me to see that Earth Day was a far more empowering event than I'd thought. Talking with Doug, I also realized that interviews could be a critical source for this project.

I ended up interviewing more than 120 people. In different ways, all allowed me to tell a richer, more compelling story. I thank, in alphabetical order, Karim Ahmed, Jo-Ann Albers, Barbara Reid Alexander, David Allan, Rick Anthony, Laurence Aurbach, Ed Beckwith, Holly Berger, Casey Black, David Boeri, Chris Bowman, Dorothy Bradley, Ben Branscomb, Peg Breen, Anne Brener, Marshall Brewer, Joe Browder, Robert Burks, Karen Buxbaum, Greg Cailliet, Cornelia Carrier, Edward Clebsch, Tom Clingman, Ross Coen, George Coling, Pan Conrad, William Cooper, Steve Cotton, Milly Dawson, Garrett De Bell, Sunni Eckhardt, Curt Freese, Ed Furia, Mike Garfield, Andrew Garling, Tee Guidotti, Bryce Hamilton, Arthur Hanson, Jim Harb, Peter Harnik, Carroll Harrington, Laurie Hawkins, Denis Hayes, Paul Hayes, John Heritage, Ed Holm, Tom Hudspeth, Cliff Humphrey, Eric Jones, Harold Jordahl, Frank Keim, Fred Kent, Linda Billings Kiser, Mary Kiss, Betty Klaric, William Kopper, Al Kraft, Richard Krantz, Rick Kunnes, Regina LaMarca, Steve Landfried, Austan Librach, Milton Love, Sam Love, Dan Lufkin, Winder Lyons, Ross McCluney, Harry Mitchell, Richard Mural, Susan Obata, Donna Olsen, Jim O'Toole, Tim Palmer, Glenn Paulson, Nancy Pearlman, Walt Pomeroy, George Potts, Larry Pryor, Edward Radatz, Carl Reidel, Pratt Remmel, Caroline Robinson, Dick Roop, Ben Rubendall, John Russell, Dale Russakoff, Mark Russakoff, Arturo Sandoval, Michael Schechtman, Steve Schmuki, Doug Scott, Paulette Setzer, Jack Sheehan, Herman Sievering, Dorothy Slusser, Mary Beth Smetzer, Alan Strahler, Dennis Sustare, Paul Swatek, Gita Talmage, Joyce Tarnow, David Trauger, Doug Turner, John Turner, Bede Van Dyke, Ross Vincent, Cameron McDonald Vowell, Gary Wakai, Nan Stockholm Walden, Mary Walton, Barry Weisberg, Rozanne Weissman, Marchant Wentworth, David Wheeler, Gordon Whirry, Rebecca Wodder, Norah Wylie, Robert Yaro, David Yetman, Jerry Yudelson, Kenneth Zapp, and Ron Zoia.

Several people also responded to e-mail queries: Dennis Bergsbaken, Gordon Bishop, Jim Boiani, Ken Cantor, Bill Cochran, Pete Gunter, Dana Kelley, Julian Koenig, Paul Link, William Menrath, Amy Pierson, Peter Sawtell, and Jack Waide.

Two archives were invaluable. The Wisconsin Historical Society has the papers of Gaylord Nelson, which include Earth Day memos, speeches, newspaper clippings, television transcripts, and much more. Because the Nelson papers were being processed when I visited, I am especially grateful to archivist Jennifer Graham for serving as my personal finding aid. The Bentley Library at the University of Michigan has a superb collection of material about the ENACT teach-in, and Malgosia Myc helped me get the most out of my time at the Bentley.

Though authors rarely acknowledge databases, I can't imagine how I could have written this book without the help of NewspaperArchive.com, a subscription collection of small and medium-sized newspapers. Before I discovered the archive, I assumed that I could only sample Earth Day coverage, and I looked at thirty-five newspapers, mostly on microfilm. The archive allowed me to get a truly national sense of Earth Day. And that was just the start. Because the archive is keyword searchable, I was able to learn much more about every aspect of the Earth Day story, from the organizing effort at the grass roots to the rise of environmental beats at newspapers.

Many Earth Day participants and relatives of participants provided invaluable source material. Steve Cotton, the media coordinator on the national Earth Day staff, was especially generous. Though he had misgivings about my project, he allowed me to use everything he'd saved from his Earth Day work. He also let me use the surviving drafts of a never-published account of Earth Day he wrote soon after the event. His archive—a box and a shopping bag!—included much that I never would have found otherwise. The same is true of the material provided by Barbara Reid Alexander, Chris Bowman, Marshall Brewer, George Coling, Ed Furia, William Menrath, Donna Olsen, Carl Reidel, Caroline Robinson, Dale Russikoff, Paulette Setzer, Tom Smith, Dennis Sustare, Gita Talmage, and Kenneth Zapp.

Many scholars, journalists, and students helped as well. Some provided material from their own research. Others e-mailed recollections of Earth Day. A few even gathered materials for me. Thanks to Scout Blum, Mary Braun, Will Bryan, Kate Christen, Ross Coen, Jack Davis, Tom Dietz, Finis Dunaway, Michael Egan, Zach Falk, Alan Glenn, Bob Gottlieb, Lorne Hammond, Jamie Henn, John Hoenig, Elana Katz, Gary Kroll, Katrina Lacher, Cynthia Melendy, Betsy Mendelsohn, Karen Merrill, Jeff Morgan, Rod Nash, Cheryl Oakes, Jim Rice, Gingy Scharff, Dave Schmidt, Terrianne Schulte, Tom Smith, Jeffrey Stine, Mark Stoll, Jay Taylor, Eric Wolfe, Blair Woodard, and Paul Wozniak.

During the five years I worked on this project, I had a chance to speak about Earth Day in a variety of venues, and I gained much from the questions and comments at those talks. I thank my wonderful hosts: Gregg Mitman, Bill Cronon, Nancy Shoemaker, LeAnne Stuver, Steven Epstein, Brian Balogh. David Robinson, Wendy Madar, Paul Milazzo, Steve Miner, David Schuyler, and Connee McKinney. I also spoke about Earth Day at Pennsylvania State University, my old home, and the University of Delaware, my home now.

In addition to hosting me when I spoke at the University of Wisconsin in 2007, Gregg Mitman and Bill Cronon hired me as a consultant for a website and two museum exhibits about Gaylord Nelson and Earth Day. That led to another wonderful visit to Madison to work with Gregg and Bill and their talented team: history graduate student Brian Hamilton, Web designer Melanie McCalmont, and Wisconsin Historical Society exhibit designer Douglas Griffin. Then I had the chance to return to Madison in 2010 for a spectacular Earth Day conference organized by the university's Nelson Institute for Environmental Studies.

At Penn State, I taught a senior seminar on Earth Day in spring 2011, and that class was a standout. Every week, I was inspired by the enthusiasm of my students: Jim Belko, Chrissy Boggs, Brad Burton, Steve Butzler, Scott Connelly, Ben Fisher, Adam Franz, Brian Jeffers, Nate Pettine, Dan Powell, Amanda Renda, Jared Shanker, Andrew Snyder, and Caitlin Yeager.

Don Worster read the first draft of every chapter, and his cheerleading and insightful comments were a huge help. Ted Steinberg, Ed Russell, Paul Sutter, and Michael Kazin offered great suggestions on the manuscript. Joanne Meyerowitz and ten anonymous readers improved the sections of chapter 1 that first appeared in the *Journal of American History*. I also thank Marc Cioc for publishing some of my thoughts on "The Genius of Earth Day" in the April 2010 issue of *Environmental History*.

Thomas LeBien acquired this book in 2007, and I very much appreciate his faith in the project. When Thomas left Hill and Wang for Simon & Schuster, Jesse Coleman of Farrar, Straus and Giroux ably stepped in as my editor. The book is much better because of Jesse's thoughtful readings. I also am grateful to the rest of the Hill and Wang/Farrar, Straus and Giroux crew.

I originally hoped to finish this book in two years, and I tried the patience of many people as that two years stretched to five. My family and friends encouraged me throughout. I dedicated my first book to Robin Schulze, and Robin was just as much a part of this book: Thanks again, my sweet, for everything.

● Index